THE CRUELEST MONTH

Spring, Nature, and Love in Classical and Medieval Lyrics

THE CRUELEST MONTH

*Spring, Nature, and Love
in Classical and Medieval Lyrics*

by JAMES J. WILHELM

New Haven and London, Yale University Press, 1965

For

KURT VILLADSEN

and

WILLIAM E. KLEB

Acknowledgments

AMONG the many teachers who have given me the linguistic training necessary for writing this book are Kurt Lewent, Clarence W. Mendell, E. T. Silk, Douglass Parker, Thomas G. Bergin, Dorothy McQuiston, and Enrico de'Negri. I owe special thanks to René Wellek and E. T. Donaldson, who read the manuscript first as a thesis and later as a book, and to De'Negri, who also read it in its final form. I gleaned a great deal of valuable information from Howard N. Porter, Donald S. Cheney, Peter Haidu, Gerrit Yates Lansing, Paul Sorel, and several of my colleagues at City University. Angel Flores was especially encouraging before and during publication. My friends Kurt Villadsen and William E. Kleb, to whom I have dedicated the work, heard most of the ideas developed here, and I must thank them especially for the opportunity they gave me to voice these thoughts in conversation.

The preparation for this book was financed in part by several fellowships from Yale University and by a United States Government Fulbright Fellowship, which allowed me a year of study at the University of Bologna.

I have acknowledged my debt to publishers in the appropriate footnotes, but beyond the call of necessity I should like to thank the following firms for their generous extension of free usage: B. G. Teubner (now of Stuttgart) for the Ovid texts; Max Niemeyer (Tübingen) for the Bernart de Ventadorn text; D. C. Heath (Boston) for Grandgent's edition of *La Divina Commedia;* and Champion (Paris) for the texts of Jaufré Rudel, William IX, and Cercamon.

All translations of the poems in the text are mine unless credited to another source.

J. J. W.

New York
October 1964

Contents

*la véritable histoire des idées et des
sentiments de cette époque ne gagne rien à
ces superfétations d'histoire extérieure.
Il faut lire ces poésies en tâchant de
s'imprégner de leur atmosphère intime, de
leur* inward form, *en suivant le fil des mots
et des métaphores jusqu'au centre intérieur
qui les a produits.*

LEO SPITZER

Introduction

THIS STUDY can be said to have originated in the awareness
of paradox in an area where I had been led to believe none
existed. I had been reading the poems of Jaufré Rudel, that
most mystical and idealistic of all the troubadours. In Jaufré,
I was prepared to find a statement of the courtly-love doctrine:
a systematic, idealized approach to love, an unqualified praise
of women. I was studying his most famous poem, "When days
are long in May" (*Lanquan li jorn son lonc en may*), which
opens with an idealized spring setting. The placing of love in
the midst of spring warmth and gladness seemed fully in accord
with an idealized attitude toward love: the microcosm joined
to the macrocosm when both are at their most brilliant moments of fulfillment.

Yet in a matter of seven lines, the spring setting had dis-
solved, and I was suddenly hurled into a world of winter ice:

> When days are long in May,
> I like the sweet songs of birds from afar,
> But when I leave them behind
> I think of my love who's far:
> I go head hanging with hope depressed,
> So that songs and hawthorn-flowers
> Mean nothing more to me than winter's ice.

> *Lanquan li jorn son lonc en may*
> *M'es belhs dous chans d'auzelhs de lonh,*
> *E quan mi suy partitz de lay*
> *Remembra.m d'un'amor de lonh:*
> *Vau de talan embroncx e clis*

> *Si que chans ni flors d'albespis*
> *No.m platz plus que l'yverns gelatz.*[1]

Furthermore, this poem, which opens on a note of happiness, ends on a note of total despair. Jaufré goes on to say that he has been cursed by a godfather so that he can never gain the thing he loves. He in turn curses the godfather for cursing him. And so the poem ends in an atmosphere of revenge and loss, as the poet states the utter impossibility of gaining the thing he is seeking.

It occurred to me that this poem raised questions of a very serious nature about the possibility of interpreting it in the light of a doctrine of courtly love—or indeed as the expression of any systematic form of belief. If this poem was written in praise of love, then it was a very curious kind of praise, ending with an almost hostile attitude toward its object: love in act. Furthermore, the ideal landscape with which the poem had opened had retreated so far from the inner world of the poet that it was, at the ending, as remote as Paradise Lost. In short, I could see that no interpretation of the poem would be satisfactory unless it could account for paradox, for a direct representation of opposite and contradictory feelings. It occurred to me that no doctrine or dogma, whether uttered by Plato, the Catholic Church, or Andreas Capellanus in his opening chapters, admits doubt or despair in its attitude toward contemplation of the Beautiful. Jaufré's poem was obviously not an expression of a firm belief; it was the expression of a man who had some sort of idealism in mind, but was totally unable to achieve it. He was not voicing opinions or ideas; he was trying to voice his emotions. In short, I came to the tautological awareness that I was reading a poem, a transcription of the emotions, and not a work of philosophy or religion. I was dealing with images, symbols, and dramatic presentation—not the logical development of ideas.

1. *Les Chansons de Jaufré Rudel,* ed. A. Jeanroy (2d ed. Paris, 1924), pp. 12–15, st. 1.

I was not so much fascinated by the over-all paradoxical treatment of love as I was by the curious handling of the images related to spring. How does one get from spring to winter in just seven lines? The whole treatment seemed directly opposed to the modern popular convention: "In the spring a young man's fancy lightly turns to thoughts of love." Was Jaufré's treatment unique, or did it have a precedent? I decided first of all to relate Jaufré's treatment of spring to other troubadour poems, especially the work of Bernart de Ventadorn, who is usually considered the formulator of courtly-love poetry. I also decided to include relevant poems of Bernart's predecessors, William of Aquitaine, Cercamon, and Marcabrun, the so-called "classical" troubadours, for an over-all picture of the period.

Then as I pursued studies of the ideal landscape, to which the spring motif is closely related, I was drawn back into the realm of classical literature for the rhetorical archetype. I was led to believe, after reading E. R. Curtius, that the pagan expression was indeed an idealized one.[2] Yet, from my own acquaintance with Latin literature, I could remember a somewhat melancholy statement about spring in the *Vigil of Venus*. I therefore decided to emphasize that long, complicated Latin poem which stands between the classical and medieval worlds. Since the *Vigil* is often considered an end of classical literature, I related it to other selected lyrics for a fuller statement.

I decided from the start to restrict my researches to the spring motif, and not the ideal landscape as a whole, since the latter involves the entire pastoral tradition. Yet I felt sure that if classical poets had idealized nature to any degree, they would have done it in terms of spring: the birth of Dionysus, the fulfillment of the world of exterior nature unclouded by any *super*natural dogma. My own preconceptions about Greco-Roman ability to merge with nature were bolstered by Curtius' assurance that the ideal landscape did indeed exist in an ideal-

2. Ernst Robert Curtius, *European Literature and the Latin Middle Ages,* tr. W. R. Trask, Bollingen Series, 36 (N.Y., 1953), esp. pp. 183–202, 106–27.

ized form in classical literature. Therefore, it seemed a simple matter to contrast the Greco-Roman rational view of the physical world with the more complicated view introduced by Christian metaphysics. Since I was primarily concerned with medieval Romance developments, I decided to emphasize Latin poetry, including Greek only for incidental purposes. Eventually I decided to consider the early Christian handling of the spring motif, largely because of the continuity of the Latin language; did the Christians, who were so utterly different in temperament, nevertheless perpetuate the basic rhetoric of the pagan era? Since the *Carmina Burana*, written in Late Medieval Latin, also employed the spring opening in numerous lyrics, I decided to include them too. I was especially interested in the relationship between these Latin poems and the contemporary Provençal troubadour poems. It was obvious that the Latin language and its Romance derivatives would manifest either a striking presence or absence of continuous rhetorical elements. I was aware that once the troubadours had written their lyrics in Provençal, the spring landscape could be observed in the early literatures of Germany, Spain, Italy, and northern France. May mornings ad infinitum. I decided to examine very briefly the developments in Italy and northern France, because these two literatures are usually considered the main avenues to modern European literature. Through these paths one approaches both Chaucer and the Italian Renaissance.

In general, I proceeded with the same methodology employed by Curtius: I was writing a history of rhetorical figures, and not a history of cultures. Only when my researches were half-completed did I discover that I was following in the footsteps of certain scholars and departing from those of others. To discuss the methodology here would be improper, for it would lead to calling a shot before it was fired. I can only say that I am deeply indebted to Curtius for treating poetry as poetry. If, in my first chapter, my findings do not accord exactly with his, it must be remembered that I have allowed myself what I consider ultimately to be the very necessary luxury of analysis, in addition to historical comparison. Yet Curtius' work is of a monumental nature, since he bridged a gap between the classical and modern worlds, and could not pause long to admire or scrutinize the details of the surrounding countryside. This study, which might be termed a critique or expansion of his chapter on "The Ideal Landscape," is very grateful for that bridge.

Abbreviations

AGWG	*Abhandlungen der Gesellschaft der Wissenschaften zu Göttingen: Philologisch-historische Klasse*
Al–A.	*Al-Andalus*
An. Hymn.	See Bibliog.: *Analecta Hymnica*
APAW	*Abhandlungen der preussischen Akademie der Wissenschaften: Philosophisch-historische Klasse*
AR	*Archivum Romanicum*
ASI	*Archivio Storico Italiano*
ASNS	*Archiv für das Studium der neueren Sprachen und Literaturen*
BSDI	*Bullettino della Società Dantesca Italiana*
CJ	*Classical Journal*
CL	*Comparative Literature*
CN	*Cultura Neolatina*
CP	*Classical Philology*
CR	*Classical Review*
CSEL	See Bibliog.: *Corpus Scriptorum*
DVLG	*Deutsche Vierteljahrsschrift für Literaturwissenschaft und Geistesgeschichte*
HJGG	*Historisches Jahrbuch* (der Görres-Gesellschaft)
JP	*Journal of Philology*
JS	*Journal des Savants*
MGH	See Bibliog.: *Monumenta Germaniae Historica: Auctores Antiquissimi*
MLN	*Modern Language Notes*
MP	*Modern Philology*

Penelope to the unrecognized Odysseus:

Just as the daughter of Pandareus, the greenwood nightingale,
sings her sweet song, when spring is new,
sitting among the dense leaves of a tree,
her rich throat pouring many a trill,
mourning her dead son, dear Itylus, whom she killed
unknowingly with a sword—son of her husband Zethus—
Just so this heart of mine sways this way and that.

ODYSSEY 19.518–24

1 The *Vigil of Venus* and the Classical Spring Lyric: A Study in Dialectic

SPRING IN THE LATIN LYRICS

HELEN WADDELL has said, "With the exception of the *Pervigilium Veneris,* the spring song hardly exists in Latin literature."[1] In one sense, this is true. If one is searching for a spring landscape as a conventional opening for a love poem (what German scholars call the *Natureingang* and French the *paysage idéal*), then he is immediately struck by the fact that Catullus, Propertius, Tibullus, and Ovid have primarily urban sensibilities. Yet in some ways the spring-song genre is totally artificial. The *Natureingang* in a troubadour poem lasts but a few lines, and is followed by a monologue that concerns the inner world of the self, just as the poems of Catullus do. The troubadour spring song is actually a love poem with a beginning set in the spring.

Catullus, however, did write a beautiful lyric in which the coming of spring is the predominant theme: *Iam ver egelidos refert tepores.* The first three lines of the poem present a more or less conventional picture of spring, with Zephyrus driving away the fury of the winter equinox:

> Now spring unthaws our long-chilled fevers
> And the madness of the winter equinox
> Grows calm before the happy western wind.

1. *The Wandering Scholars* (7th ed. London, 1949), p. 222. But see Georg Luck, *The Latin Love Elegy* (London, 1959), p. 69 for Tibullus' use of nature; also, for the history of the love vigil and the basically unhappy motif of the shut-out lover, Frank O. Copley, *Exclusus Amator: A Study in Latin Love Poetry,* Philol. Monographs of Am. Philol. Ass., 17 (1956).

But does the coming of spring inspire Catullus with thoughts of love? Does it make him aware of his closeness to nature? No. He wants to run from the fertile cornfields of hot Nicaea, flee to the shiny cities of the Greeks. He becomes sentimental about Rome, about friends, about friendship (*amicitia,* not *amor*); essentially, he wants to replace nature with society.

Ovid also wrote a spring poem, but it is contained in his *Tristia* (3.12), the poetry of his exile. In this case, the external conditions of the poet's life have a direct bearing upon the poem. Ovid begins by painting an ideal landscape with Zephyrus and a flower-filled meadow, singing birds, and laughing girls and boys. Then his tone shifts suddenly. He thinks about spring in Rome, with the theater opening and athletic games beginning. Finally the whole picture dissolves. He returns to his barren life on the Black Sea, where "the winter ice is barely dissolving in the spring sun": *at mihi sentitur nix verno sole soluta* (27). Suddenly the joy of spring leads to wintry despair.

We go to Horace expecting a conventional attitude toward spring probably because Horace is noted for his common sense. We expect a lovely spring song with a garden orchard and Mount Soracte looming off in the background, with wine and wit and a few words of wisdom. Indeed, Horace has left us three spring odes. One is the fourth ode of his first book, *Solvitur acris hiems.* This poem opens promisingly enough with Favonius and the spring coming to replace the bitter winter weather. In the fifth line, Venus or Love enters the picture, followed by the nymphs and graces. It is time to deck the head with myrtle and flowers, time to sacrifice a sheep or goat to the god of the woods. Here at last, we feel, is the classical pagan picture of spring, with the world of man brought firmly into accord with the world of nature. One expects the splendor of the pagan ethos, in which polytheism verges upon pantheism; matter, godhead, and nature seem one. Unfortunately, this poem is the celebrated ode on death. It shifts abruptly in the thirteenth line to a description of the way

4

Pale Death (*pallida Mors*) strikes the cottage of the humble peasant and the palace of the king. It thus presents two very different points of view, and although the death stanzas come last and make the more lasting impression, they do not cancel out what has gone before. This poem's structure is strikingly similar to Horace's *Diffugere nives* (4.7), where a brilliant picture of trees tossing their heads, rivers brimming over verdant banks, and nude graces dancing in the company of nymphs is shattered by a description of oncoming winter. Horace therefore urges Torquatus to abandon his dreams of immortality, and the ode ends with allusions to Hippolytus and Theseus, who were finally trapped in the cold, shadowy realm of death.

A third Horatian spring ode (4.12) employs a similar technique. Spring's companions, the warm breezes, push sails over the seas, and meadows abound with flowers. Then in the second strophe a traditional spring myth creeps in:

> That unhappy bird is making her nest,
> tearfully mourning Itys, eternal shame
> of the house of Cecrops, for ill avenging
> the barbarous lust of kings.

> *Nidum ponit Ityn flebiliter gemens*
> *Infelix avis et Cecropiae domus*
> *Aeternum opprobrium, quod male barbaras*
> *Regum est ulta libidines.*

Suddenly the tragedy of Philomela-Procne emerges in the midst of spring joy. These ambiguous birds cause Horace to think of death:

> But put off delay and desire for gain
> and, remembering the black fires, while you can,
> mix a little foolishness with wisdom:
> it's good to be foolish at the right time.

> *Verum pone moras et studium lucri*
> *Nigrorum memor, dum licet, ignium*

5

> *Misce stultitiam consiliis brevem:*
> *Dulce est desipere in loco.* (25–28)

Yet this poem blends melancholy with the joy of *dolce far niente*. The foolishness is not completely detached from the wisdom; the fear of death, the black fires, is not totally isolated from the sweetness (*dulce*) of life. The two elements abide in an unresolved tension.

Horace has had a strong influence upon the development of the spring topos. If one examines the three opening lines from one of the *Carmina Burana,* he can see the derivative qualities of later expressions of the spring motif:

Omittamus studia,	(*pone moras et studium lucri,* 25)
dulce est desipere,	(*dulce est desipere in loco,* 28)
et carpamus dulcia.	

Carpamus dulcia ("let's seize what's sweet") is an echo, one thousand years later, of that most famous of all Horatian cries: *carpe diem* ("seize the day"; 1.11.8). Without analyzing the *Burana* at this point, one might stress the fact that the Horatian cry is not one of sheer hedonism, as it is sometimes interpreted. Horace says: live to the full (not necessarily to excess); life is brief; make the present count, without worrying about mysteries that no man will ever understand. It is a superb statement of classical agnosticism, a rejection of mysticism. Later generations will find it difficult to perpetuate the Horatian point of view with taste.

The word *carpere* (to pluck, snatch, or gather in) is interesting in the Horatian usage because it is frequently used with flowers. Days are to be gathered the way flowers are gathered. The Horatian awareness of life's beauty and its accompanying fragility is implicit in that single word. Later poets of the *Latin Anthology,* in which the *Vigil of Venus* is contained, fastened upon this connotation and expanded it into a full-blown metaphor. Man's life was seen in the same perspective as the life of a rose. No distinction was drawn between man and nature; nature, if anything, was humanized. Florus told the whole life history of a rose in five quick lines:

> Once some roses were born in the rush of pleasant
> spring;
> The first day they showed their points;
> The second, their pyramids swelled to a greater bud;
> The third day came baskets; the fourth day finished
> Their toil. They die today unless they're plucked in
> the morning.

> *Venerunt aliquando rosae per veris amoeni*
> *Ingenium: una dies ostendit spicula florum,*
> *Altera pyramidas nodo maiore tumentes,*
> *Tertia iam calathos; totum lux quarta peregit*
> *Floris opus. pereunt hodie, nisi mane leguntur.*[2]

In this poem, the underlying metaphor becomes a thought (*consilium*), and it is frightening: a thing of beauty is *not* a joy forever—alas! Florus' treatment is in some ways more subtle than Horace's, since Florus never really draws the parallel between man and the rose. Yet at the same time, Florus' work is not so poetically exciting, because the poet does not transmit to the reader a sense of the fervor of spring and the joy of life, as Horace does. Florus has frequently been nominated as a candidate for writing the *Vigil,* but none of his work shows the dramatic intensity of the larger poem.[3]

An idyll sometimes attributed to Ausonius makes explicit what Florus merely implies.[4] This poem (*Ver erat*) begins with a poet walking in his garden among the budding roses. He comments upon their lush beauty, and then considers

2. *Poetae Latini Minores, 4: Anthologia Latina,* ed. E. Bährens (Leipzig, 1882), 279.

3. The *nodo . . . tumentes* (3) is compared with *nodos tepentes (Perv. Ven.,* 15) to establish Florus' authorship of latter; indeed, *tepentes* is often emended to *tumentes* through the comparison.

4. Text in *Perv. Ven.,* ed. P. Pithoeus, I. Lipsius, and others (Hagae Comitum, 1712), pp. 24–25. Cf. Ausonius, *Opuscula,* ed. R. Peiper (Leipzig, 1886); see Waddell, p. 6.

THE VIGIL AND CLASSICAL LYRIC

their plucking or "rape" (*rapinam*, 35). The fact that such beauty should be so perishable causes him to cry out to Nature against this gross injustice:

> I complain, O Nature, that the flower's beauty's so brief.
> Soon you steal from our eyes the gifts you've given them.

> *Conquerimur, Natura, brevis quod gratia florum est.*
> *Ostentata oculis illico dona rapis.* (41–42)

Then he brings the life of the virgin rose into direct comparison with the life of a young girl; he ends by warning:

> Gather your roses, girl, while the flower's young and youth is new,
> And remember: your years are also hurrying by.

> *Collige, virgo, rosas, dum flos novus, et nova pubes*
> *Et memor esto, aevum sic properare tuum.* (49–50)

It is doubtful that a technique can be carried beyond this point of metaphoric expression and total explication. The last line echoes an inscription found on a tombstone near Benevento:

> Live well. Hurry on. This will happen to you.[5]

When we consider the treatment of spring in Latin lyrics, we are drawn inexorably toward a consideration of time, love, death, and disaster. Greek lyrics do not seem to be different. Unfortunately very few complete poems survive from the classical lyric age, but among these is Ibycus' celebrated "Cydonian Spring" (*Eri men hai te Kudoniai*).[6] This poem opens

5. *Carmina Epigraphica: Anth. Lat. sive Poesis Latinae Supplementum,* 2, pt. 1, ed. F. Bücheler (Leipzig, 1930), 43.
6. *Poetae Melici Graeci,* ed. D. Page (Oxford, Clarendon Press, 1962), no. 5, p. 149. One striking exception is Meleager of Gadara, *Epigram* 110, ed. F. Gräfe (Leipzig, 1811), pp. 35–36, which mentions love, spring, and poetry as inextricably related factors; it contains the most graphic spring picture in Greek lyric poetry, with colorful flowers, singing birds, blossoming trees, and even a joyous nightingale and swallow (16–18). Although its form shows a

8

on a lively note, with quinces growing in a green garden, a brook, blossoms budding—in short, one of the small "ideal landscapes" that have appeared throughout the course of western lyric poetry. But a bolt strikes in the ninth line—*Threikios Boreas,* "Boreas, the cold North Wind from Thrace." Yet Boreas is not really a wind at all; it is a psychic calamity sent by Aphrodite into the poet's heart and is felt there all year round. The transition from the external garden of bliss to the interior frenzy of the poet, the intrusion of the winter wind Boreas into the domain of Zephyr, show us once again that the classical attitude toward spring and love constantly compels us to consider their opposites. Let us now turn to a consideration of the *Vigil of Venus* for a synoptic picture of the spring motif.

THE VIGIL OF VENUS

Tomorrow he will love who has never loved;
 tomorrow he who has loved will love again.   1
Spring is new, the spring of bird-song; in the spring
 our earth was born.
In the spring hearts come together; in the spring the
 birds all mate.
And the trees undo their tresses to the husband rain.
Tomorrow the lovers' coupler in the forest shade 5
Will weave green mansions from the myrtle boughs.
Tomorrow Dione lays down laws, terrible from her
 high throne.
Tomorrow he will love who has never loved;
 tomorrow he who has loved will love again.   8

---

marked similarity to some of the *Carmina Burana,* one would scarcely attempt to assert it as a direct rhetorical antecedent. Other lyrics mention spring (e.g., Simonides, *Poetae Melici Graeci,* Frag. 92, p. 304), but are fragmentary. A Locrian folk song (Frag. 2, pp. 450–51) is interesting for the dark qualities related to the appearance of the swallow in the spring, but is more useful to the anthropologist than the critic.

Tomorrow's the day when Father Heaven held his
    marriage: 59
he made the whole year out of his springtime showers,   6o
falling as husband Rain to the lap of his lovely wife,   61
mixing seeds to nourish all in her broad body.   62
Then the Sea from its foamy ball, from Saturn's
    floating blood,   9
In the middle of sky-blue legions and squads of two-
    legged horses   10
Made Venus shivering-wet from the shower-sprayed
    foam.   11
She herself rules mind and matter with inward-
    stealing spirit.   63
The creatress governs all with her secret strength.   64
Over the land, the heavens, over the deep-dug sea   65
she sows her seed-path in a straight and uncut course,   66
ordering the world to know the ways of birth.   67
Tomorrow he will love who has never loved;
    tomorrow he who has loved will love again.   68

She herself with jeweled flowers paints the purpling
    year;   13
With the breath of the Western Wind, swells
    trembling bosoms
into blossoming buds; she sprinkles the sparkling
    dewdrops,   15
those glistening waters left by the winds of night.
Look! those tears are trembling in their downward-
    falling force:
each little drop's a world trying to check its fated fall.
Look! those dark-red flowers are confessing their
    inner shame:
The tears that the stars let fall on tranquil nights   20
Will strip those virgin breasts from their red, wet
    cloaks.
Venus in the morning will tell the dewy roses to wed:

Roses made from the blood of the Paphian, made
    from Cupid's kisses,
made from jewels and flames and the sun's red rays.
Tomorrow they'll cast off the shame that lurks in
    their fiery cloaks
as one by one they take their marriage vows.
Tomorrow he will love who has never loved;
    tomorrow he who has loved will love again.   27

The goddess tells the nymphs: go to the myrtle
    groves;   28
my son will be your friend. Yet nobody can believe
That Love will take a holiday (if he carries his
    arrows).
Go, nymphs! He's thrown away his weapons. Love's
    taking a holiday.
Venus told him: go unarmed. Venus told him:
    naked, go!
Leave that quiver, leave those arrows, leave that
    torch aflame.
But listen, nymphs, be careful. Cupid's a handsome
    boy.
Even naked he has weapons that can thoroughly
    destroy.   35
Tomorrow he will love who has never loved . . .

Diana, with your blushes, Venus sends you all her
    girls,
Asking a single favor: leave us, virgin born at Delos,
leave our forest free from bloody hunts of beasts.   39
Let the trees with green shadows cover the freshening
    flowers.   58
Venus would gladly invite you if she could bend
    your modesty;   40
Venus would ask you to come if you weren't the
    Virgin Queen.

Soon for three nights you'll see us wandering with
    happy songs
hand in hand throughout your holy thickets,
wearing crowns of flowers in your myrtle mansions.
Ceres will be there; so will Bacchus; and the god
    of poetry.   45
We must hold the whole night back, keeping vigil
    with our songs.
Venus, rule our forests! You, Diana, go away!
Tomorrow he will love who has never loved . . .

Venus wants her court covered with Hybla's flowers;
She, our judge, will hand out laws with the Graces
    at her side.   50
Hybla, give her flowers; give whatever the year
    gave you.
Hybla, wear a coat of flowers, wide as the fields of
    Etna wear.
Girls from the countryside are coming; girls from
    mountains too;
Girls from groves, girls from forests, girls who live
    in brooks.
The mother of the winged boy tells them all to have
    a seat.   55
She warns them: never trust in naked Love.
Tomorrow he will love who has never loved . . .

She herself took her Trojan offspring to the land
    of Latium;   69
she gave the girl Lavinia in marriage to her son,
took the blushing Vestal, gave her to the god of war;
she herself arranged the wedding of Sabines with
    men of Rome,
to make the Ramnes, make Quirites, and for the race
    of Romulus

make the future father Caesar and the nephew
    Caesar too.
Tomorrow he will love who has never loved . . .   75

Desire makes our country fertile; it feels the spell
    of love.
Love, the son of Venus, is himself a country boy.
Yes, Cupid was born in a meadow, then suckled at
    her breast.
She brought him up on the fragile kiss of flowers.
Tomorrow he will love who has never loved . . .   80

Look! the bulls and cows are stretching beneath the
    broomplants,
each one safely held in the marriage bond.
Look! the bleating sheep in shadows are meeting
    their mates,
and the goddess is ordering the birds: don't be silent.
Noisy swan-songs are echoing stridently through the
    swamps.   85
The wife of Tereus is singing in the shade of a
    poplar tree.
You'd think she sang love's measures with her
    melodious voice;
You'd never think she mourned a sister wronged by
    her husband's rape.
She is singing. I am silent. When will *my* spring ever
    come?
When will *I* be like the swallow, with my days of
    silence done?   90
I have lost my Muse by silence. Apollo never looks
    my way.
So Amyclae, in its silence, lost in death its silence too.
Tomorrow he will love who has never loved;
    tomorrow he who has loved will love again.   93

PERVIGILIUM VENERIS

Cras amet qui numquam amavit, quique amavit cras
    amet.   1
Ver novum, ver iam canorum, vere natus orbis est,
vere concordant amores, vere nubunt alites,
et nemus comam resolvit de maritis imbribus.
cras amorum copulatrix inter umbras arborum   5
inplicat casas virentes de flagello myrteo:
cras Dione iura dicit fulta sublimi throno.
Cras amet qui numquam amavit, quique amavit cras
    amet.   8

Cras erit quom primus Aether copulavit nuptias: 59
ut pater totum crearet vernus annum nubibus,   60
in sinum maritus imber fluxit almae coniugis,   61
unde foetus mixtus omnes aleret magno corpore.   62
[cras amet . . .]

Tunc cruore de superno spumeo pontus globo   9
caerulas inter catervas, inter et bipedes equos,   10
fecit undantem Dionen de marinis imbribus.   11
ipsa venas atque mentem permeanti spiritu   63
intus occultis gubernat procreatrix viribus,   64
perque caelum perque terras perque pontum
    subditum   65
pervium sui tenorem seminali tramite   66
inbuit, iussitque mundum nosse nascendi vias.   67
cras amet . . .   68

Ipsa gemmis purpurantem pingit annum floridis;   13
ipsa surgentes papillas de Favoni spiritu
urget in nodos tepentes; ipsa roris lucidi,   15
noctis aura quem relinquit, spargit umentes aquas.
en! micant lacrimae trementes de caduco pondere:
gutta praeceps orbe parvo sustinet casus suos.   18
[cras amet . . .]

En! pudorem florentulae prodiderunt purpurae:　19
umor ille, quem serenis astra rorant noctibus,
mane virgineas papillas solvit umenti peplo.
ipsa iussit mane ut udae virgines nubant rosae:
facta Paphies de cruore deque Amoris osculis
deque gemmis deque flammis deque solis purpuris
cras ruborem, qui latebat veste tectus ignea,　25
unico marita voto non pudebit solvere.
cras amet ...

Ipsa nymphas diva luco iussit ire myrteo:
it puer comes puellis; nec tamen credi potest
esse Amorem feriatum, si sagittas vexerit.　30
ite, nymphae, posuit arma, feriatus est Amor!
iussus est inermis ire, nudus ire iussus est,
neu quid arcu, neu sagitta, neu quid igne laederet.
sed tamen nymphae cavete, quod Cupido pulcher est:
est in armis totus idem quando nudus est Amor.　35
cras amet ...

Conpari Venus pudore mittit ad te virgines.
una res est quam rogamus: cede, virgo Delia,
ut nemus sit incruentum de ferinis stragibus,　39
et recentibus virentes ducat umbras floribus.　58
[cras amet ...]

Ipsa vellet te rogare, si pudicam flecteret;　40
ipsa vellet ut venires, si deceret virginem.
iam tribus choros videres feriatis noctibus
congreges inter catervas ire per saltus tuos,
floreas inter coronas, myrteas inter casas:
nec Ceres nec Bacchus absunt, nec poetarum deus.　45
detinenda tota nox est, perviglanda canticis:
regnet in silvis Dione! tu recede, Delia!
cras amet ...

Iussit Hyblaeis tribunal stare diva floribus:
praeses ipsa iura dicet, adsidebunt Gratiae.　50

15

Hybla, totos funde flores, quidquid annus adtulit;
Hybla, florum sume vestem, quantus Aetnae campus
   est.
ruris hic erunt puellae, vel puellae montium,
quaeque silvas, quaeque lucos, quaeque fontes
   incolunt:
iussit omnes adsidere pueri mater alitis;   55
iussit, et nudo, puellas nil Amori credere.
cras amet . . .

Ipsa Troianos nepotes in Latinos transtulit: 69
ipsa Laurentem puellam coniugem nato dedit:
moxque Marti de sacello dat pudicam virginem:
Romuleas ipsa fecit cum Sabinis nuptias,
unde Ramnes et Quirites proque prole posterum
Romuli patrem crearet et nepotem Caesarem.
cras amet . . .   75

Rura fecundat voluptas, rura Venerem sentiunt;
ipse Amor, puer Dionae, rure natus dicitur.
hunc, ager cum parturiret, ipsa suscepit sinu:
ipsa florum delicatis educavit osculis,
cras amet . . .   80

Ecce! iam subter genestas explicant tauri latus,
quisque tutus quo tenetur coniugali foedere.
subter umbras cum maritis, ecce! balantum greges:
et canoras non tacere diva iussit alites.
iam loquaces ore rauco stagna cygni perstrepunt: 85
adsonat Terei puella subter umbram populi,
ut putes motus amoris ore dici musico,
et neges queri sororem de marito barbaro.
Illa cantat, nos tacemus. Quando ver venit meum?
Quando fiam uti chelidon, ut tacere desinam?   90
perdidi Musam tacendo, nec me Apollo respicit:
sic Amyclas cum tacerent perdidit silentium.

*cras amet qui numquam amavit, quique amavit cras
amet.**

*Reprinted with permission from *Pervigilium Veneris, The Vigil of Venus*,
ed. Cecil Clementi (3d ed. Oxford, Basil Blackwell, 1936). My translation. I
have included the opening refrain omitted by Clementi; it occurs in all three
manuscripts. Also, I have omitted the refrain after 88.

Aside from being the most complete spring poem of the
classical era, the *Vigil of Venus* is one of the most mysterious
poems in Latin literature. It comes down to us like a queen
in tatters, in three manuscripts which are all apparently corrupt.[7] The problems surrounding the text are so enormous
that a critic must choose between printing the poem as it
stands in one of the manuscripts, re-editing the poem completely, or accepting one of the many edited versions.[8] In any
case, he can never be sure that he is dealing with the work as
it was originally written. He cannot approach the poem looking for a strictly logical development of theme; he has only a
vast system of images and metaphors—sometimes arranged in
strophic blocks—from which chaos he can abstract order.[9]

The *Vigil* is not mysterious simply because of its tortured
textual history. Its author is unknown, and such diverse poets
as Catullus, Seneca, Tiberianus, Florus, and Apuleius have

7. It is important to note that the MSS span the medieval time period:
Codex Salmasianus, which forms the bulk of the *Latin Anthology* (*S;* c. 7th,
8th century; found 1615 by Claude de Saumaise); Codex Thuaneus (*T;* c. 9th,
10th century; owned by Jacques Auguste de Thou), also called Pithouaneus
for Pierre Pithou, who based his *editio princeps* of 1577 upon it; Codex San-
nazarii–Vindobonensis (*V;* copied from a lost archetype in the sixteenth century
by Jacopo Sannazaro). Scholarship summarized in Clementi, *Bibliographical
and Other Studies on the Perv. Ven.* (Oxford, 1913).

8. The four major faults: 58*S* stands alone between two refrains; *Tunc,* 9*S*,
can refer only to *vere,* 3 (but see n. 19 below); *ipsa,* 63*S*, has no antecedent (see
n. 18 below); the chronology in 69–74 is unclear unless *matrem,* 74*S*, is emended
or 73–74 are shifted before 70.

9. In adopting the text of Clementi's 3d edition with minor emendations,
I incline toward the opinion of E. K. Rand, "Sur le *Perv. Ven.*," *REL, 12*
(1934), 84. Cf. the conservative text of R. Schilling, *La Veillée de Vénus* (Paris,
1944), and the drastic stanzaic patterns of J. W. Mackail, "The *Perv. Ven.*," *JP,*
17 (1888), 179–91.

17

been suggested.[10] Its date of composition is likewise unknown, but it seems to have been written at some time between the second and fourth centuries.[11] The language of the poem has distinct Romance overtones, in which the Latin preposition *de* assumes possessive meanings proper to the Italian *di* or French *de; toti* (whole, entire) approaches *tutti* or *tous* (all), and *mane* (in the morning) is near *domani* or *demain* (tomorrow). There is no real internal evidence for dating the poem accurately, although a number of intriguing theories have been proposed.[12]

To some extent, the history of the poem in modern scholarship seems to have been influenced by Walter Pater's *Marius the Epicurean*.[13] Pater's romantic use of the *Vigil* (attributing it to a dying poet who heard the call of the love festival coming to him over the waters and the fields) caused people to think of the poem in terms of an historical author. Since no author was mentioned in the manuscripts, scholars tried to find one to match this romantic ideal. The *Vigil of Venus* became the *Dying Gaul* of Latin literature: the symbol of a waning pagan age. In the sense that any great work of art symbolizes the age in which it was written, this comparison has some validity. There does seem to be a great deal of what is commonly called "Hellenic failure of nerve" in the texture of the poem, a quality that Bury described as "so fresh and so artificial."[14] Aside

10. See Clementi (1936), pp. 75–90. The two most plausible candidates are Florus, cited by Rand, p. 93, and Schilling, pp. xxii f.; and Tiberianus, cited by J. A. Fort, *Perv. Ven. in Quatrains*, preface by J. W. Mackail (Oxford, 1922), p. 15.

11. This time limit is now generally accepted; see Rand, pp. 92–93; Fort, pp. 10 f.

12. E.g., L. Raquettius reads *Romoli* (74S) as Romulus Augustulus and *nepotem* as Julius Nepos in "De Auctore Carminis *Perv. Ven.* Inscripti," *CR*, *19* (1905), 224–25. I concur with J. B. Bury: "I have little doubt that the Caesar meant is either the original Augustus or the original Iulius," in "On the *Perv. Ven.*," *CR*, *19* (1905), 304.

13. *Marius the Epicurean, His Sensations and Ideas* (2d ed. 2 vols. London, 1885), *1*, 112–21.

14. P. 304.

from the fact that the *Vigil* was a favorite translation piece in the nineteenth century (when some translators did not have the courage to append their names to their work), there is a kind of Swinburnian quality to the diction. A rose in the poem is not just a beautiful flower to be woven into a garland for a Horatian banquet; it is not the product of Italian sun and soil, with a certain decorative use; it is a mystical compound of Venus' blood, Cupid's kisses, jewels, flames, and the rays of the sun (23-24). The technique is not one of *la nature pour la nature;* it is *la nature pour l'art.* The poet's hand hovers over the landscape in a more obvious way than it does in Homer.[15]

Turning to the beginning of the poem, we notice at once certain unusual qualities. It opens on a note of incredible promise: "Tomorrow he will love who has never loved; / tomorrow he who has loved will love again." The poet insists on the verb *amare*—four occurrences of the word "love" in a single line of poetry, where Ovid and Vergil, even at their most dramatic moments, ordinarily permit themselves just two. Aside from the very startling phenomenon that the line can be read either accentually or quantitatively (in either case, the stress at the caesura falls on *amavit*), there is an implication in the line that one seldom finds in Catullus: an awareness of a universal desire for love existing outside the limits of the self. This opening line is nothing less than a call to the whole of humanity, since all of humanity must necessarily be a member of one of the classes distinguished on one side of the caesura.

Yet the poet has just begun. Saturated with the notion of love, he proceeds to saturate his hearer with a feeling for spring. In lines 2 and 3, the word *ver* occurs no fewer than five times; in both lines, it receives the full stress that is always given to the fifth foot in a seven-foot trochaic line. The word "love" is again prominent in the third and fifth lines (*amores*

15. For a balanced discussion, see Werner Jaeger, *Paideia: The Ideals of Greek Culture,* tr. G. Highet (2d ed. N.Y., Oxford University Press, 1945), *1,* 3-56.

and *amorum,* respectively). A student of Latin literature is immediately struck by these repetitions. Either the poet is hopelessly deficient in avoiding metrical and verbal excess, or he is pursuing a deliberate scheme. When the "tomorrow" of the first line crops up again in the fifth line, and the entire first line recurs as a refrain, we are inclined to give the poet the benefit of the doubt. A lesser hand would perhaps have lacked the courage to organize a poem in such a daring way.

In the first strophe the narrator has, in fact, sent his reader a cryptic telegram: spring . . . love . . . tomorrow. It is the kind of poetic organization that may seem somewhat naive, yet is very effective. We need only glance at Clementi's bibliography of translations to see just how effective this call has been. In one sense, the organization is totally different from a four-word poem on the same subject by Ezra Pound (based on an imaginary fragment of Sappho):

> Spring . . .
> too long . . .
> Gongula . . .[16]

Pound's poem is tour de force, mystery for its own sake; Gongula might be construed as a monster; it is not a beautiful name to the English ear, but it happened to be the name of one of Sappho's friends. Pound's poem is meant to be ambiguous: to leave the reader with a vague sense of expectation and despair. The *Vigil,* at least in its opening, leaves no doubt whatsoever. It has some of the martial vigor of an early Christian hymn: when the sun rises tomorrow He will come! As a matter of fact, the meter of the *Vigil,* the trochaic septenarius, dates back to the marching songs of Julius Caesar's legions and is unquestionably well-suited as a vehicle for the Latin language.[17] With respect to the meter, then, this poem is a

16. "Papyrus," *Personae: Collected Poems of Ezra Pound* (N.Y., New Directions, 1926, 1954), p. 112.
17. *Fragmenta Poetarum Romanorum,* ed. E. Bährens (Leipzig, 1886), pp. 330–32.

return to, rather than a departure from, a long-standing popular tradition.

The parallel with a Christian hymn holds even further when we learn that a divinity is being invoked: appropriately, Venus; although the poet waits until line 37 to call her by her Latin name (indeed, many lines further in Clementi's rearranged version). Generally she is referred to by *ipsa* (63, 13, 14, etc.), which has a regal, deferential connotation: "she herself." The poet also calls her Dione (7, 11, 47, 77), and he is strongly biased in favor of Greek expressions throughout (*throno*, 7; *chelidon*, 90). However, there can be very little confusion about her identity or the fact that she dominates the poem.[18]

The constant repetition of words and phrases as leitmotifs seems at first glance to be quite foreign to classical Latin literature, which syntactically is noted for its balancing of disparate elements. Vergil used refrains in his *Eclogues* (e.g., 8), but never composed a long poem around such obvious principles. Rhetorically, we are approaching the standard poetic methodology of the Middle Ages, in which repetition functions as assonance and eventually evolves into rhyme. In fact, rhyme (supposedly the great invention of medieval poetry) is already observable in the classical *Vigil:*

> *Ver nov*um, *ver iam cano*rum, / *vere nat*us *orb*is *est,*
> *vere concor*dant *amo*res, / *vere nu*bunt *alit*es.   (2-3)

In this hymn to Venus we can hear the music of many very diverse kinds of hymns to come. Musically, the poem stands between two worlds; it is easy to understand why the work cannot be dated.

In some ways the images of the poem are more exciting than the music. The third and fourth lines are striking for their

---

18. One of the basic flaws disappears through this repeated usage (see n. 8); the poet uses *Illa*, 89, to refer to a different feminine subject, Procne.

personifications. The birds are getting married; the grove is undoing her hair to the husband rain (one is tempted to capitalize both "grove" and "rain"). The term *comam resolvere* ("to undo the hair") derives from Roman marriage ceremonies. Once begun, the personification becomes still another way in which the poem is held together. Myrtle bowers in the forest are houses (*casas,* 6); sea-horses form blue legions of soldiers (*catervas,* 10); the buds of roses are breasts (*papillas,* 14–15); dewdrops are tears (*lacrimae,* 17). The trend culminates in an entire strophe (19–26), when red roses are portrayed as blushing virgins whom Mother Venus has ordered to marry. They must throw off their cloaks (*peplo,* 21) and fiery chastity belts (*veste ignea,* 25) and take the solemn vows of matrimony.

There is also personification in lines 59 to 62 (which Clementi shifts behind line 8), but it is of a very different order. The personification in that strophe is drawn directly from traditional Greco-Roman mythology. It is part of whatever mythopoetic factors were present when the Greek religion was being shaped. This objective, dogmatic presentation of the Marriage of Heaven and Earth clashes with the subjective mythologizing of the poet in the surrounding strophes, and may account for the tendency of editors to shift the lines forward or backward. This strophe and the one describing Venus in her traditional role (69–75) seem out of place in the subjective world of the poem; our poet is far more interested in romance than religion. The ineptness of lines 59 to 62 has struck almost every editor of the *Vigil.* Line 62, for example, contains one of the infrequent spondees in the poem: *aleret* (sometimes emended to *alit*) *magno corpore.* Salmasius was among the first to point out that these verses are an obvious imitation of Vergil's *Georgics* 2.325–27:

> Then the almighty Father Heaven in fertile showers
> Descended into the lap of his joyous wife; his great seed,
> Mixed in her great body, nourishes all.

Tum pater omnipotens fecundis imbribus Aether
Conjugis in gremium laetae descendit, et omnes
Magnus alit, magno commixtus corpore, fetus.

Perhaps the poet of the *Vigil* had trouble fitting Vergil's dactylic hexameter into his seven-foot line; at any rate, he knew his Vergil well.[19] The poet continues to use a traditional mythology in lines 28 f., Cupid and nymphs; but at the same time, it is not an easy matter to distinguish between the mythological and the human. The god Cupid is a *puer*, a boy; the nymphs are *puellae*, girls. Yet it is difficult to say whether the girls in line 29 are semidivine nymphs or "just plain girls," some of whom are obviously going to take part in the festival. Furthermore, although Cupid is traditionally pictured as a mischievous little boy, the poet dwells on this mischief to the point where the god seems more human than divine. In other words, it is hard to say whether "that festival tomorrow" is now being mythologized or a mythological scene based upon past festivals is being humanized. This distortion of time and identity is merely an extension of the personification of roses and trees in the lines already examined. The natural and the supernatural seem to merge.

In line 37, which is roughly the middle of the poem according to Clementi's rearrangement, Diana, the goddess of chastity and wild groves, is urged to depart. Lines 37 to 48 form a consistent plea against chastity and shame. Virginity is castigated; love as sensual passion, as empirical fact, is idealized. (The Christian age will reverse these terms by idealizing the Virgin Queen Mary and castigating Venus, who will linger on as lower-case *venus*, "lust.") And so Venus gains more and more glory at the expense of her fellow goddess; Diana cannot be forced by the laws of nature to take part in the ceremony the way the roses in lines 19 to 27 were commanded to

19. The vague reference of *Tunc* (9) to *vere* (3) has a parallel in *Georgics* 2.323–25.

know the miraculous ways of birth (the *Homeric Hymn to Aphrodite* assures us of Artemis' immunity to love); therefore, she is simply urged to depart. Yet despite Diana's absence, the poet assures us that this festival will not be a gross orgy, for the Graces, the God of Poetry (Apollo), Ceres (the grain goddess of fertility), and Bacchus (regenerative Lord of Wine) will be among the guests. The festival is a communion of the numinal and phenomenal; as a result, the gods are humanized and the humans who partake are deified. It is hard to imagine such a divine *fête champêtre* in the *Odyssey*, for example, where the gods speak more as superior personae than as direct participants in the human drama. The scene is more Renaissance than Homeric; we imagine Botticelli's Graces locked in a sylvan dance. The gods themselves seem to have overriding symbolic meanings (Graces, Poetry, Bread, and Wine); they are almost allegorical figures, incapable of any dramatic actions that would sully their idealized forms.

Then occurs a line that might well have haunted later ages: "We must hold the whole night back, keeping vigil with our songs" (46). The night is good; the dawn is evil. The traditional equation of deity with light, the underlying solar-myth symbolism of Indo-Iranic mythology, is here stated in inverse terms; the Christians will destroy the romantic involution and restore the religious equation. Although the imagined scene becomes brighter as visualized through a dream, the poet maintains his control; he assures us again that he is merely projecting himself into the future; the whole affair takes place *tomorrow*.

Yet in lines 49 to 56, tomorrow seems to be at hand. The poet imagines Venus calling her Court of Love into order. At the same time, the artistic scene hovers between the imaginary and the real. The goddess will hand out her decrees at Hybla, which is a field or peak in Sicily; but Hybla is also a geographic location in the dream world of Theocritus and the romantic pastoral. Etna (or Enna?) is a real volcanic peak in Sicily; yet both Etna and Enna belong to the mystical world of the

Persephone myth. The dramatic field of the poem is elusive. Are the farm girls who are coming from the countryside real girls? We might well imagine some Sicilian *contadine* assembling to discuss some "love question" in a late-pagan Court of Love. But then in line 54 we encounter "girls who live in brooks"; dramatic realism dissolves, and we are thrown once again into a blurred world of the romantic imagination that has evolved from primitive animism; the *genius loci* here is not a Sicilian shepherdess but an underlying natural principle that has been personified. Suddenly Queen Venus orders all the girls (who were merely in the act of coming) to have a seat. Has the festival begun? Before our question is answered, the goddess utters one of the most important lines of the poem: "never trust in naked Love" (56). A curious thing for the love-goddess to say! These words, which sound so chilling in the middle of an idealized eulogy of love, will find a haunting echo in the close of the poem. Even back in lines 29 to 35, when we learned that playful Cupid had dropped his lethal weapons, we were told that love was as dangerous naked as armed. There the military symbolism mixed with sexual symbolism was funny; but here Venus' words strike the first clear minor-key tonalities that will dominate the last strophe of the poem.

The events summed up in lines 69 to 75 seem to be a digression, for they interrupt the tribunal. This, however, is a very vexing part of the poem, since line 58 lies utterly detached in the manuscripts. Perhaps the traditional portrait of Venus ought to be placed near the traditional account of the Marriage of Heaven and Earth (instead of pulling lines 59 to 68 forward as Clementi does), yet even with this change, there is bound to be an interruption. Venus makes her curious statement about love, and suddenly Venus is idealized as the tutelary protector of the Roman state. The poet's treatment is not particularly original, recalling both the general treatment of the *Aeneid* and the opening lines of Lucretius' *De rerum natura*, but it serves the poet's purpose well. He is intent on considering Love in every conceivable aspect: as goddess, as philosophical principle, as accident or act. In one sense, his changing attitude toward the goddess, whom he abstracts or humanizes as the spirit moves him, is but one reflection of his attitude toward everything in the poem. For example, as soon as he finishes his discussion of Venus as divine persona, he suddenly reduces her to an abstraction: *Rura fecundat voluptas, rura Venerem sentiunt* (76). This line is almost an equation: *Venus* (love) equals *voluptas* (desire). Yet in the next line he changes his technique and treats her as the human, loving mother of Cupid, suckling her son at her breast. Similarly Cupid or Amor, whose name also means "love," seems to usurp some of the functions of his mother. In the totally subjective world of the poem, it is pointless to look for objective distinctions. This fact, more than any other, may account for the impossibility of establishing a perfectly sound text unless a new manuscript is discovered.

The turning-point in the poem occurs in line 81. Suddenly the festival that is supposed to take place tomorrow and that was always hovering upon reality seems to be taking place today: "Look! the bulls and cows are stretching beneath the broomplants." The scene that the poet was envisioning comes alive, and he is drawn into it. The poet actually hears the birds singing (*canoras alites,* 84) that he had merely painted abstractly back in line 2. These are the traditional sweet-singing lovebirds who haunt medieval poetry. In the next line, however, they are replaced by swans—and the swan-song is a song of an entirely different nature. Indeed, their intrusion into the picture is obvious: they are raucous and talkative (*loquaces ore rauco,* 85). Then they are followed by one of those ambiguous birds of spring lyrics, the swallow. But the poet does not call her the swallow when he hears her cry; he calls her the wife of Tereus (*Terei puella,* 86), showing that he has immediately thought of her mythical character (has perceived her true character), and is not the least bit deceived by the beauty of her visual image (*chelidon* or "swallow" occurs in line 90) or by the beauty of her song. In fact, he tells us that her song is deceptive: "You'd think she sang love's measures with her melodious voice; / You'd never think she mourned a sister wronged by her husband's rape" (87–88). The dramatic effect of the contrasts can only be pointed out with reference to the Latin:

> *ut* pu*tes* motus a*mor*is *or*e dici musi*co,*
> *et* neg*es* queri *soror*em de mari*to* barba*ro.*

The interior rhymes are soothing and imitate the deceptive song of the bird; the beginning and end rhymes clash, thus accomplishing musically what the poet is trying to transmit verbally: that the paradoxical situation of the swallow (a thing of beauty that has somehow become defiled) extends in some way into the recesses of his own mind.

Then, without any break such as Clementi indicates (no break is called for in any of the manuscripts), the whole complicated relationship between the poet, his poetic creation, and the world of external reality is brought into focus by the contrast of: "She is singing. I am silent" (89). At last the narrator, whose presence can be sensed throughout the poem by means of his subjective techniques, steps into the picture himself. The second half of the line underscores his presence: "When will *my* spring ever come?" (*Quando ver venit meum?*) Then, "When will *I* be like the swallow, with my days of silence done?" (*Quando fiam uti chelidon, ut tacere desinam?*) The translation betrays the original in two respects: the English pronoun cannot be the last word in the sentence, and hence a major emphasis is lost; furthermore, the Latin "cease being silent" is, by its very inversion, a stronger poetic device.

After line 89, the poet dominates the poem entirely. The festival seems to have melted away—a mere figment of the imagination. All we are left with is the narrator, who keeps asking questions about himself. And what peculiar questions they are! He says, in the 89th line of a 93-line poem, that he is "silent." Then he condemns himself for this silence by saying that Apollo, the lord of poetry, never favors him. The irony, of course, is that he has just written ninety of the most memorable lines in Latin literature. Then, after yielding to a charge that he himself has made, he draws a simile between himself and the town of Amyclae (either the Laconian or Italian Amyclae; both were associated with variations of the cry-wolf myth), quietly accepting the implicit conclusion: just as Amyclae lost even its silence in death by being silent in life, so his silence will end in death.

Then the refrain, which was lost in the tonalities built around the word *tacere,* comes quietly back: "Tomorrow he will love who has never loved; / tomorrow he who has loved will love again." This time, however, the zest and assurance of the opening line are gone. Some critics would read the closing line as a bitter, ironic comment; others see it as the expression of a "passion of regret."[20] I prefer to think that the invocation to the goddess has by this time become a genuine prayer.

The total effect is extraordinary. No Latin poet ever created a world of such profound beauty and then suddenly, almost inexplicably, rejected it. To understand the poem fully, we are driven to know the meaning of the word *tacere.* What did the poet's silence consist of? The word cannot mean "silence" in the literal sense. That interpretation would force us to consider the poet as someone intolerably modest. Furthermore, the personal outcry of line 90 forces us to reject such an overweening poetic conceit as an explanation. Neither can we accept another literal meaning—the one suggested by Pater's fiction—that the poet is actually dying. If that is true, then why the joy and exultation during the greater part of the poem? The poet does not say that he is actually dying; he merely suggests the notion of death through his simile. To force an exterior explanation upon the consciously interior working of the poem is to destroy the texture that has been created.

20. E.g., *Aphrodite* . . . , tr. F. L. Lucas (Cambridge, 1948), pp. 37 f.

Only the poem itself can hold the key to its mystery. The poet creates a totally subjective view of nature and love. He sees love as a cosmic principle that binds together the natural world, coupling beasts and fish and roses and boys and girls and the whole order of creation. He re-creates a vision of universal harmony that is so realistic (in his terms) that he is lured into his fiction. He even hears the birds that are part of tomorrow's dream. But once inside his portrait, he realizes that he is an outsider: that art is not life, that idealism is not reality, that when the play or the visual scene dissolves, the rest is silence. The world of the self can be enlarged—indeed, extended here over the whole order of creation; the microcosm and macrocosm can join for ninety magic lines; but when the creative self finds the real self in his fiction, that fiction no longer exists. The poet is thrown back into a world of brutal reality, of barbarous husbands and raucous swans, and the vision is gone.

Or is it gone? The line that closes the poem is identical with the line that begins it. The work is circular. Most readers will not want to begin reading the poem once they have finished it, but inevitably they will be drawn back to the opening words and the promise inherent in them. The vision does not exclude the comment upon the vision; the reality of the poet's situation does not cancel out the reality of his dream.

If we call the *Vigil of Venus* the most beautiful spring love lyric in Latin literature, then we must be prepared to define beauty in a way that somehow includes terror, love in a way that includes the absence or even the opposite of love, and spring in a way that includes the "winter ice" of Jaufré Rudel's vision. In short, nothing less than a definition that admits paradox will account for the statements in this poem.

The *Vigil* is in many ways unique in Latin literature. In language and composition, it is obviously somewhat removed from the classical styles of Vergil and Ovid. Yet we can detect a similarity of theme in the ambiguous way that it approaches nature and love. To examine the Latin love lyric even in general terms lies beyond the scope of this study, which is primarily concerned with the spring motif. Yet, in passing, the following lyric lines seem to have some bearing on the problem:

SAPPHO: I don't know why I'm running (in circles). I have two thoughts (purposes, intents).

ouk oid' otti theo. dicha moi ta noemata.[21]

ANACREON: I'm in love, yet I'm not in love. I'm mad, yet I am not mad.

ereo te deute kouk ereo. kai mainomai kou mainomai.[22]

CATULLUS: I hate and I love . . .

odi et amo . . .[23]

OVID: What chases me, I run from; what runs from me, I chase.

quod sequitur, fugio; quod fugit, ipse sequor.[24]

Maximus Tyrius noted that Sappho caught the whole paradox of love in a single word: *glukuprikon*, bitter-sweet.[25]

Paradox was very much a part of the classical attitude toward love. It was not consistently portrayed in a detached, rational manner: a prelude to automatic fulfillment, an operation conducted on a pleasure-pain principle, the "plastic plus

21. *Poetarum Lesbiorum Fragmenta*, ed. E. Lobel and D. Page (Oxford, Clarendon Press, 1955), Frag. 51, p. 39.

22. *Poetae Melici Graeci*, Frag. 83, pp. 210–11.

23. 85.1.

24. *Am.* 2.19.36; see also 3.14.39.

25. For Sappho, *Poetarum Lesbiorum Fragmenta*, p. 92; Maximus (ed. H. Hobein, p. 232) further cites Diotima's speech (*Symp.* 203–04), where Love is called the son of Plenty and Poverty, to show his paradoxical nature.

immediate satisfaction."[26] After the studies of Hermann Fränkel and others, it is possible to discuss the poems of Catullus and Ovid in terms of illusion and disillusion—in short, to approach them as poems and not as transcriptions of an actual experience.[27] Love in classical lyrics is usually treated as something experienced (as opposed to something imagined or envisioned), but there is still a difference between dramatic realism and historical reality. We do not have to know who the real Lesbia was; she has become the paragon of every Roman *belle dame sans merci.* The love poetry of any age would be utterly incomprehensible if it did not draw from a transcendental level of idealism for its primary inspiration. In Greco-Roman poetry, from Sappho's "Marble-throned, undying Aphrodite" to Ovid's *Art of Love,* this idealism springs from the religious sphere of Aphrodite-Venus and her divine son Cupid-Eros. But although Venus and Cupid were divinities, they were worshiped far more by poets than by preachers or prophets; the religious symbolism of love (arrows, nets, wounds, potions, and cures) soon became the personal, private symbolism of lyric poets.[28] Ovid codified these loosely bound mystical symbols into a half-serious, half-comic private mystique in his *Art of Love* and his lyric poems. Catullus,

26. Guido Cavalcanti, *Rime,* ed. and tr. E. Pound (Genova, 1931), p. 2. Classical rationality also praised by Lucas, p. 38; a bleaker point of view expressed by C. S. Lewis, *Allegory of Love* (N.Y., 1958), pp. 4–12.

27. *Ovid: A Poet between Two Worlds* (2d ed. Berkeley-Los Angeles, University of California Press, 1956); e.g., p. 21: "The identities of the two lovers have been merged in a mystic union." See also Godo Lieberg, *Puella Divina* (Amsterdam, 1962); Kenneth Quinn, *The Catullan Revolution* (Melbourne, 1959); Erich Reitzenstein, "Das neue Kunstwollen in den *Amores* Ovids," *RMP, 84* (1935), 62–88; Luck, esp. pp. 11–16, 59–61, 69–70, 152–71. For the antibiographical approach, see esp. Archibald W. Allen, "Elegy and the Classical Attitude toward Love: Propertius I, 1," *YCS, 11* (1950), 253–77, and the various contributions in *Critical Essays on Roman Literature: Elegy and Lyric,* ed. J. P. Sullivan (Cambridge, Mass., 1962).

28. For partial documentation, see Appendix; also, Wilibald Schrötter, *Ovid und die Troubadours* (Halle, 1908); J. P. Sullivan, "Cynthia Prima Fuit: A Causerie," *Arion, 1,* pt. 3 (1962), 34–44.

however, was the great portrayer of love in act. His collection of poems proceeds from the semidivine Lesbia who can transform any man who just sits near her into a god, to the less-than-human Lesbia who "now in the highways and alleys of the city / rolls the grandsons of great-souled Remus."[29] The ladies of Latin lyrics (Lesbia, Corinna, Cynthia) exist within the shadows of Venus, the ideal embodiment of feminine, passionate love. If they ultimately fade away into those shadows, it is simply because they are also "real" and are therefore subject to death, dissolution, and corruption—the legacy of the flesh.

At this point, we might very well generalize about the role of the lyric poet in classical literature. It is obvious that none of the poets already considered has taken pains to force the basic emotions he has expressed into an idealistic mold. None of them, for example, has approached spring as the birth of Dionysus-Bacchus; none of them has adopted the Dionysiac attitude toward death, nature, and love. Yet we know that the Eleusinian mysteries and rites of Dionysus were centered around spring festivals, and we surmise that immortality was very much a part of these rites.[30] Furthermore, none of these poets has resorted to an idealized system of philosophy. There is no mention of reincarnation or regeneration through nature. In short, none of these poets has been in the least doctrinaire. They have all spoken from the self as it relates to the external world. They do not look at nature (Greek *physis,* from *phyein,* that which grows—and hence withers; Latin *natura,* from *nascor,* that which is born—and hence dies) in the light of any transcendental teaching. This would seem to be the inherent genius of classical lyric poetry, for, as Werner

29. 51.1–2; 58.4–5.
30. In the main, I accept Cornford's sharp contrast of Apollonian-Olympic and Dionysiac-Earth Mother impulses: *From Religion to Philosophy* (N.Y., 1957), pp. 144 ff. The less anthropological Guthrie acknowledges the mystical-rational competing tendencies: *The Greeks and Their Gods* (Boston, 1954). The fullest statement of Greek mysticism occurs in E. R. Dodds, *The Greeks and the Irrational* (Berkeley-Los Angeles, 1951).

Jaeger has said, the Greek lyricists "did not see nature as an objective or aesthetic spectacle, like the shepherd in Homer who gazes with joy from the mountain peak upon the splendour of the midnight stars; they felt that the changes of sky and season . . . the cheering breath of spring, reflected the changing emotions of the human soul, and that earth and sky echoed and strengthened their cries of love and grief."[31]

It is interesting to note that two critics working in different periods arrived at the same conclusions about the origin of lyric poetry. Bruno Snell, accounting for the birth of Greek lyric poetry in the cities of Ionia, says that early Greek poets "discovered that a feeling may be divided against itself, distraught with an internal tension; and this led to the notion that the soul has intensity, and a dimension of its own, viz. depth."[32] Theophil Spoerri, commenting on the origin of troubadour poetry, said: "A love that fulfills itself becomes an act. The object comes into the foreground; the subjective expression disappears. The poet does not speak any more; he acts. But unfulfilled Love moves with its force the whole man, upsetting him all the way into the depths."[33] Both critics explain lyric poetry in terms of self-expression and paradox, factors already observed in lyrics that deal with spring.

Spoerri's interpretation is especially provoking because it ignores popular distinctions between "classical" and "romantic" love. Spoerri says simply that if love finds its object, poetry ends with marriage or consummation. The epic, which

31. *Paideia, 1,* 132; for an excellent general statement of lyric origins, see C. M. Bowra, *Greek Lyric Poetry from Alcman to Simonides* (Oxford, 1936), pp. 1–15. Although the epithalamion and threnody are characteristically considered lyrics, I would group them thematically with "choral hymns," reserving "lyric" for the more secular function. What acts are more sacramental in nature and less open to inquiry than marriage and death?

32. *The Discovery of the Mind,* tr. T. G. Rosenmeyer (Oxford, Basil Blackwell, 1953), p. 301.

33. *ZRP, 60* (1940), 304: "*Eine Liebe, die sich erfüllt, wird zur Tat, das Objekt tritt in den Vordergrund, die subjektive Bewegung verschwindet. Man spricht nicht mehr, man tut. Aber unerfüllte Liebe bewegt mit ihrem Drang den ganzen Menschen, wühlt ihn auf bis zur Tiefe.*"

is a consciously idealized work of art, may follow this development through to its logical end: Odysseus reunited with Penelope in Ithaca; Dante reunited with Beatrice in Paradise. However marriage (absolute fulfillment) is death to lyric poetry, is the end of romantic love, whether the lover be Ovid or Sappho or Bernart de Ventadorn. In a sense, the finest lyric poetry begins with some unattainability on the part of the object, with a tension between what is wanted and what is not had. Socrates was keenly aware of this paradox when he defined Love in the *Symposium* as lack, not fulfillment.[34] Denis de Rougemont is correct when he says that the history of western love poetry is not a history of marriage; but he is perhaps reaching for intangibles when he attributes this phenomenon to Celtic, Catharistic, or other esoteric sources.[35] Spoerri suggests more plausibly that it is not human nature to idealize or desire what one already possesses.

We can say, in relating the statements made above to the theme of spring, that if any Roman poets sincerely believed in life after death and a metaphysical reality imposed over the physical world, they did not convert their lyric poems into hymns. Indeed, even the *Homeric Hymns* are striking for their distinctions between divinity and humanity, although in other respects the worlds are coterminous. Catullus' *Hymn to Diana* (34) shows the practical Roman attitude toward religion, the desire for good works, good results (*bona . . . ope*, 23–24). If we are searching for an idealization of nature in classical lyric poetry, our search is fruitless. Polytheism is not pantheism; godhead and man are not one.[36]

However, the lyric poet is not the only kind of poet, and we might now consider other poems where the author is consciously imposing philosophical, religious, or romantic ideals

34. 200B–201C.
35. *Love in the Western World*, tr. M. Belgion (N.Y., 1940; rev. 1956).
36. The study of Wilhelm Ganzenmüller, *Das Naturgefühl im Mittelalter* (Leipzig, 1914), draws on a similar conclusion: "*So fand man in der Natur nur ästhetische, formale Werte oder—das eigene Ich*" (p. 9).

on his treatment of nature. In one sense, this examination is a digression, for we have already examined the lyric domain, which is the proper subject of this study. However, the poet of the *Vigil* drew heavily upon nonlyrical treatments of Venus and spring in the early part of his poem. In order to evaluate the achievement of the *Vigil*, it is worthwhile to examine some of these poems.

OLYMPIC RELIGION AND REALITY: THE SEARCH FOR AN IDEAL SPRING

In Hesiod, we find a treatment of spring that is free from paradox. In his *Works and Days*, the poet relates two different accounts of the origin of man, and these accounts are illuminating. One explains the creation of man by Prometheus, the theft of fire, and Zeus' revenge: "To pay for that fire, I'll give him an evil (gift)" (57). The gift is Pandora, woman. The practical dualism of this account is obvious; it gives evil a substantial basis in woman, and is close to literal interpretations of man's undoing through Eve. However, in line 106, Hesiod decides to tell another story about how gods and men sprang from a *single* source. Here is monism, replacing dualism; here is the notion of a *chruseon genos* (109), a golden race of men living in an Earthly Paradise. This Golden Age is gone, but the memory of it lives on in Hesiod's continuous view of nature, the harmony of the yearly round of seasons.

The dire old peasant from Boeotia was not a great poet, however. When he starts to talk about the joy of spring, his first thoughts are those of a practical man of the soil: "Plow in the spring" (462). To be sure, he mentions the beautiful flight of a swallow (568; a visual image, not a mythic reminder, as in the *Vigil*), but his poetry dissolves in a lecture on how to prune a vine. Actually, Hesiod does not seem to like the spring at all. He has to work too hard. He prefers the summer, especially June, because the crops are growing and he can stretch out under a tree and drink his wine (582–96). His final view of woman is likewise conditioned by a keen eye for the practical: "First of all, get a house, a wife and a plow-ox" (405).

Yet if Hesiod did not idealize nature, he supplied a general framework that more poetic poets could utilize. Vergil's *Georgics* are a bold recreation of the Golden Age in terms of Augustus' Italy. Like Hesiod, Vergil regards nature in terms of a realistic annual cycle. Since his poem is patently political, the Roman poet states quite unqualifiedly that Italy is now the land of "perpetual spring": *Hic ver adsiduum* (2.149). Vergil's great portrait of spring (2.319–42) has already been mentioned, since the poet of the *Vigil* knew those lines by heart. Indeed, Vergil's account of the marriage of Heaven and Earth became such a fixed topos that even the ninth-century heretical Christian philosopher Scotus Erigena cited those lines to account for the creation of matter through divine causes.[37]

Yet Vergil's portrait is not without disparate elements, even if it does manage to avoid paradox. "Birds singing on trees" are alternated with "bulls going after Venus (love)":

> *Avia tum resonant avibus virgulta canoris,*
> *Et Venerem certis repetunt armenta diebus.*
>
> (2.328–29)

Finally the whole picture, beautifully hyperbolic as it is, fades away in some lines that treat the manuring of a field. There is no apparent correlation between this picture of spring and the human psyche—only, possibly, a gasp at the wonder of nature, conditioned in turn by an awareness that, even if this is the Golden Age, men still have to toil and plow the fields. Augustus' world empire has to be fed. In the last analysis, Vergil's idealism is fully tempered by his practicality.

Ovid carried the circular-nature poem to its logical conclusion by writing a calendar poem, the *Fasti*. The fact that he

---

37. *De divisione naturae* (*PL 122*, col. 712).

left it unfinished may tell us something about his own feelings on the subject. Aside from the artificiality of the genre, the poem is hopelessly sedulous in its attitude toward the house of the Caesars. The exiled poet wrote it as a kind of penance (1.13): "Let others sing of Caesar's arms; I sing his altars" (*Caesaris arma canant alii; nos Caesaris aras*). The poet begins in January and decides to devote one book to each month of the year. Yet, with his characteristic interest in romantic detail, he often digresses into myths that are not really central to his thesis.

Book 4, the book of April, treats Venus' month, and lines 55 to 58 contain a capsule family history of the Caesars and their descent from the goddess, mentioning also Rhea Silvia, Romulus, and Aeneas. These lines may have furnished the poet of the *Vigil* with a thumbnail sketch for his portrait in lines 69 to 74. Yet the most important thing about Ovid's spring portrait is that it firmly binds together the related notions of spring, love, and poetry. The rhythm of the opening lines of the *Vigil* is close to Ovid's.

There is no time better suited for love than the spring:
in the spring the earth is glistening, in the spring
   the fields are loosened.

nec Veneri tempus, quam ver, erat aptius ullum—
vere nitent terrae, vere remissus ager.   (4.125–26)

Ovid's portrait is about as idealized as any in Latin literature. It is thoroughly romantic, yet it is also thoroughly abstract; the ideal situation is never related to any individual. We know, from the poem of the *Tristia* already considered, how Ovid himself reacted toward spring at this point in his life.

The dark side of spring comes back again and again in the myths of the *Fasti:* the rape of Rhea Silvia (3.11 f.), the rape of the Sabines (3.167 f.), the rape of Proserpina (4. 419 f.), the rape of Flora (5.183 f.). These little portraits of violence modify and enlarge upon the idealized picture that they enclose.

37

In the story of Flora, Ovid's romantic narration strays into realism:

> It was spring. I was wandering. Zephyr saw me. I ran.
> He followed. I fled. He was stronger than I was.
> Boreas gave his brother full rights for the rape.
>
> (5.201–03)

Once again we see the winter wind Boreas coupled with the spring wind Zephyr; but here the paradoxical coupling becomes a full-fledged irony: those two competing winds are actually brothers! In Flora's case, however, the story has the traditional happy ending of romance. She becomes the goddess of flowers and through her divinity enjoys the perpetual spring of the Golden Age (5.207): "I enjoy spring forever: forever the most glistening part of the year" (*vere fruor semper: semper nitidissimus annus*). But even this portrait does not completely escape the taint of violence, for we learn that Flora "first created flowers out of blood": *prima Therapnaeo feci de sanguine florem* (5.223). Then, when we recall that the myths of Narcissus and Hyacinth, two traditional spring flowers, contain the hidden seeds of violence, we might return to the *Vigil* and notice various undertones that were present in that poem before they erupted in the song of Procne.

For example, Venus herself was born from the castrated body of Saturn, lord of that bygone golden realm. The flowers in line 17 are crying for the loss of their virginity; the dewdrops left by the winds of night are tears. The roses in line 24 are made out of the blood of the Paphian. The forest in which the love-rite is going to take place must not be bloodied by Diana's hunt (38). The rape of Rhea Silvia is recounted in line 70; the rape of the Sabines in line 72. The whole poem is tinged with dimly perceptible strains of discord; but these strains are not consciously expressed until the poet hears the fateful cry of the swallow. This cry and its terrible meaning are as old as the *Odyssey,* in the passage quoted as the inscription for this chapter. Penelope heard the call of the nightingale, and her "heart was swayed this way and that" (*hos kai emoi dicha thumos ororetai entha kai entha,* 19.524) between the two poles of love and despair, fulfillment and loss.[38] We might at this point wonder how these myths involving rape, lust, revenge, and murder got attached to beautiful flowers, birds, and the most beautiful of all the seasons. But the answer to that question probably lies in the realm of social anthropology. It is enough for us here merely to point out the fact that these discordant elements exist, and that they have had an immense influence on poetry dealing with nature and love. The ambiguous qualities of the nightingale and narcissus have a direct correlation with the ambiguous feelings expressed in classical poems about spring. If I insist on this point now, it is for two reasons: first, I cannot see that the point has been adequately stated in rhetorical studies of the so-called "ideal" landscape; and secondly, the classical statement has a direct bearing on all medieval and modern statements.

It seems to me that Curtius and Wilhelm Ganzenmüller, in tracing an ideal landscape in classical literature, are correct in pointing out the basic elements of a tree, a grove, a brook, and some birds as the kind of rhetorical grouping that goes directly into later literature.[39] Yet if we begin to examine these landscapes a little more closely, they do not seem so ideal. The tracing of any rhetorical tradition must combine analysis with historical comparison. It is possible for a later poet to skim off the superficial rhetorical elements of an earlier poem for his own use; but this study is not so much concerned with rhetorical similarities as it is with similarities of total form.

---

38. There are two versions of the nightingale myth, aside from the Latin transferral of names for Philomela and Procne; see "Luscinia," Pauly-Wissowa, *Real-Encyc.; Meta.* 6.424 f. Homer is using a less popular version in which Aedon (literally "nightingale"; not the Greek Procne nor Roman Philomela), attempting to slay another's child, accidentally slew her own. See Albert R. Chandler, "The Nightingale in Greek and Latin Poetry," *CJ, 30* (1934), 78–84.
39. Curtius, pp. 183–202; Ganzenmüller, ed. cit.

Homer's influence on the creation of the bravura landscape
has been authoritatively sketched by Curtius.[40] Homer is the
father of the "lovely place" (*locus amoenus*) of Theocritus,
Vergil, and scores of later writers of medieval romantic epics.
As the Olympic religion began to lose its radiance in the shadows of Hellenic romance, the "lovely place" of nature became
more simply a "place for love"; Servius' commentary on the
Aeneid spelled out the conceptual relationship between natural beauty and love by etymologically linking *amor* and
amoenus.[41] Homer's little goat-island or the gardens of Phaea-
cia, real places set in the middle of the stormy sea of being,
eventually became gardens of bliss for Daphnis and Chloe.
His remote Islands of the Blessed, the ideal land of death,
were brought nearer to the world of reality by Vergil's Elysium
in the *Aeneid*. The pastoral tradition was moving closer toward the shadows of romance and mysticism, and these shadow-
lands were moving closer toward reality; eventually, when
the time came, the classical pastoral tradition would merge
completely with the Hebraic-Christian pastoral motif that lies
at the heart of early Christian expression: "The Lord is my
Shepherd." As the Apollonian masculine-oriented vision of
objective reality yielded to romantic, subjective statements,
artistic creations mirror the passing of world sensibility toward the feminine-centered Dionysiac urge of the earth-
mother cults; this tendency might be said to culminate, as
Erich Neumann suggests, in Apuleius' account of the ascent
of Psyche (Soul, a feminine principle) into the Olympic
pantheon.[42] At any rate, we will find that Christian poets
could relate Vergil's Elysium to the Christian Paradise and his
Golden Age of the *Georgics* to the Garden of Eden without

40. Pp. 185 ff.
41. *Comm. in Verg. Carm.* 6.638; 5.734; cf. *Satyricon*, 131: *Dignus amore locus.*
42. *Amor and Psyche*, tr. R. Manheim, Bollingen Series, 54 (N.Y., 1956). For a general statement of the change, see Franz Cumont, *Oriental Religions in Roman Paganism* (N.Y., 1956).

the slightest feeling of conflict. Romantic mystery foretold the coming of vital mysticism.

Homer's view of nature, as conveyed by the Shield of Achilles, is circular, like Hesiod's, and objective. It is a pastoral interlude in the epic vein, a haunting vision of human and natural concord glimmering out of the chaos of war:

And the renowned smith of the strong arms made on it a meadow
large and in a lovely valley for the glimmering sheepflocks,
with dwelling places upon it, and covered shelters,
and sheepfolds.[43]

Yet we might examine one small Homeric landscape that is often considered objectively "ideal," merely to show the ambiguous treatment of nature that culminates in the *Vigil of Venus.*

Calypso's garden (5.63 f.) is a place of perpetual spring or summer. Yet the birds perching in the trees are owls, falcons, and chattering sea-crows—all birds of prey, without the bittersweet qualities of the swallow and nightingale. The meadows around the garden are rich with violet and parsley (72–73). Parsley (*selinon;* Latin, *apium*) is an interesting flower. The Liddell and Scott dictionary says, for example, that "victors at the Isthmian and Nemean games were crowned with chaplets made of its leaves."[44] However, it was also attached to a dead man's door in ancient Greece.[45]

Vergil exploited the ambiguous quality of the plant in *Eclogue* 6, when Gallus, a living man, is gathered up by the

---

43. *The Iliad of Homer,* tr. R. Lattimore (Chicago, University of Chicago Press, 1951), p. 391 (18.587–89). Homer often contrasts the brutal reality of war with the natural serenity of spring: 2.87–93, 467–73; 8.306–07.

44. *Greek-English Lexicon, Abridged* (Oxford, 1949), p. 632.

45. For a somewhat similar analysis, see William S. Anderson, "Calypso and Elysium," *Essays on the Odyssey,* ed. Charles H. Taylor, Jr. (Bloomington, 1963), pp. 73–86. Earlier work by W. Kranz, "Die Irrfahrten des Odysseus," *Hermes, 50* (1915), 93–112, and Hermann Güntert, *Kalypso* (Halle, 1919). See also Adam Parry, "Landscape in Greek Poetry," *YCS, 15* (1957), 3–29.

41

Muses at Helicon and "crowned with bitter parsley": *floribus atque apio crinis ornatus amaro* (68). This poem, narrated by the drunken Silenus, is a curious mixture of transcendentalism, metamorphosis, life in death, and a real character placed in a make-believe Arcadia. In his *Eclogues,* Vergil often accomplishes in the third person what the poet of the *Vigil* does in the first: he contrasts realism and idealism, creating a totally subjective picture of external nature in which Messianic visions are blended with reality (*Ecl.* 4) or the vital love of Gallus becomes a living death (*Ecl.* 10). Calypso's garden eludes classification in the same way. If we see it as a Garden of Bliss, that is just a superficial view. It is also a garden of lust, death, prey—and Odysseus abandons it as soon as he can.

Vergil's pastorals are intriguing because the total form of the poetry resembles that of the *Vigil.* Bruno Snell's masterful analysis of the *Eclogues* has called attention to this subjective, romantic handling.[46] Vergil's shadowy worlds are not clearly the worlds of spring, but it is interesting to note one of the poet's most extraordinary uses of paradox in *Eclogue* 10. There Vergil puts a beautiful love lyric into the mouth of Gallus, who is wasting away with love. The lyric gains momentum until it reaches its culmination in that most supreme of Vergilian lines: "Love conquers all; and me—let me yield to Love" (*Omnia vincit Amor: et nos cedamus Amori,* 69). Then the poet steps into the picture he has created and exhorts Gallus to rise up and put love aside: *Surgamus!* (75). In one sense, he tries to cancel out everything that Gallus has said, to destroy Gallus' romanticism by a call to reality. Did he succeed? We need only think of the inscription on Chaucer's Prioress' brooch to observe the continuity of the dialectic.

The poems discussed in this section (the *Fasti,* the *Georgics,* the *Works and Days*) supply us with as objective an attitude toward spring as we can find. Yet there is no unmodified ideal-

46. *Discovery of the Mind,* pp. 281 ff. See also Charles Paul Segal, "Nature and the World of Man in Greek Literature," *Arion,* 2, pt. 1 (1963), 19–53, esp. 42–51.

ization in these works. At best, there is an acceptance of nature's bounty, with no small consideration of her utility. In Ovid's *Fasti* there is a certain amount of idealization, but that is qualified by the brutal portraits around it. It is to Ovid's *Metamorphoses* and Claudian's *De raptu Proserpinae* that we turn for two great romantic representations of spring, youth, and love.

FROM RELIGION TO ROMANCE: OVID AND CLAUDIAN

In the first few hundred lines of his *Metamorphoses,* Ovid contrasts a real and an ideal spring much more clearly than Hesiod did. The ideal spring is part of the Golden Age, and is gone forever: "Spring used to be everlasting" *(ver erat aeternum,* 107). An ideal spring for Ovid was already a thing of the past; it is a religious conception, just as the Garden of Eden is a religious conception. Even in the Silver Age it was gone, for then Jupiter shortened the length of the old-time spring. Modern spring, the "real" spring of lyric poetry, is merely one of the four seasons:

> Jupiter shortened the bounds of the old-time spring
> and through unequal winters and summers and falls
> and brief spring divided the year into four parts.

> *Iuppiter antiqui contraxit tempora veris,*
> *perque hiemes aestusque et inaequales autumnos*
> *et breve ver spatiis exegit quattuor annum.*
>
> (116–18)

There is little point in idealizing what is brief and passing, and in the *Metamorphoses* Ovid does not do this. He rushes on to the flood with Deucalion and Pyrrha, immersing himself in a world of nature gone mad, with fishes swimming on mountains. When he pulls himself out of these horrors, he descends into a totally subjective view of nature that is not unlike the one depicted in the *Vigil,* where the mythic and

43

real seem to join. In the Ovidian scheme, gods, men, and nature are sometimes indistinguishable (*panta rhei*: everything flows). Most of the *Metamorphoses* seems to take place in a dark forest of the soul where everyone and everything is searching for a self: some definition whereby it can rise above the natural chaos. It is a *selva scura* without a Golden Bough. It is not surprising that an ideal spring never penetrates this forest. Nor is it really surprising that the finest tale in the *Metamorphoses* is the story of Narcissus, which concerns the tragedy of self-love. Since so much of classical poetry has been discussed in terms of self-love (Aristotle's *philautia*), it is perhaps worth analyzing Ovid's treatment of the subject as a critique contained within the bounds of classical literature.[47] The curse was put on Narcissus by a rejected lover: "May he love himself—and not gain the thing he loves" (*sic amet ipse licet, sic non potiatur amato, 3.405*). It is a terrible curse; indeed, it is not totally unlike the curse that a nameless godfather put on Jaufré Rudel:

> And so my godfather cursed me:
> That I'd love and not be loved.

> *Qu'enaissi.m fadet mos pairis*
> *Qu'ieu ames e no fos amatz.*[48]

Finally we encounter Narcissus sitting on a bank above a pool. The landscape around him is one of the least ideal landscapes in Latin literature: "The pool was clear and crystal; but no shepherds approached it, no kids, no flocks, no birds, no beasts; no branch ever fell from the trees; grass grew around it, sprinkled with moisture; no sun ever entered to warm the wood" (3.407–12). This is a natural scene that is frightening for the very absence of nature. Without our even knowing it, Ovid has introduced us to the lonely inner world of his hero.

47. Fränkel's *Ovid* attacked the prevailing notion, largely through the *Amores*; he also noted, "In general, the character of the *Metamorphoses* is romantic and sentimental" (p. 81).
48. *Lanquan li jorn*, 48–49.

The boy is described as he sees himself in the pool: with an ivory neck (*eburnea colla*) and rosy, snow-white body (*in niveo mixtum candore ruborem*), terms that Ovid usually applies to women.[49] As the boy keeps staring at himself, he is caught in a terrible sequence of tensions, for "while he is seeking himself, he is sought; while he kindles himself, he burns": *dumque petit, petitur, pariterque accendit et ardet* (426). Suddenly the poet cries out: "Fool! Why are you running after false images in vain? What you're seeking is nothing; what you love you are losing. It's just the shadow of a reflected image . . . It has no substantial reality. With you it comes and it goes" (432–36). Narcissus tries to embrace that shadow and drowns; he is then carried off to the Underworld, where he gazes at himself while crossing the muddy Styx. Then as a kind of retribution, his flower, the narcissus, sprouts up to become his spring memorial. Thus the traditional happy ending of romance, extracted from the redemptive features of an earth cult, dispels the implied tragedy of psychic realism.

One thousand years later, Bernart de Ventadorn took this little myth of self-love and adapted it to the relationship between a man and a woman:

> I lost all power over myself,
> I wasn't mine from the moment on
> When she let me look into her eyes,
> Into a mirror I like so well.
> Mirror, since I first saw myself in you,
> Deep sighs have murdered me,
> And I lost myself the way
> Handsome Narcissus lost himself in the pool.

> *Anc non agui de me poder*
> *ni no fui meus de l'or'en sai*
> *que.m laisset en sos olhs vezer*
> *en un miralh que mout me plai.*

49. E.g., *Am.* 3.2.42; 3.7.7–8.

45

miralhs, pus me mirei en te,
m'an mort li sospir de preon,
c'aissi.m perdei com perdet se
lo bels Narcisus en la fon.[50]

The lines of both poets are extraordinary. Ovid's handling shows a depth of feeling that is often denied to classical love poetry; Bernart's shows a perception of the nature of love (with potential danger to the self) that is not usually granted the troubadours. In this myth, the two worlds meet. Hermann Fränkel's sensitive study, *Ovid: A Poet between Two Worlds,* has done a great deal to promote a deeper analysis of all of Roman poetry. The persistent notion of Ovid as the whimsical, self-willed lover of the *Amores* is gradually being recast into the broader perspective of Ovid as the great perpetuator of western romance.

The way Ovid is drawn into his portrait again suggests the *Vigil of Venus.* The poet creates an imaginary world so real that he tries to enter it himself; he shouts at his character, giving advice (giving, as a matter of fact, Platonic advice about the danger of attributing reality to a world of shadows, *umbrae*), but to no avail. The myth grinds on; Narcissus goes to the land of the dead. He is resurrected every spring to join Tereus, Philomela, Procne, and Itys to remind the world of the beauty and the fragility of the earthly estate. The story was once a part of Olympic religion; with Ovid, it is freed into the wider, more universal world of romance.

In Claudian's *De raptu Proserpinae,* another religious myth of spring is subjected to a full-scale romantic interpretation. It is the story of Proserpina, a myth that is bound up with all the mysterious forces of life and death. It is significant that no Greek ever set out to tell the story the way Claudian told it. Perhaps the doors of the Eleusinian mysteries were not to be so easily opened. It is also significant that Claudian never finished his task.

50. *Can vei la lauzeta mover,* 17–24.

The heroine Proserpina lives in an idealized fantasy world, in the vale of Enna in Sicily. This valley is the paragon of all idealized landscapes. Claudian catalogues the various trees (2.107–11) and flowers (2.128 f.) so authoritatively that Geoffrey Chaucer can imitate him centuries later.[51] Yet a dark shadow broods over the entire landscape. Pluto, the lord of death, has marked Proserpina for his bride. While her mother Ceres is gone, Pluto persuades Venus, Minerva, and even Diana (who is here the goddess of wild groves, not the patroness of chastity) to lure the girl into the valley, where she is to be abducted to the realm of death. In order to assist in the abduction, Enna itself begs Zephyrus (*Pater o gratissime veris*, 73: "most pleasing father of spring") to inspire flowers in the fields. The same undertones of violence that lurk in the *Vigil* are also lurking here. The roses shine with bloody splendor (*sanguineo splendore*, 92). The two famed spring flowers, Hyacinth and Narcissus, are conspicuous (131–36). Claudian adds, by way of parenthesis, that Hyacinth was born at Amyclae, the city of the *Vigil*. Just as she does in the *Vigil*, Venus exhorts the disguised goddesses and the virgin to enjoy themselves (119 f.). Then the violence that is everywhere implied breaks loose:

> Beyond her companions, the one great hope of the grain
>   goddess
> burns with a fierce desire to pluck; now she stuffs
> her laughing basket, osier-twined, with spoils of the field;
> now she weaves herself a flowery crown—not knowing!—
> the fatal coming of the bed. (137–41)

Claudian's most poetic moments come after the rape has been committed: the vale of Enna, the Earthly Paradise, becomes a wasteland; Hell becomes, by complete inversion, an Elysium. The entire land of death, not just the fields of Elysium or the distant Islands of the Blessed, at last knows a genuine spring.

Claudian's portrait of nature is perhaps the ultimate secular

51. *Parliament of Foules*, 176 f.

expression in classical literature of the mystical view of death-in-life and life-in-death. It is unfortunate that Claudian never went on to write the most dramatic lines of his epyllion, the lines in which his heroine would rest somewhere between the land of the living and the land of the dead. The poem ends abruptly with Ceres beginning her search, lighting a torch on Mount Etna (hence the perennial confusion between Etna and Enna in line 52 of the *Vigil*). Then it strays off, the way the river does in that listless, meandering poem *Amnis ibat;* or the way Ausonius' Moselle seems to flow on forever without a beginning or an end.

On the way to Hell, Pluto tells Proserpina that the land of the dead is a land of gentler west winds and perpetual flowers (2.288–89). Claudian assures us that "the whole of Nature was joyously awaiting the birth of new gods" from this pair: *iam laeta futuros | Exspectat Natura Deos* (2.370–71). Indeed, we feel, it was. By Claudian's time, the myths seem played out; their poetic enactments were no longer finished; many of the poets were silent. Claudian's Hell resembles the literal Christian Paradise. Claudian exploits the dramatic inversion for all it is worth, but does not really seem to appreciate its paradox. After all, he is telling a myth that everyone knows, a thousand years or more after its prime. Perhaps he merely stopped because he was bored. At any rate one feels at the end of the *De raptu* that he has reached more than the end of a poem.

There is one other large poem in Latin literature that touches on spring and love and that has had a direct effect on the rhetoric of the *Vigil;* it is Lucretius' *De rerum natura.*[52] Because it is a philosophical poem, we expect to find love treated in a systematic manner. Yet not even the poetic philosopher can escape ambiguity with regard to love. The Venus of Lucretius' invocation is a goddess, the patroness of the Roman state. She is also a philosophical principle that binds the spheres together. These are two of the ways in which the *Vigil*

52. Cf. Lucretius 1.2–3, 17–18, and *Perv. Ven.* 5–6, 65; 1.7–13 and 2–8.

sees her. Yet once Lucretius becomes involved with his atomic theory, love can be little more than an illusion, an emotion that tingles the atoms, a disaster, something to be shunned. In the fourth book of the *De rerum*, the word *nequiquam* (in vain) provides a dominant motif (e.g., 4.1110, 1133). The praise of love that opens the poem is balanced by dispraise once the problem is analyzed psychologically. Love as theory, as abstraction, is beautiful; but in practice, as Petronius once said, *Foeda est in coitu et brevis voluptas.*

THE FORMATION OF TWO TOPOI: THE EPIC AND LYRIC SPRING

It was now the beginning of the spring, the snow was gone, the earth uncovered, and all was green, when the other shepherds drove out their flocks to pasture, and Chloe and Daphnis before the rest, as being servants to greater shepherds. And forthwith they took their course up to the Nymphs, and that Cave, thence to Pan and his pipe; afterwards to their own oak, where they sat down to look to their flocks, and kiss and clip insatiably. . . . The soft breath of Zephyrus and the warm sun had brought some . . . [flowers] . . . forth; and there was then to be found the violet, the daffodil, the primrose, with other primes and dawnings of the spring. And when they had crowned the statues of the Gods with them, they made a libation with new milk from the sheep and from the goats. They began too to play on the pipe, and to provoke and challenge the nightingale with their music and song. The nightingales answered softly from the groves and, resuming their long intermitted song, began to jug and warble their Tereus and Itys again.

LONGUS, *Daphnis and Chloe*[53]

There are thus two springs in classical literature: the ideal spring of epic and narrative romance (Ovid's *ver aeternum;*

53. 3.12; tr. G. Thornley and M. Hadas (N.Y., Pantheon: Random House, 1949), pp. 108–09.

49

Vergil's *ver adsiduum*) and the "real" spring of lyric poetry
(Ovid's *ver breve*). Rhetorically, they are almost identical, because the lyric spring with its landscape seems to descend from
the epic springs of Homer and Hesiod, as Curtius has indicated.[54] Yet the functions of these landscapes differ according
to the operation of the genre in which they are enclosed. The
bravura landscapes in Homer's *Odyssey* or Longus' romantic
novel form lyric interludes in which various nooks in the natural world seem to be bits of heaven on earth. In this sense,
the pastoral tradition is closely connected to the epic vision
of the whole. That is why in this study I have avoided the epic-
bucolic or pastoral antithesis employed by Huizinga and
Empson, preferring the more neutral yet more inclusive term
"lyric" to signify the epic contrast.[55] For example, I have
treated Vergil's *Eclogues* and the *Vigil of Venus,* which
abound in pastoral imagery, as lyrics composed around a built-
in dialectic; yet I consider *Daphnis and Chloe,* which also
abounds in pastoral imagery, a romantic prolongation of the
epic narrative, a tale told entirely in the third person and
working toward a monistic restitution of things, as opposed
to a realistic examination of the shadows that lie between human ideals and reality. The medieval definition of comedy
and tragedy as basic underlying modes of expression is formed
around the simple concepts of fulfillment and nonfulfillment,
and it is this definition that I have employed up to this point,
equating the lyric with tragedy and the epic with comedy.[56]
Of course these bold definitions leave much to be desired, but
in the main the terminology of the artist Dante is much
simpler and much more flexible than that of the philosopher
Aristotle, who based his concepts on an empirical analysis of

54. P. 185: "With Homer the Western transfiguration of the universe, the
earth, and man begins. Everything is pervaded by divine forces."

55. J. Huizinga, *The Waning of the Middle Ages,* tr. F. Hopman (N.Y., 1954),
p. 39: "The themes are few in number, and have hardly changed since
antiquity; we may call them the heroic and the bucolic theme."; William
Empson, *Some Versions of Pastoral* (London, 1950); also Curtius, p. 187.

56. Locus classicus: Dante, *Epistula* 10.10.

plays. As far as "Greek tragedies" are concerned, the medievalist would view *Oedipus Tyrannos* as a true tragedy, but *Oedipus at Colonus* as a Divine Comedy, since the apotheosis of the King of Thebes is one of the high points of Greek mystical expression; both plays compose the epic view.[57] Although the landscapes of narrative romance are idealized on the surface in classical literature, dark undertones can be felt even in the most sublime and religious of Greek epics, the *Odyssey*. Gods mingle with men in the broad world of nature and even share the same beautiful nooks, but the distinctions between divinity and humanity are usually clearly drawn. Aphrodite is, as Richmond Lattimore says, the perfection of the essence (*virtus, arete*) of Helen; yet Helen is but an imperfect copy of the divine archetype; she will die, but Aphrodite is, as Sappho said, *athanat'*, deathless.[58] Therein lies the tragic crux of the matter. Aphrodite is the transubstantiation of Helen's essence, its divinely enduring perfection; Helen is not a consubstantial part of that perfection. The metaphysical aspects of Olympic religion tend ultimately to define humanity and thereby to distinguish. They do not usually, as in Christianity, work toward universal communion; they do not always join. The poet of the *Vigil* becomes a part of the cosmic order of things; then he fades away into the shadows.

Only in the hermetic worlds of late Hellenic romance do we sense the conquest of time and the human condition. The

---

57. See Snell, p. 43: "It is generally agreed nowadays that the various poetic genres which make up the literatures of the West, the epic, lyric poetry, and drama, coexist side by side." In terms of generic distinctions, it may be preferable to regard dramatic literature as a third component with epic and lyric; tragedy and comedy may then be considered *tones* which permeate the three divisions. However, the close relationship between drama and the epic vision of the whole is spelled out in any history of Greek literature; both are fundamentally religious in nature, at least in their origins, although the dramatic may work toward humanistic tragedy and realism. The lyric in its religious phase is the hymn, which also descends from or is contemporaneous with the epic, as I have defined it. The prose novel (Petronius, Fielding) is a late development, the realistic grandchild of the epic (Homer, Dante).

58. *Iliad*, tr. Lattimore, p. 54.

spring that is just beginning in the passage from Longus seems to be perennial. It will come back again and again. The novel ends with the lovers, who are protected by the God of Nature, Pan, locked in each other's arms after several stormy trials and perilous pursuits. The plot stops short of marriage because, as Spoerri suggests, possession marks the death of romance; marriage must be the end of fantastic illusions and the beginning of a realistic attitude toward adjustment. In the *Odyssey*, Odysseus treats Penelope with great love and respect—but he also makes sure that she has not betrayed him; he is not misguided by any romantic illusions about her weaving. We could search medieval epics for one small sign of this rather realistic devotion of a man to his wife and, as De Rougemont has pointed out, have trouble finding it. If the Church sanctified the sacrament of marriage, Christian poets of romance were singularly unimpressed.

The epic poet may utilize the framework of a religious system, as Homer conceives crafty Odysseus under the divine tutelage of Athena, the goddess of wisdom, or as Dante gradually surrenders his ego to ideology. Yet the greatest epics are not woven around the straight-hewed strand of the hero; musically, they are composed of many voices; the dissonant, negative cries of Elpenor, Menelaus, Dido, Helen, Paolo, Francesca, and Brunetto Latini supply the minor-key tonalities to the comic symphony conceived in a major key. The dialectic in epic is gradually suppressed for a vision of the whole: Odysseus survives the sea and Circe to put Ithaca (the Earthly Paradise as Polity) in order; Aeneas puts Dido and other distractions aside to pave the way for the Golden Age of Augustan Rome; Daphnis and Chloe escape pirates and panderers to lie in the sensual Paradise of mystico-sexual union; Charlemagne's army under God routs the heathen Saracens to save the Christian Empire (the Earthly Paradise as Polity again); the good knight in medieval romances defeats the bad one and wins the Grail or his lady or both; the quester in the *Roman de la rose* dispels the evil graces of society and at last gets a sniff of his precious flower in the new pagan-Christian Garden of Delight. Philosophically, the epic is constructed upon a dualistic principle that resolves itself into monism. Modern cowboy movies with their tediously identical plots are debased versions of the same general technique.

Allegory is a friend of the epic sensibility because allegory is the conceptual spelling-out of free-flowing dramatic elements, *une explication des principes,* a classification of the competing forces of light and darkness. (The consistent conceptualization of heroes and savior gods as solar forces merely underscores the religious origin of the epic form of art.)[59] We do not need to account for medieval allegory by going to the *Battle of the Soul (Psychomachia)* of Prudentius, where the passive virtues subdue the aggressive vices (how Prudentius struggles to make Patience, sitting on her monument, overcome Rashness!).[60] We must go beyond the *psychomachia* (soul-war) to the *machia* (war) of Homer; we must step back from Christian "virtue" (a psychic principle) to classical *virtus,* "manliness." The world sensibility may shift from the masculine virtues of the Homeric warriors (where Prudentius' Rashness would be tempered into Courage) to the feminine virtues of Prudentius (Humility, Meekness, Patience), but the battle rages on, and the good, however defined, always manages to carry the day. What separates a Homeric warrior from a medieval knight like Roland is not merely the classical portrayal of the splendid but touching death of Achilles in the horror of war as opposed to the glorious death of the Christian soldier fighting for the right (the curious Christian-Germanic idealization of war that Curtius, sitting in the ruins of Germany in the 1940s, pointed out), but a far more complicated vision of life that does not lend itself to erecting a dramatic structure

59. For the epic-religious interaction, see Joseph Campbell, *The Hero with a Thousand Faces,* Bollingen Series, 17 (N.Y., 1949); for a Christian interpretation of Homer, see Hugo Rahner, *Greek Myths and Christian Mystery,* tr. B. Battershaw (London, 1963), pp. 281–390.

60. Lewis, p. 69, commenting on *Psych.* 125 f.

between good Greeks and bad Trojans.[61] In the *Iliad,* we feel something for the death of the enemy Hector. In the *Song of Roland,* we feel no sympathy at all for the Moors, those cardboard forces of darkness aligned against the legions of light. It remained for Dante, an intellectual bourgeois who utterly ignored the Northern European chivalric tradition, to write the complex Christian epic in which we sympathize with the lost Francesca even while she is being condemned.

The allegorical method begins, as Bruno Snell has pointed out, with the gods of polytheism conceived as material personae who embody certain universal competing tendencies: Love (Venus), Justice or Wisdom (Minerva), Courage (Mars), etc.[62] Their competition and their multiplicity overrule the simplicity of monotheistic representation. One simply cannot ally himself with the Good in an unexamined way, because he cannot be sure whether the positive side in any question is represented by Aphrodite, Athena, Zeus, or Hera. For example, is love always good? Consider the Judgment of Paris. Even in the *Aeneid,* where Venus is the supreme power, the romantic love of Dido is a major obstacle to the foundation of order. Then, as the Olympic gods begin to lose their objective reality, their essences must be *recreated* in order to be perceived. The Romans, who adopted their religion almost wholesale from the Greeks, had to pursue the myths psychologically and realistically (as in Ovid's analysis of Narcissus, an earth-cult principle who becomes a psychic force: narcissism)

61. P. 185: "[Homer] reflects the view of life of a knightly ruling class. But the heroic ideal is not conceived tragically, heroes are allowed to feel fear, like Hector, and war is an evil. This the Christian-Germanic Middle Ages will no longer allow." Yet if the Greek heroes feel fear, and if war is evil, and death is the "one dark shadow [that] hangs over this happy world," why is the death of Achilles not tragic? Certainly Achilles' appearance in the *Odyssey* as a specter can hardly be said to show him as satisfied with the natural course of things. Every death in a world that "does not yet know the chthonic" (ibid.) must suggest unfulfillment in the afterlife, despite the fulfillment of a heroic ideal in the present life.

62. Snell, pp. 306–09; for another authoritative account, see Jean Pépin, *Mythe et allégorie* (Paris, 1958).

54

in order to discover their meanings—an act that the great historian of Christian dogma Adolf Harnack has defined, with reference to the philosophy of the Hellenic Age, as "romanticism."[63] Objective religious interpretation yields to subjective romantic reinterpretation; valid mysticism (the Persephone myth) becomes the romantic mystery of a little girl who is raped in a meadow (Claudian's Proserpina). When a mystical religion such as Christianity overcomes the competing chthonic religions (Magna Mater, Dionysus, Isis, Persephone) and sanctifies the long-suppressed consubstantiation of divine and human forces that the Apollonian gods generally forbade (except to such paradigms as Hercules and Oedipus), then Vergil's Elysium is a true prototype of the Christian Paradise; his Golden Age can serve as a model for the Garden of Eden; his Prophetic Eclogue becomes a true prophecy; Claudian's joyous Underworld acquires universal dogmatic reality.

This digression on the epic occurs here because I shall ignore its continuation in medieval literature until it crops up again in North France and Italy many centuries later. C. S. Lewis has traced the latter part of this tradition with exactness: gods are rationalized by Stoics; complex divine forces are reduced to philosophical concepts; these concepts are then adapted by Neoplatonic and Christian poet-philosophers, and ideas are "enlivened" in the treatises of Macrobius, Martianus Capella, Boethius, Alanus de Insulis, and Bernard Silvestris.[64] Lady Philosophy and Mr. Philology are the epic heroes of the Dark Ages. It requires many centuries for Christian monism to admit a two-dimensional character even in a consciously idealized work of art. Plato had suggested that we keep our eyes firmly fixed upon the good; Augustine and the early Church Fathers agreed wholeheartedly.

63. *Outlines of the History of Dogma, Abridged,* tr. E. K. Mitchell (Boston, 1957), p. 35. See Segal, esp. pp. 42–51.
64. For Lewis, see above n. 26. Snell's account of the origin of allegory is more penetrating, since it shows the interaction of religious and philosophical concepts in classical times.

In defining the epic, I have attempted to define the lyric, for I am calling a lyric essentially everything that an epic is not: psychic inquiry as opposed to kinetic questing; a statement of dualistic principles without resolution in monism; the preference of the contradictory first-person to the teleologically conceived third-person; life presented as a mystery composed of paradoxes (with the outcome essentially tragic) rather than comic assumption within a framework of belief. The juxtaposition of spring and winter that we have observed in classical lyrics dealing with the spring motif merely mirrors the many paradoxes concerning life and love that lie at the heart of the finest Greco-Roman lyric poetry. We find no happy spring songs in this domain, except as facets of the religious or romantic sensibility. Even when these landscapes do occur in the larger works, they are frequently flawed. The Greco-Roman religion was vitally concerned with reality; it had no consistent metaphysic with which to shroud the paradoxes of the physical world.

Yet despite the bitter-sweet tonality of the classical attitude toward love and nature, Greek and Roman poets bequeathed a valuable ideogram to later generations of poets, an ideogram that could be interpreted in many different ways. They linked the spring to youth, poetry, and romantic love, an archetype that is probably as old as human consciousness itself. We will go to Ovid's *Art of Love*—the great treatise that embodies the praise of love with the dispraise of love (*remedium amoris*)— for the last and fullest statement of this rhetorical grouping:

> And now, right now (*iam nunc*) remember your coming
>   old age
> So no lost time will slip away from you.
> And while you can, now (*etiamnunc*) while you're living
>   the years of springtime (*annos vernos*)*,
> Play! for the years are flowing like water.
> The wave that passes will never flow back.

*Heinsius; *veros*, Merkel-Ehwald

The hour that passes can never return.
You must use your time; time runs with nimble feet,
And what's good now will not be good later on.
These violets that are withering I saw in their bed;
This thorn was once a graceful garland I was given.
There'll come a time when you, who shut out your lovers,
Will lie a cold old woman in the wasted night.

(3.59–70)

This passage is worth keeping in mind, for it is capable of inspiring the melancholy of the later *Latin Anthology* as well as the joy of the *Carmina Burana*. Like the positive and negative aspects of the love dialogue within the treatise itself, this passage touches upon both tonalities. When love is linked to time and when spring is detached from the perfect circle of the seasons, not viewed as one of Four Quartets composing the epic whole, it is perhaps fated to become the cruelest month.

We must turn to one of the few surviving fragments of Orphic hymns to uncover a world view that successfully destroys the essentially tragic nature of a realistic vision of life, that consistently idealizes nature and gives an utterly comic (in the Dantesque sense) meaning to death:

Exalted, all-ruling Kore, bounteous in fruits,
Clear-shining one, horned, the one and only desired of all
    mortals;
The bringer of springtime, when thou art pleased with
    the sweet-smelling meadows,
When thou dost let thy heavenly form be seen
In the green, fruit-bearing growth of the field,
And art set free for the gathering of the mighty harvest
    sheaves . . .
Hear, O blessed goddess!
Let the fruits of the earth spring forth
And grant us peace alway, sound health, and a prosperous
    life;

Then at last, after a hale old age,
Lead us down to thy realm, O Queen,
And to Pluto, the Lord of all.[65]

This beautiful hymn can be heard across the ages, even though
the rites of Proserpina have long since vanished. The contrast
of Claudian's humanization of the goddess and the hymn's
essentially objective treatment is obvious. The hymnologist
never injects himself into the poem, except for the inclusive
and elusive "us" of the singers. The poem is patently idealistic
and dogmatic; it will admit no doubt about the goddess' ability
to perform the services required of her. It is beautiful in the
way that any work implying perfect order can be beautiful.
Spring growth and autumn harvesting (symbolically, life and
death) are coupled without any awareness of paradox. The
natural order of life is calmly transcended. The manner in
which this is done is so serene that the hymn would seem to
be totally unaware of any tension between life and death,
mortality and immortality. If anything, death comes last, is
"natural," and is in every way to be desired.

At first glance, the Persephone hymn might appear to resemble the shield of Achilles, where scenes of blossoming nature are juxtaposed with scenes of harvesting and death. Yet
the shield is a fragment of a larger poem, an island of peace in
a sea of war. The shield itself contains the "two cities of man":
scenes of joy and despair that jar the heart. It is also one of
the instruments provided for Achilles' death. The Persephone
hymn, on the other hand, stands alone, quietly resolving the
negative aspects of life within the positive. When the contradictory elements of life are suppressed by or subsumed within
the positive, the lyric dialectic is destroyed, and we have a
hymn, which is a vital part of the epic sensibility, a divine
comedy in abbreviated form.

When we examine the *Vigil of Venus* in the light of the

65. F. C. Grant, ed. and tr., *Hellenistic Religions: The Age of Syncretism*
(Indianapolis, Liberal Arts Division: Bobbs Merrill, 1953), pp. 110–11.

classical tradition, we are struck by its inclusiveness. The poem combines the methodology of a hymn to Venus with the lyric "I"; it thus creates a tragi-comic synthesis that makes its basic structure almost impossible to define in conceptual terms. The first 80 lines of the poem are a portrait of universal order created by a loving goddess. If the poem goes on to reject that vision, this rejection stems from the poet's insistence on his presence in the universe. He makes personal demands about the conjunction of idealism and reality that no religious worshiper or philosopher is entitled to make. Belief for the poet is not enough. He seems to reject the ultimate reality of his vision because it does not have a direct bearing upon the self. That is why he has left the world what is much more a lyric than a hymn. In dealing with the *Vigil,* then, we must not settle for a contrast between paganism and Christianity, and then interpret the poem historically. We must not consider the poet a man waiting in the shadows of a twilight world for the Gospel of Christ. He had the Gospel of Venus. The contrast is not between the poem and something outside the poem; it is between the contradictory elements within the poem: belief and non-belief, speech and silence, love and death, dreams and reality; the poem, in its total form, is a statement of these conflicts. It is the embodiment of a mystery.

In a great work of art, we must be prepared to acknowledge the fusion of the epic-hymnal with the lyric as I have defined them; we must be ready to face the tragi-comic synthesis. This is apparently difficult to do, for "paradox" to many people means "confusion," especially, as Leo Spitzer moaned, to the nineteenth-century scholars working in the positivistic, neo-Kantian tradition.[66] Long after the Symposium had ended and Alcibiades wandered away in a drunken haze, Socrates made a great aesthetic and philosophical point that none of the stragglers could understand: a man who can write tragedy should also be able to write comedy.

66. *L'Amour lointain de Jaufré Rudel,* Univ. of No. Car. Studies in Romance Langs. and Lit., 5 (1944), 42–44.

The interaction of secular and religious themes is of paramount importance to any study that approaches medieval poetry. We have found that interaction in the classical love lyric; we will find it throughout the remainder of this study. Classical poets compared man's life to falling leaves and cut roses. Spring in the *Vigil* is as much the season of death as of birth. Yet Jesus and the nameless poet of the Persephone hymn saw man's life in terms of the sowing and harvesting of wheat.[67] In the perpetuity of the grain, they saw the perpetuity of mankind; for them, both spring and autumn were seasons of glory. In classical literature, the tragic-paradoxical view predominates, although the viewpoint of mystical resolution was also present. At about the year 400, and for several hundred years thereafter, the history of the spring song becomes the history of the Easter hymn. One aspect of the human psyche waxes; the other wanes. The pale Galilean had conquered.

67. Matth. 13:1–9, 24–30, 31–34; 6:26 f.; Marc. 4:26 f. All biblical citations are from the Vulgate, unless marked *RSV* in text or quoted in English.

Don't go outside. Truth dwells in the inner soul.

noli foras ire; in interiore animae habitat veritas.

ST. AUGUSTINE

It's no crime to love, because, if it were,
God would never have bound even divine things with love.

Non est crimen amor, quia, si scelus esset amare,
nollet amore Deus etiam divina ligare.

CARMINA BURANA

2 Early Christian Hymns to the *Carmina Burana*

Early Christian Hymns: A Metaphysical Thesis

THE "Hymn at Cock-crow" by the fourth-century poet Prudentius ushers in the new age of Christian poetry:

> The bird, the messenger of dawn,
> Sings out the light is near,
> And Christ, the rouser of our minds,
> Now calls us back to life.

> He shouts: "Take up your beds,
> You sick, you sleepy, lazy ones:
> And chastely, rightly, soberly,
> Keep watch, for I am near."

> *Ales diei nuntius*
> *Lucem propinquam praecinit,*
> *Nos excitator mentium*
> *Iam Christus ad vitam vocat.*

> *Auferte, clamat, lectulos,*
> *Aegros, soporos, desides:*
> *Castique recti ac sobrii*
> *Vigilate, iam sum proximus.*[1]

The poem opens on a note of martial vigor and assurance. The rhythm is iambic dimeter, a meter well suited for marches and processionals. It is a somewhat difficult meter for sustained poetry because there is a sense-pause at the end of almost every

1. *Cathemerinon* 1.1–8: Prudentius, *Carmina*, ed. T. Obbarius (Tübingen, 1845), p. 3.

line. Since each line contains only four feet, the poet must say a great deal in a very limited time sequence if he employs the meter correctly. Prudentius puts the short, choppy rhythm to good advantage by charging it with vital language. The words have a telegraphic quality; they veritably shout at one from the page. They are written to be sung in unison, *alta voce*.

At first glance, Prudentius' poem may seem far removed from the realm of classical Latin literature. Yet it does bear certain resemblances to the *Vigil of Venus*. In both works, the poets summon divinities which are to emerge from the shadows and create a world-order. Both poems begin with birds singing, immediately creating a scene drawn from external nature. The world of the *Vigil* was set in an atmosphere of spring, in which the poet was also waiting for the dawn of tomorrow's festival. In the Christian world, Easter services are traditionally held at dawn; hence the alba and spring song tend to fuse. Dawn is to the day what spring is to the year: a time of rebirth, a moment of reawakening. Stylistically, Prudentius' hymn also shows a tendency toward strong internal rhymes (particularly in the sixth and seventh lines), a feature abundantly revealed in the *Vigil*.

Yet despite these similarities, Prudentius' poem departs immediately from its pagan counterpart when a common rooster announces the coming of the dawn.[2] This simple barnyard creature has no place in Latin nature poetry, the realm of the aristocratic nightingale, swallow, and hawk. Furthermore, Prudentius' god appears suddenly in the fourth line. The goddess of the *Vigil* spoke only through the poet's expectant visualization of the future; as far as the poet himself was concerned, she never did appear. Prudentius' god not only ap-

2. The sacramental nature of the rooster was established in Matth. 26:34, 74–75; for earlier use, see Job 38:36, Prov. 30:31. Conceptualized by Ambrose, *Hexaemeron* 5.24 (*PL 14*, col. 240); given the significance of "castrated" martyr by Isidore, *Etymologiae* 12.7.50 (*PL 82*, col. 466). For the opposing figure of the lustful cock, see Eustathius (*PL 53*, col. 949).

pears but announces that he is near; his voice will brook no despair.

Then the Christian poet effects a time distortion much like that observed in the *Vigil,* when tomorrow's festival suddenly seemed to be beginning today. Christ says, "I am near." The rooster sings about a light that is near. Dawn seems about to break, or is perhaps already breaking. Yet Christ also says: "Keep watch." A vigil or all-night watch would imply a long time span, as in the classical *per*vigilium. A problem therefore arises: how can we keep vigil all night when the dawn is already upon us?[3] Furthermore, are we sleeping *(soporos)* or are we listening to the cock crow? We seem to be not only sleeping, but dead, for Christ in line 4 is summoning us back to life *(vitam).* But if we hear Christ's voice and the rooster's call, if we respond to some marvelous moment that is about to break upon us, how can there be time to "live soberly and chastely and uprightly"? How can we compress a whole lifetime of virtue into a very few moments? There is a compelling urgency about this poem: hurry up, it's time. We might think: no, it's already too late. Yet the god of the poem says: it's never too late; I'm near. In Prudentius' work, nearness and distance, time and space begin to lose their usual meanings. The earthly "reality" of this poem is intentionally unreal. Even the rooster seems to be more than a mere rooster.

The Christian poet will not let us assign arbitrary meanings to his symbols. He tells us quite clearly what they mean:

> That voice by which the birds all crow
> Standing under that very peak
> A little before the light breaks through
> Is but the image of our Judge.

3. The notion of life as a constant sequence of vigils was developed in Ps. 62:1: *"Deus Deus meus ad te de luce vigilo,"* and 7–9, 91:3; Is. 21:6–12; Job 7:4. Cf. Bernard, *Sermones in Cantica Canticorum* 17 *(PL 183,* col. 856): *"Vigilandum proinde, et vigilandum omni hora, quia nescimus qua hora Spiritus venturus sit, seu iterum abiturus."*

> *Vox ista, qua strepunt aves*
> *Stantes sub ipso culmine,*
> *Paulo ante quam lux emicet,*
> *Nostri figura est iudicis.*   (13–16)

The rooster is a metaphor (*figura*) or figurative image for Christ. The words that Christ spoke in the second strophe were a translation into human terms of the animal's crowing. Therefore, the rooster has no reality in and of himself; he has reality only insofar as Christ speaks through him. Prudentius forces his reader to attach broader meanings to the very simple visual images of his poem. First, he equates the individual with the genus: the one rooster is seen in the light of all roosters; by extension, the one coming dawn is equated with all coming dawns. Secondly, the generic classification drawn from nature is lifted to a level where it acquires superior meanings that are not evident from an empirical analysis of the physical world: all earthly roosters are divinely ordained harbingers of Christ; by extension, all earthly dawns point toward the One Great Dawn or awakening that is to come. Objects derived from the world of natural reality become *meta*phors; natural reality itself begins to assume *meta*physical, universal meanings.

Prudentius continues to spell out these meanings in no uncertain terms:

> This sleep that's given us in time
> Is but the image of endless death.

> *Hic sompnus ad tempus datus*
> *Est forma mortis perpetis.*   (25–26)

There is no need to wonder how Prudentius felt about the all-night festivities of Venus. He equates night and sleep with evil, sin, lack of consciousness, yielding to the emotions. He equates day and light with goodness, toil, chastity, and sobriety. It is a mechanical, two-dimensional structure, in which the single dimension of goodness is heavily accented. The day always comes to drive away the night, and thus we have a symbolic proof of an order in time that assures us of a supernatural order beyond time. Yet quite unconsciously Prudentius has created a puzzling situation. If the One Dawn always drives away the One Night, then how, in the lines cited above, can death be said to be eternal? The poet is caught up in the symbolic war that he has created through his use of the traditional symbols of light and darkness. The poet wants desperately to portray the conquest of the light, but he cannot forget those shadows; he cannot forget those sleeping ones who have not responded to the rooster's call. In fact, they are the ones who create the dynamic development in his poem. For after opening on a note of complete assurance, the poet breaks into a fervent prayer just three strophes from the end of his poem:

> Weeping we cry to Jesus
> With prayers and sobriety;
> His anxious supplication
> Forbids the chastened heart to sleep.

> *Iesum ciamus vocibus*
> *Flentes, precantes, sobrii,*
> *Intenta supplicatio*
> *Dormire cor mundum vetat.*   (81–84)

Jesus had spoken in the second strophe of the poem. Now, in a matter of 80 lines, he seems very far away, so far that he can be reached only by prayers. The joyous moment of dawn that was about to break in the opening lines of the poem seems far away too. The poet is weeping. The world of the here and now, however much it may be foreshadowed by a world to come, is a vital part of this poem.

Prudentius tries very hard to dispel the elements which are creating conflict. In fact, in his final strophe he accomplishes this rout of paradox through the grammatic implication of a prayer:

> Thou Christ, shake off our slumber,
> And break the shackles of the night,
> And loose for us our ancient sin
> And usher in the newborn light.

> *Tu Christe sompnum dissice,*
> *Tu rumpe noctis vincula,*
> *Tu solve peccatum vetus*
> *Novumque lumen ingere.*　　　　　　　　(97–100)

Prudentius strongly implies that the Light will win and Darkness be forever banished. Yet logically and structurally, the darkness is there unto eternity. The problem of evil—the great bugaboo of western monistic philosophy and monotheism—remains a problem, even in the face of triumphant Christian idealism. Prudentius struggles to make his belief come out right and manages it through a prayer. Yet it is his struggle for expression, not the statement of his belief, that enables us to discuss his hymn as a lyric poem.

What ultimately sets Prudentius' work apart from the *Vigil*, where the poet yielded the self to darkness and death, is the Christian poet's insistence that his own self and everything else in his poem make sense only when considered from a metaphoric point of view. The poet of the *Vigil* would not surrender the self for a moment to a religious vision or his own fiction; Prudentius finally collapses in the arms of Christ. Even if we read the last occurrence of the refrain in the *Vigil* as a prayer, the goddess Venus is never attributed with the powers that Prudentius assigns to Christ. Venus is a force *of* nature; Christ is a force *above* it speaking *through* it. The conflict in the *Vigil* arose between the poet's self and nature; in Prudentius, it arises between two different natures: the natural and the supernatural. Prudentius does not grieve for himself, but for his fellow man: "Love thy neighbor as thyself." Christian charity, an impassionate principle aligned with virtue, has replaced passionate *amor*.[4] The love festival is now in the hands of the Virgin King and Queen.

The "Hymn at Cock-crow," with its continuation of a dramatic structure in a new mystical climate, is typical neither of Prudentius' poetry nor of other early Christian hymns. The difference can be observed in a dawn hymn by St. Ambrose, the father of western Catholic hymnology:

> Splendor of the fatherly glory,
> bearing the light out of the light,
> O light of light and fount of light,
> O day that lights our day.

> *Splendor paternae gloriae*
> *De luce lucem proferens,*
> *Lux lucis et fons luminis*
> *Diem dies illuminans.*[5]

Out of the fifteen words used in this single strophe, Ambrose selects nine words that either connote or denote light. He will not even admit an image of darkness for the sake of expelling it, as Prudentius did. He erects a mystical structure by compounding abstractions. Ambrose is trying to define God, the good Creator, the Supreme Virtue, through the personage of the Son. Instead of creating Christ as a dramatic character involved in a drama, Ambrose conceives him as an absolute, idealized image. He thus avoids paradox, personification, and dramatic conflict by keeping his eyes fixed firmly upon an absolute Good. Ambrose achieves total mysticism with complete simplicity. As a Christian mystic, he leaves nothing to

---

4. Classical definition by Augustine, *De doctrina Christiana* 3.10.16: *"Charitatem voco motum animi ad fruendum Deo propter ipsum, et se atque proximo propter Deum: cupiditatem autem, motum animi ad fruendum se et proximo et quolibet corpore non propter Deum."* Also, of course, 1 Cor. 7, which marked the death of pagan "romance."

5. *An. Hymn. 50*, no. 5, pp. 11–12, st. 1; for a statement of Prudentius' achievement, see Aimé Puech, *Prudence* (Paris, 1888), pp. 86–101.

be desired; as a poet, he omits all the elements that modern critics are accustomed to associate with poetry. Ambrose strikes us as an advanced thinker; he impresses us as a poetic craftsman largely because he seems to be an innovator. Yet Ambrose, like most early Christian writers, was interested in poetic art only as it influenced his belief. He wrote hymns under stress and duress, to help his congregations add courage to their faith.[6] His hymn is a marching song for the Church Militant; his goal was Heaven.

Yet Ambrose's mystical bent is not common to all men or to all Christian poets. Prudentius himself created a spring land-scape based primarily on classical rhetoric:

> Then he orders them in lovely fields
> to live, in leafy-haired places,
> where perpetual spring smells sweet,
> where in four flowing rivers the water
> bathes swiftly the many-colored fields.

> *Tunc per amoena vireta jubet*
> *Frondicomis habitare locis,*
> *Ver ubi perpetuum redolet*
> *Prataque multicolora latex*
> *Quadrifluo celer amne rigat.*[7]

Yet the scene described in these lines is not contemporary. It is the Garden of Eden, the Christian garden of former perfection that corresponds with the pagan Golden Age.[8] Like

6. Augustine, *Conf.* 9.7 supplies the historical background; also, Ambrose, *Ep.* 21.34 (*PL 16*, col. 1017).

7. *Cath.* 3.101–05: *Carmina*, p. 12.

8. Gen. 1–3. For an early commentary aligning Adam with Nous and Eve with Aisthesis, see Ambrose, *De paradiso* 15 (*PL 14*, cols. 311–14); for bird lore, *Hex.* 5.12 (ibid., cols. 222 ff.). The Hebrew pastoral tradition runs throughout the Old and New Testaments, but is dominant in the Psalms (e.g., 22, 64:9–14, 103:10–24, 106:33–38). The good man or state is often likened to a flowering vine or tree (Ps. 91:13–16, 95:11–13; Is. 11:1; Os. 10:1, 14:7; Jer. 11:16; Joan. 15:1–11; Apoc. 22:1–2). For the basic elements, which resemble the classical picture, see D. W. Robertson, Jr., "The Doctrine of Charity in Medi-

Ovid, Prudentius does not mourn long over the loss of *ver perpetuum*. He damns Eve (as Hesiod damned Pandora), rejects the Vergilian notion of an Earthly Paradise under a temporal ruler (City of Man), and ends his poem by stating his hope of reaching Heaven (City of God). The Celestial Paradise of the future was of far more interest to Prudentius and most Christians than the paradise of the present or past. In another hymn, Prudentius paints that coming Paradise for us. He creates a truly ideal spring landscape by using traditional pastoral images, drawn partially from a Vergilian Elysium and from the language of Genesis and the Psalms:

> The busy shepherd calls back
> (the lost sheep) and, driving off wolves,
> carries it on his shoulders
> back to the open sheep-pen.

> He restores it to green pastures
> and fields where no thorn shakes
> with rude burrs, no thistle thick
> with spikes covers the seed,

> But where there's a forest thick
> with palms, and the grasses' bent
> heads know spring; the eternal
> laurel shades a glassy brook
> for the living.

> *Inpiger pastor revocat lupisque*
> *Gestat exclusis humeros gravatus,*
> *Inde purgatam revehens aprico*
> *Reddit ovili:*

---

aeval Literary Gardens," *Speculum, 26* (1951), 24–49. Some differences in plant and animal species help to classify the rhetoric: the nightingale is not Hebraic; the cedar is not Greco-Roman, etc. Robertson later qualified this essay: *A Preface to Chaucer* (Princeton, 1962), p. 92, n. 67, because of its "polarities." Cf. the usage of Rahner, pp. 72–73.

CHRISTIAN HYMNS TO THE *BURANA*

Reddit et pratis viridique campo,
Vibrat inpexis ubi nulla lappis
Spina nec germen sudibus perarmat
Carduus horrens:

Sed frequens palmis nemus et reflexa
Vernat herbarum coma, tum perennis
Gurgitem vivis vitreum fluentis
Laurus obumbrat.[9]

But again, this landscape has no application to the present. It can be understood only metaphorically, as the dawn poem was interpreted. The picture owes a great deal to the Psalms: The Lord is my Shepherd . . . He makes me lie down in green pastures. Yet the laurel tree and the visual scene in the third strophe are Vergilian. In these verses, the Hebraic and Greco-Roman pastoral traditions meet. Both are given their due, but the Hebraic metaphoric approach is here dominant. Let us spell out these terms and arrive at the parable or sum of equations:

> The shepherd is the Lord.
> The sheep is the lost Christian.
> The sheepfold is the Church.
> The green pastures are Heaven.[10]

The picture exists ultimately in terms of these superior meanings. Vergil's pastoral fantasy-land may blend in with Christian mysticism, but the light of God drives out the shadows just as the truth of Christ expels paradox. The mystical qualities that pervade the Vergilian world are the only true values in the Christian scheme. Prudentius' setting is not Arcadia or Sicily seen through a glass darkly. It is in some ways far more

9. *Cath.* 8.37–48: *Carmina*, pp. 32–34.
10. See Rabanus Maurus, *De universo* (*PL iii*, cols. 9–614); e.g., col. 201: *"Pecora autem aliquando peccatores, et qui voluptatibus dediti sunt"*; col. 203: *"Ovile ovium Ecclesia est"*; ibid., citing Joan. 10: *"Pastor, Christus."* One becomes aware of the danger of ascribing dogmatic meanings to animal symbols, for most are ambiguous: even the raven can signify Christ (col. 252)!

remote than those subjective worlds of the imagination. Yet at the same time, Prudentius' pastoral scene is immanent and real. The loving shepherd and the lost sheep have a homely quality; they are as simple and effective as the crowing rooster. The aristocratic tendencies of classical literature come to an end with Prudentius. A farmer or shepherd is not romanticized by the Christian poet; they are taken at face value, and in the orderly routine of their lives the poet sees the enactment of universal law. Yet, of course, the literal side of the rhetoric is unimportant, although we may sense the paternal nature of God as the kind shepherd. The perennial laurel and the intrusion of the word *vivis* (for the living) forbid us to interpret the scene realistically. Perennial life can occur only in a Christian Paradise; this little codified metaphor or parable has meaning only insofar as it relates to that other world. Yet in Prudentius' time, that other world was the world of true reality.

Thus, the Christians perpetuated the classical epic notion of an ideal spring in two ways: they interpreted the lost Christian garden in terms of the lost pagan Golden Age; they suggested a future garden to match the blessed fields of Elysium. But what became of the "brief spring" of classical lyrics? What about youth, spring, and romantic love, the world of the here and now (Ovid's *etiamnunc*)? The answer is quite simple: the Christians did not write lyric poems as I have defined them. They wrote *hymns,* consciously idealized works of art, usually addressed to divinities. None of the Christian poets in the age of Augustine created a garden of the personal imagination; none of them sang about the coming of spring in Alexandria or Rome and the effect that it had upon his soul in purely personal terms. Lyric expression waned; epic wholeness ruled. And their epic narratives? Officially, they had only one plot, one narrative: *To Biblion,* The Book.

In the fourth and fifth centuries, Christian poets were trying to make the Old and New Testaments palatable to the sophisticated Vergilian taste of the upper classes. St. Jerome's laconic Latin translation had to be embellished, and Vergil's *Georgics*, already cited for its influence upon the *Vigil*, supplied the inspiration for descriptions of the Garden of Eden and the Creation. For purposes of comparison, we might recall three of Vergil's most memorable lines:

> *Hic ver adsiduum* ...   (2.149)
>
> *Vere tument terrae, et genitalia poscunt.*
> *Tum pater omnipotens fecundis imbribus Aether* ...
>
>   (2.324–25)

When we examine a hymn on the creation written by the early fourth-century Roman noblewoman Proba, we find: *tum pater omnipotens* and *vere tument terrae et genitalia semina poscunt.*[11] As late as the sixth century, Avitus beautified his description of the Garden of Eden with the words: *Hic ver adsiduum.*[12] Raby has called attention to recurrent Vergilian echoes in Dracontius' *Hymn in Praise of God* and Marius Victor's *Alethias*, a poetic paraphrase of the Book of Genesis.[13] Vergil's perpetual spring under Augustus could blossom again in any European monastery, no matter how far north. Peculiarly enough, the Roman Paradise Gained supplied the rhetorical framework for the Christian Paradise Lost. Yet this new tradition of adaptation was doomed to failure. These poetic paraphrases of the Bible did not supplant either Vergil or St. Jerome. Vergil went on being read as Vergil; his portrait of the Earthly Garden of Bliss as a facet of reality could be imitated without being perpetuated in spirit. Certainly the flowering Italy of the Caesars had no bearing upon the Christian Paradise to come. The sobriety of all the early hymns (in the Latin world, but not necessarily the Byzantine) overruled Oriental opulence, even as a just reward.

11. *Cento,* 64, 75: *CSEL 16,* ed. C. Schenkl, p. 573; paralleling Gen. 1:4–16.

12. *De mundi initio,* 222: *MGH 6,* pt. 2, ed. R. Peiper, p. 209; see also 46–48, p. 204.

13. F. J. E. Raby, *History of Christian-Latin Poetry* (2d ed. Oxford, Clarendon Press, 1953), p. 97 (Dracontius), p. 77 (Victor).

What did the return of spring's warmth mean to an early Christian? On the surface, nothing. Augustine spoke for the whole Church in its early phases when he said, in one inscription quoted for this chapter, "Don't go outside." We can perhaps understand these words better when we realize that even in Augustine's lifetime, people were still celebrating the rites of Dionysus, Venus, Maia, Flora, and Proserpina. Later these rites went underground, but James Frazer could still find traces of them throughout Europe in the twentieth century. Spring could mean to Augustine only what the dawn meant to Prudentius: every spring was but the shadow of the one spring; every rebirth of the physical world was but a sign of the one great rebirth in Christ. Christ's passion and resurrection took place in the spring, and this miracle was imposed over the more obvious empirical fact that trees were leafing again and birds were singing. Christian contempt for natural phenomena (*contemptus mundi*) is best illustrated by a remarkable hymn written by Paulinus of Nola, who died one year after Augustine:

> Spring opens the voices of birds; but my tongue
> considers the birthday of Felix my spring . . .
>
> *Ver avibus voces aperit, mea lingua suum ver*
> *natalem Felicis habet.*[14]

Felix' birthday occurs in the winter, but does this bother Paulinus? Not at all. He paints a spring landscape over the snow, insisting, "Sadness and the winter of the soul, with cares forced aside, have left our hearts" (*Cedit pulsis a pectore curis / maeror, hiems animi,* 7–8). Then Paulinus prays to God to be transformed into a nightingale (*philomena*), so that he can sing a varied song: sometimes happy, sometimes shrill, sometimes almost tearful (*quasi flebile carmen*). Paulinus welcomes the ambiguous voice that cut across the heart of Penelope. He

---

14. *Carmen* 23, 1–2: *CSEL 30*, pt. 2, ed. W. von Hartel, pp. 194–206.

will take the bird's tragi-comic strains and turn them into a monistic praise of God, just as he will turn winter's ice into spring warmth. Paulinus' hymn is one of the most remarkable in western literature because of its complete mystical inversion. Through sheer strength of belief, Paulinus achieves what the poet of the *Vigil* had only prayed for: he makes his dream reality. He believes, and all things are possible for him.

A new spirit breathes over this early Christian poetry: all losses are restored and sorrow ends. Spring qua spring is nothing; spring qua Easter is everything, and there is only one word to express its miraculous effect upon the soul: *gaudium,* joy, a word that one almost never finds unqualified in classical expressions of the spring motif.[15] Even in the Orphic "Hymn to Proserpina," which best expressed the mystical resolution of contradiction, joy and life were not presented as single facets of experience: they were quietly coupled before being quietly resolved in terms of mystical idealism.

The Christian Easter hymns, however, are anything but quiet. The iambic dimeter marching beat insists on a resolution that barely admits a contradiction:

> When Christ arises from the tomb,
> He returns victorious from the depths,
> and puts the tyrant into chains
> and opens up His Paradise.

> We ask You, author of us all,
> in this Your Easter joy,
> from every violence of death
> to keep Your people safe.

> *Cum surgit Christus tumulo,*
> *Victor redit de barathro,*
> *Tyrannum trudens vinculo*
> *Et reserans paradisum.*

15. For scriptural usage, see Gal. 5:22; also general tone of Ps. 64, 67, 83, etc.

> *Quaesumus, auctor omnium,*
> *In hoc paschali gaudio*
> *Ab omni mortis impetu*
> *Tuum defendas populum.*[16]

This hymn, frequently attributed to St. Ambrose but more reliably dated in the sixth century, shows the totally new attitude toward spring that has entered western literature. For one thing, the word "spring" never appears in the poem; it is replaced by Easter (*pascha*), a word of Semitic origin. Greek words from the New Testament (*barathro, paradisum,* ultimately Persian) vie with Latin words. There is no landscape in the hymn at all. The whole poem is but a single-purposed affirmation of Christ's resurrection, of the triumph of life over death. The phrase *in hoc paschali gaudio* can be taken as a motto for the poem, and it serves as a leitmotif in other Easter hymns.

Another hymn from the same period combines the alba or dawn poem with the spring poem and begins with a natural setting:

> The light of dawn is growing red
> and heaven shouts its praises,
> the world has joyous jubilee,
> while groaning Hell is howling.

> *Aurora lucis rutilat,*
> *Caelum laudibus intonat,*
> *Mundus exsultans iubilat,*
> *Gemens infernus ululat.*[17]

Yet the light of the sun (a natural image) disappears immediately in the personification of jubilant heaven. The metaphysical redeemer appears in his terrestrial role as a most powerful king (*rex fortissimus*), and the world is bathed in the

---

16. *An. Hymn. 51,* no. 83, p. 87, sts. 6–7; for authorship and dating, Raby, *Christian-Latin Poetry,* p. 41.
17. *An. Hymn. 51,* no. 84, p. 89, st. 1.

"clear joy of Easter" (*Claro paschali gaudio*). The poem ends
with a promise on the part of the worshipers to sing Christ's
praise forever.

Christian joy reached a peak of expression in a long poem
by Venantius Fortunatus (d. c. 610) which produced the Easter
processional *Salve, festa dies*.[18] Venantius accomplishes on a
grand scale what Prudentius and the anonymous hymnologists
merely suggest with quick strokes. He creates a full-blown picture of a spring landscape that can rival any found in Ovid
or Vergil. Indeed, it contains echoes of both these pagan poets.
Gradually, however, Fortunatus transforms the scene, image
by image, into the metaphoric meanings inherent in all the
pieces. As in Prudentius, the light is a symbol of Christ; but
Christ is also implied by everything else in the poem—the
growing grass, the flowers, the trees, the birds:

> Behold! the God who was crucified reigns through all:
> all created things offer prayer to their Creator.

> *qui crucifixus erat, deus ecce per omnia regnat,*
> *dantque creatori cuncta creata precem.* (37–38)

The hymn avoids the Christian anathema of pantheism
through the correct use of a preposition: God rules through
(*per*) all things; not in them. The most striking use of Christian idealism occurs in Venantius' handling of Philomela:

> from now on the nightingale tunes the instruments to
>   her reeds,
> and the air is sweeter, stricken by her song.

> *hinc filomela suis adtemperat organa cannis*
> *fitque repercusso dulcior aura melo.* (29–30)

The classical Philomela (her name is sometimes altered to
Philomena through a Romance dissimilation of liquids) is finally freed from her pagan heritage of bloodshed and loss. She
is no longer the beautiful but miserable prey of Tereus, as the

18. *MGH 4*, pt. 1, ed. F. Leo (1961), pp. 59–62, 39 f.

poets of Greece and Rome knew her. She is now among the lower-case species of the bird kingdom who, along with Prudentius' rooster, are harbingers and symbols of Christ. Perhaps the whole story of Christian adaptation of pagan symbolism is foreshadowed by the "conversion" of Philomela. In the seventh century, Eugene of Toledo (d. 658) wrote an entire poem to the nightingale without once hearing the ambiguous strains that Paulinus of Nola heard and welcomed.[19] Eugene says to the bird: "Don't be silent, don't be silent" (*Nolo tacere velis, nolo tacere velis*, 18) and, unlike the poet of the *Vigil*, is totally unconcerned about his own silence; for, as Eugene says at the close of his poem, "all good things are conferred by Christ upon those who serve him" (*qui praestas famulis haec bona grata tuis*, 20). The nightingale's song and the poet's hymn are both songs of praise to their maker. About two hundred years later, at the height of the Carolingian Renaissance, Paulus Albarus wrote another nightingale poem and ended with a very similar line: *qui nobis famulis gaudia tanta dedit*.[20]

The happy nightingale is a heritage of early Christian hymnologists. The joyous spring, however, measured in terms of the individual and the external world, is not. The Christian does not see himself pitted against the world of nature; he sees the entire natural world pitted against or subsumed by a supernatural world. Usually the hymns will admit no conflict whatsoever; they see the two worlds in absolute conjunction. The Christians did not write idealized spring songs; they wrote joyous Easter hymns, and the change from the word *ver* (spring, a process of the natural world) to *pascha* (Easter, a

19. *MGH 14*, ed. F. Vollmer, no. 33, p. 254. See Raby, "Philomena praevia temporis amoeni," *Mélanges Joseph de Ghellinck* (2 vols. Gembloux, 1951), 2, 435–48. The medieval etymology of *philomela* (*philos*, "friend," plus *melos*, "song": hence, "lover of song" or "friendly song") helps to account for the change; see Eugene, no. 30, p. 253: "*Sum noctis socia, sum cantus dulcis amica, / nomen ab ambiguo sic philomela gero.*" The other meaning, "friend of darkness" (*melas*), was not exploited, probably because of its negative symbolism.

20. *PLAC 3*, ed. L. Traube, pp. 126–27, 18.

miraculous event that has no bearing whatsoever upon the workings of nature) is a monumental step that affected every area of life. The Greek and Roman lyric poets saw only the world outside the window bursting into leaf and flower; they contrasted that growing world outside with themselves and found that they were merely growing older. But age, time, and death were robbed of their tragic meanings by Christ. Augustine, Prudentius, and Ambrose have their eyes fixed on a world that Catullus and Horace never depicted. To the Christians, the world outside is merely the Creation, the phenomenal world, all that is fleeting and passing. Above it and infusing it is the Creator, the numinal world, all that is permanent and divine. There is a bridge across that gulf, and that bridge is the love of the personalized Logos, Christ (*charitas*). The poetry of the next thousand years depends upon the existence of these two worlds.

At the beginning of the Christian tradition, the physical values are sacrificed to the metaphysical. Ultimately, it makes no sense at all to compare a Christian hymn to a pagan spring song. The Christians constantly import a level of meaning that is absent in pagan expression. For example, the Easter dawn hymn is most startling when compared to an Ovidian alba, such as *Amores* 1.6 or 1.13. The secular lover Ovid thrives in the adulterous night that Prudentius condemns: "run slowly, you horses of the night!" (*lente currite, Noctis equi,* 1.13.40). The dawn is envious (*invida*), a thing to be despised, because it robs the lover of his loved one. Ovid's albas also exist in a tension between light and darkness, and the light, which to the secular romantic lover is evil, always seems to win. Ovid's poems are tragi-comedies. He knows perfectly well that he cannot reverse the processes of nature, yet he comically tries to place himself above them.

The early Christian hymns, on the other hand, are always divine comedies. The darkness and shadows have little or no substantial or dramatic existence. The inevitable return of the light is the fulfillment of God's promise that divine law, and not man, rules the universe. The great power of a hymn such as that cited above by Venantius Fortunatus does not lie in any abiding tension between the light and darkness. It lies in the inevitable, almost mechanical, way that the light gradually pervades the scene; the way traditional images such as trees and birds and flowers are gradually revealed as living proofs of Christ's eternal presence. Venantius says: you can't reverse the processes of nature; they are divinely ordained. The beauty of his poetic landscape is not in its visual form, but in its *figura,* its figurative meaning: it is the creation of a loving God. This God, and no human being, is the proper object of all earthly love: *Amicitia enim mundi huius fornicatio est abs te (Conf.* 1.13).

It might seem from the preceding statements that the Christians destroyed paradox and tragedy; but this is not entirely true. Most of the poems examined here were composed under the influence of Ambrose, whose theological certainty precluded drama and doubt. Yet the greatest poet of the age was Augustine, who wrote poetic prose. His *Confessions* record the struggle of the saint to escape the world of the flesh. In this sense, Augustine perpetuated the romantic agony by condemning it and lifting its propositions to a metaphysical plane.

Erich Auerbach has discussed the manner in which the slings and arrows of outrageous Cupid are lifted out of the secular Ovidian arena and transferred by the Christians to a higher level; the way the "suffering" of love (Greek *pathos;* Latin *passio)* is an emotion to be shunned in ancient poetry, but one that cannot be escaped.[21] Yet at the time of Augustine's writing, "passion" had already become the *passio Christi,* the greatest and noblest suffering in love that the world had ever known. Christ changed the notion of the old Roman agony by supplying himself as an idealized end. As a result,

21. "*Passio* als Leidenschaft," *PMLA, 56* (1941), 1179–96; see also Frank, *St. Augustine and Greek Thought* (Cambridge, Mass., 1942). The antifeminist tradition from Juvenal to Jerome had been pointed out long before, esp. by E. K. Rand, *Founders of the Middle Ages* (Cambridge, Mass., 1928).

the western world suddenly had two distinctly dogmatic concepts: *amor mundi,* the love of this world; and *amor Dei,* the love of God.[22] Mystics who extolled the love of God over the love of a human being eventually tended to humanize God or Christ, and thus transferred the age-old symbolism of love to a metaphysical plane; the old Roman agony with its bitter-sweet refrains thus became the Romantic Agony after centuries of modification. Actually the methodology consisted of two operations. First, human love was condemned:

> For even in my youth I sometimes burned to glut myself in hell, and I dared to wander in the forest of various shadowy loves, and my beauty withered and I stank openly before Your eyes, because I was pleasing myself and wanting to please the eyes of men. . . . And what did I delight in except loving and being loved? (*Conf.* 2.1, 2)

Second, the love of God was idealized, but not in Ambrosian abstractions; it was humanized through the traditional symbolism that lies at the heart of western Indo-European expressions of love:

> Who will let me rest in You? Who will let You enter my heart and make it drunk so that I can forget my sins and embrace my One and Only Good, who is You? . . . Say to my soul "I am your health". . . . I shall run after Your voice and catch hold of You. O, don't hide Your face from me. Let me die so that, not really dying, I can see Your face. (*Conf.* 1.5)

If we change the capitalized pronouns to lower case in this second passage, we have the spirit of the *Liebestod* that some modern critics of the later Middle Ages would like to attribute to Mohammedanism, druidism, or Albigensianism. Sometimes the truth is so obvious that it seems extremely subtle. Auerbach merely posed the question: did six hundred years of

22. Developed by Mario Casella, "Poesia e storia," *ASI, 96,* pt. 2 (1938), 3–63, 153–99.

orthodox mystical Christianity not have any effect on secular poetry when people finally began to write it?

Actually, the process was not invented by Augustine or the Christians; it may be described as a typical Platonic denigration of matter (*hyle*) and idealization of spirit (*nous*). Yet Plato had far more effect upon Augustine and the Christians than he had upon classical poets. Once the Neoplatonic spirit is loosed in the world, it sets Augustine's Platonic dialogues and *Confessions* far apart in spirit from the ancient lyrics of Sappho and Catullus (despite the continuity of basic symbolism). It becomes one of the strongest binding forces of mystical Christianity, linking Augustine's dialogues with a personal God to the mystical tracts of Richard of St. Victor, the Platonizing school at Chartres, and the even later love lyrics to God written by St. John of the Cross:

> O living flame of love,
> Which softly penetrates
> Into the deepest center of my soul!
> Because you're never shy,
> Finish it now if you will:
> Break these cloths for our sweet encounter!

> O healing that's so soothing,
> Gash that's freely given,
> O hand so soft, O touch so delicate!
> You savor of eternal life
> And pay my every debt!
> And killing, you turn my death to life.[23]

A summary of Auerbach's work at this point would lead to a lengthy digression involving the entire range of love symbolism from Sappho to the *Confessions*. In the Appendix, I have assembled various isolated symbols that were given broad coinage by Ovid (simply because he is the Aquinas of classical love poetry), perpetuated by hymnologists or Christian mystics

---

23. *Oh llama de amor viva*, 1–12.

in the new idealized metaphysical sphere, and returned to secular expression in the later Middle Ages. It seems incredible that nineteenth-century philologists could not (or would not) see the relationship between the language of love as used by a Christian Neoplatonic like Richard of St. Victor or St. Bernard, and the very same vocabulary employed by the troubadours: faith, hope, love, worship, service, suffering. Richard applies the terminology to God, the troubadours to women.[24] The Christian Neoplatonic tradition of portraying the love of the divine in the language of human love begins with Augustine.[25] It runs directly counter to the sober, somber rhetoric of most early hymns, but begins to acquire momentum in post-Carolingian hymnology.

Certainly the theory of the interaction of religious and secular expression is proved by the way that the early Christians treated the *Cantica Canticorum* (Song of Songs).[26] To the modern reader, this body of Hebrew lyrics may seem to consist of patently sensual love poems written at the time of Solomon. Whether or not they were actually composed with a metaphysical frame of reference in mind is immaterial; the fact remains that they have been subjected to a purely secular interpretation throughout the course of Christianity. In the age of Augustine, when the values of human love are denigrated and when love lyrics cease to be written for several hundred years, how is a Christian supposed to read these lyrics

24. Richard, *De praeparatione animi ad contemplationem: Benjamin Minor* (*PL 196*, cols. 1–64) and *In Cantica Canticorum* (196, cols. 405–524), which culminates in a prayer to Mary; Bernard, *Sermones in C. C.* (*PL 183*), esp. cols. 810 (on kissing and secrecy); 815 (passion); 856 (love-vigil); 870 (stages of ascension from the "carnal" image of Christ to the totally spiritual); 890 (ecstasy); 1183 (doctrine of love-service and attainment of honor; the soul purifies itself through love and acquires the virtue of the loved one).

25. Auerbach cites such recurrent mystical expressions as: *ebrietas spiritus, suave vulnus charitatis, gladius amoris, pax in Christi sanguine, surgere ad passionem*, etc. (p. 1186 et passim).

26. For a synoptic interpretation, see Cornelius a Lapide, *Commentarii in Sacram Scripturam* (Lyon-Paris, 1864), *4*, 371–750.

of the Holy Book? The answer, of course, is: allegorically, metaphorically, as almost everything except orthodox theology was read. Augustine says in his commentary on the poems that the woman addressing her lover must be interpreted as the Church (or human soul) crying out for salvation; the man or bridegroom is Christ or God.[27] In other words, the entire sphere of love, with all its circumjacent sexual symbolism, can be read on a metaphysical level. Need it be said, then, that the poetic composition in this ethos will partake of the soul and essence of ambiguity?[28]

Naturally, the allegorical or metaphoric method was a salvation for Christianity in its formative phases; Christian priests and theologians could turn the least promising pagan dross into gold. One is most consciously aware of the value of such an operation in reading a late-medieval treatise such as the *Ovide moralisé*, where the sexual aberrations of Narcissus, Hero and Leander, and Daphne are treated in two ways, mirroring the twofold treatment of love by Augustine. First, these love affairs serve as moral lessons: Leander deserved to drown in the stormy sea of life because he overestimated the value of earthly love. Second, they serve as metaphoric tableaux with direct Christian overtones: Leander is the striving Christian soul swimming to Hero's lighthouse, which is Heaven, through the stormy temptations of reality.[29]

St. Augustine is the key to the next thousand years of history. The saint himself in his *Confessions* assures us that when

27. Augustine, *Speculum (De divinis scripturis), CSEL 12,* ed. F. Weihrich, pp. 74–75: *"Ecclesia quippe, in qua utique sumus, his verbis exhortatur filias suas . . . ipsa est ager dei fructuosissimus"* (p. 74) and *"Christus quoque ipse ibi dicit: Pulchra es, amica mea, suavis et decora"* (p. 75). Cf. Bernard, *De diligendo Deo,* 3.7 et infra (*PL 182,* col. 978); also Curtius, p. 122.

28. Robertson, "Doctrine of Charity," p. 28: "The fact that the word love (*amor*) could be used for either Charity or cupidity opened enormous possibilities for literary word-play."

29. 4.3587–731; for *"fole amour,"* 3587–663; for Hero as *"divine sapience,"* 3664–731; ed. C. de Boer (Amsterdam, 1920).

he looked at the letter he was slain.[30] Under his aegis Christianity triumphed as an intellectual tool because it could suppress the paradoxes of the natural world; and in triumphing it created a whole new sphere, one might even say grammar, of thought. Latin words in Christian poems rise above the meanings ascribed to them by Romans:

> They bring the standards of the King,
> there shines the Mystery of the Cross.

> *Vexilla regis prodeunt,*
> *fulget crucis mysterium.*[31]

Is the king Caesar? Of course not. He is The King, Christ. Is the cross a punishment for criminals? No. It is the instrument of world salvation. The modern use of capital letters in the translation indicates the pervading air of mysticism with which Christian expression begins. As W. T. H. Jackson has said, in his history of medieval literature, every word in the above poem by Venantius Fortunatus has two meanings.[32] Any critical study that continues past the age of Augustine must be prepared to acknowledge symbolism, metaphoric raising, allegory, and ambiguity. To ignore the enigmatic nature of existence in early Christian expression is to be blind to the overriding world of essences that imbues the physical world with its "real" meanings. Without that superior world of essence, *factus eram ipse mihi magna quaestio,* one returns to a world of paradoxical questions.

From Augustine on, we pursue a tradition of orthodox mystical resolution within the One or the Good. There is a brief philosophical interlude in the ninth century when the

---

30. *Conf.* 5.14; see also 6.4, based on 2 Cor. 3:6. Naturally Augustine did not deny the literal meaning: *Civ. Dei,* 13.21 (on Garden of Eden).

31. *PL 88,* cols. 95–96. For poems with drawings of birds, animals, and mystical figures superimposed, see Rabanus Maurus, *De laudibus Sanctae Crucis* (*PL 107,* cols. 133–294).

32. *The Literature of the Middle Ages* (N.Y., 1960), p. 220. See Rahner, pp. 46–68.

great Neoplatonist John Scotus Erigena refuses to accept the standard Augustinian equation of God and Good, and redefines God as the "contradiction of contradictions":

For God is not properly, but only metaphorically, called essence, truth, wisdom, etc.; instead he is called *super-essential*, being more than truth, more than wisdom, and similar things.[33]

Scotus was condemned by later philosophers and theologians who, like many nineteenth-century scholars, equated paradox with confusion.[34] Yet his words haunt the poetry of the post-Carolingian era, for they encompass a world view that embodies paradox and that I have linked to the lyric sensibility. After Scotus come poets in abundance; Scotus is himself a poet in prose, for, as Helen Waddell has suggested, every Neoplatonist is at heart a poet.[35] Yet Scotus is also a *vox sola in deserto*. The Church preferred the far more comprehensible monistic position of Augustine, who made clear-cut distinctions between good and evil, the Creator and the Creation, and who placed the metaphysical world and City of God above the physical world and City of Man. Until St. Thomas Aquinas and the Aristotelians of the thirteenth century began to reexamine the cosmos and endow the physical world with a great deal more reality, Augustine's view prevailed.[36] At times in the *Confessions* and *The City of God* Augustine praised both worlds, largely through the quotation of the Psalms.[37] But in the main, early Christian descriptions of spring, nature, and human love have only metaphoric values.

33. *De div. nat. (PL 122,* col. 460).

34. Alfred Jeanroy, *La Poésie lyrique des troubadours* (2 vols. Paris, 1934), *1,* 89, where a "*création paradoxale*" is considered "*confuse jusqu'à l'absurdité.*"

35. *The Wandering Scholars,* p. 56 (about Scotus).

36. See Maurice de Wulf, *Philosophy and Civilization in the Middle Ages* (Princeton, 1922), pp. 62–98.

37. E.g., *Conf.* 7.13. See Marjorie Hope Nicolson, *Mountain Gloom and Mountain Glory* (Ithaca, 1959), p. 47.

A Suggestion of Dialectic: The Carolingians and After

St. Augustine died in 430, twenty years after the Vandals had clattered over the walls of Rome and the last vestiges of the pagan paradise on earth had crumbled. The religious poetry analyzed in the preceding section was written over the clamor of a bewildering array of ephemeral rulers drawn from Ostrogothic, Visigothic, Vandal, Gepid, Lombard, and other Germanic stock. Yet a definite subcurrent runs freely beneath the mystical tidal wave. Once again one is drawn back to the *Vigil of Venus*. That little poem was tucked among the pages of purely pagan poetry in the *Latin Anthology*, which was compiled for Vandal kings, possibly a good century after Augustine's death. There is every reason to believe that some of the anonymous (and inferior) poems in the *Anthology* were written at the same time that Augustine was turning his eyes toward the Heavenly City. In the seventh and eighth centuries, that undercurrent runs so deeply that it is barely discernible; it emerges, however, about the year 800 when Charlemagne was crowned Emperor, and, for a century at least, the Earthly Paradise seemed to be restored in northern Europe. In the year of his coronation, an unknown hand wrote a poem praising Aachen as the second Rome and King Karl as the new Augustus.[38] In the ninth century, Irishmen, Anglo-Saxons, Franks, and other Germanic peoples combined to grace northern Europe with something that can be called a literary renaissance.

The notes of a secular spring were sounded once again in a curious little debate-poem called the "Conflict of Winter and Spring," formerly attributed to the Englishman Alcuin, who was Charles' literary advisor.[39] Lovely Spring tries to persuade Dire Winter to allow the return of the cuckoo, a bird that seems to enter spring literature by way of the British Isles.

38. *PLAC 1*, ed. E. Dümmler, pp. 366–79. The poem is sometimes attributed to Angilbert.
39. *PLAC 1*, pp. 270–72.

Although the bird involved is North European, the judge of the contest is Palemon, a stock Mediterranean drawn from the pastorals of Vergil and Theocritus. Palemon resolves the debate by crying:

So let the cuckoo come! . . .
You now, my sweet love, are a most welcome guest for all!

Et veniat cuculus . . .   (46)
Tu iam dulcis amor, cunctis gratissimus hospes.   (53)

His words ring out beyond the context of the poem. In purely secular terms, the lush beauty of spring has been chosen over the ascetic harshness of winter. Palemon's invitation to the bird ("now, my sweet love") is echoed later in the opening line of one of the most famous of all the *Cambridge Songs:* "Come now, my sweet love" (*Iam, dulcis amica, venito*). The point at which the woman replaces the bird is but a mere shift of genders away.

Alcuin himself wrote two poems in which birds symbolize human beings. E. S. Duckett has shown, with reference to Alcuin's correspondence, how the abbot called his pupils by bird names. Alcuin's "Lament on the Departure of the Cuckoo" actually tells the story of how a young man named Dodo, but probably nicknamed Cuckoo, "fled the haunts of religion and learning in the springtime of his youth."[40] Similarly, his poem about a lost nightingale would seem to be a symbolic mask for the story of a young man who fled the abbey at Tours for a life in sunny Italy.[41] These two poems are extraordinary, for they mark a period of personal mythologizing and private symbolism. The nightingale in classical literature was part of a fixed myth that had evolved from a

40. *Alcuin, Friend of Charlemagne* (N.Y., 1951), pp. 153–54.
41. Dodo or another student is undoubtedly masked in the Nightingale Poem: *PLAC 1*, pp. 274 f. For a purely literal interpretation, see Raby, *History of Secular Latin Poetry in the Middle Ages* (2 vols. Oxford, Clarendon Press, 1934), *1*, 184.

kind of primitive consciousness that connected the bird with
grief, misery, and loss. Philomela (or Procne, since there was
a confusion) had a dogmatic connotation. The Christians proceeded to strip her of her mythic meaning and merge her into
the bird kingdom with roosters, where she was just another
harbinger of Christ. Alcuin somehow manages to combine
both methods in a totally original way. The boy who lurks
under the image of the bird has surrendered himself to the
pleasures of the flesh, and is hence lost. Yet, as a creature of
God who once sang so beautifully in the abbey choir, he still
fills Alcuin with a sense of wonder at the Creator's creation:

> Your plumage was poor, but not your song.
> Broad tones issued from your narrow throat:
> A sweet melody, varied in the Muses' mode,
> With constant hymns to your Maker on your lips.

> *Spreta colore tamen fueras non spreta canendo,*
> *Lata sub angusto gutture vox sonuit,*
> *Dulce melos iterans vario modulamine Musae,*
> *Atque creatorem semper in ore canens.*   (7–10)

In this poem pagan loss and acceptance of tragedy vie with
Christian joy and certainty of a good end. The Muses and the
Maker brush shoulders without any conflict; rhetorically, they
are at home. Yet there is a very definite conflict of emotions: a
feeling of the loss of something beautiful in tension with the
belief that nothing beautiful is ever really lost. The human,
personal element is present in the feelings of the poet and in
the characterization of the bird that is a boy. For example, in
the seventh line, the bird is reproached for its plumage, yet
the nightingale in classical lyrics was never criticized for its
appearance. (In later medieval poems, however, such as "The
Owl and the Nightingale," it was.) In the first two lines of the
poem, Alcuin says that "a jealous hand took you away from
my bushes." Literally, these lines make perfectly good sense;
someone might very well steal a nightingale for its song, if

Alcuin actually had a pet bird in his abbey at Tours. Yet the
disturbed calm of the poet exerts itself in the use of that human word "hand" (dextra). This is no ordinary bird-snatcher.
The over-all personification works gradually to the surface in
such lines as:

> O, you were far too happy! You who had
> The name of God on your lips both night and day.
> Not food, not drink, not the company of birds
> Was sweeter to you than your odes.   (15–18)

Now the nightingale is primarily a night-bird in the world of
romantic poetry; to Germanic Europe, it is a bird of shadow-
land (e.g., German Nachtigall). Actually the bird sings all day
long, but Alcuin is hardly correcting a poetic fallacy here; he
is stretching the terms of a poetic conceit to cover the personal
history of a choirboy who sang at matins and vespers. Similarly,
the nightingale in poetry and in fact is fond of singing; but as
an animal it is also fond of eating and drinking. We are not
dealing so much with an idealized bird here as we are with an
idealized devotee of the arts. The boy literally had the name
of God on his lips while singing Church hymns; a bird could
have it only metaphorically. The nightingale furthermore is
a lonely creature who does not like "the company of birds";
but neither did the boy like the other "birds" in Alcuin's
abbey if he left it. In short, the poem is a tissue of interwoven
symbolic fiction. It offers little evidence that Alcuin knew very
much about nightingales per se; but he was keenly aware of
the temptations of the flesh.

Alcuin does not employ the metaphoric process of Prudentius, who took figures from the natural world and endowed
them with figurative meanings on a transcendental level. Alcuin takes an image from the natural world and humanizes it,
thus employing a subjective romantic technique not unlike
that of the Vigil. Yet his handling is highly original. For example, Alcuin does not use the traditional mythological name

for a nightingale: *philomela-mena*. He uses the unmytholog-
ical Classical Latin word *luscinia*, thus cutting off from the
very first line both the classical and Christian associations.
His poem ultimately owes little to the *Vigil* or Eugene of
Toledo in its rhetoric; it is a blend of these two strains, and
thus something new. Alcuin's confidence in his mode of expression shows through in these extraordinary lines:

> Why should I wonder that seraphim and cherubim
>   Praise the Thunderer forever, when you could do the
>   same?

> *Quid mirum, cherubim, seraphim si voce tonantem*
>   *Perpetua laudent, dum tua sic potuit?*

The Thunderer suggests Juppiter Tonans far more than Augustine's Deus Creator. The cherubim, however, are firmly
Christian. Alcuin mixes the two as unconcernedly as he
blended the Maker with the Muses. The poem ends with a
prayer that the nightingale may be safe, but it is not the kind
of prayer that destroys conflicting elements for the sake of a
vision of the whole. Alcuin is obviously aware of the fact that
the young man may be damned.

The Cuckoo Poem is very much like the Lost Nightingale
Poem, and contains these similar dramatic lines:

> May our cuckoo not perish; may he come back in the spring,
>   and coming, sing for us joyous songs . . .

> If he lives, let him come; let him run to our safe nest;
>   may no crow tear our cuckoo apart with his vicious claws.[42]

We are back in a world where vicious crows (or barbarous
husbands and raucous swans) can disturb the safe little nest
at Tours; where the world of outer reality can intrude upon
an inner sanctity but not destroy it. The tension between these
two worlds is very real; so is the kind of idealism that clings

42. *PLAC I*, pp. 269 f., 13–14, 19–20.

to the voice of the lost nightingale, a kind of idealism that arouses in the reader a feeling of compassion. Raby's cursory judgment of Alcuin ("He was a great teacher, if a mediocre poet") is hardly fair.[43] Alcuin's poetry should not be compared to his educational pursuits. In the Cuckoo Poem, Alcuin calls himself Menalcas, the name of a shepherd drawn from the pastoral poems of Vergil and Theocritus. When a Christian *pastor* (priest or shepherd; the word is ambiguous in Medieval Latin) can call himself by a pagan shepherd's name, then culture has indeed reached a point of development where a two-dimensional view of reality is again possible.

It is interesting to note that the historical subject of the Lost Nightingale Poem is a boy, but all the adjectives describing him depend on the word *luscinia* and are therefore thrown into the feminine gender. This transposition of gender will crop up again and again in this study. Women in Provençal poetry are traditionally called *midons* (Milord); in the *Carmina Burana* a lady is called *mea dux*. On the other hand, in the poetry of Guido Cavalcanti, or indeed in any mystical poetry in which the poet identifies himself with his *anima,* as in the poems of St. John of the Cross, a male poet becomes feminized. Furthermore, Ivo of Chartres tells us in a letter that Bishop John of Orléans was the subject of numerous love poems written by his disciples in which he was always addressed by the Ovidian name Flora.[44] These points are mentioned not because it is important to know that a boy named Dodo is Alcuin's nightingale or that Bishop John is Flora in many medieval poems, especially since there are very few gossips like Ivo of Chartres to supply us with historical titbits. Yet it is important to be aware of the risk involved in making generalizations about the culture existing outside the poetry from the poetry itself, which is highly ambiguous. If

43. *Oxford Book of Medieval Latin Verse* (Oxford, Clarendon Press, 1959), p. 466; hereafter cited as *Oxford*.

44. For discussion with sources, see Hennig Brinkmann, *Geschichte der lateinischen Liebesdichtung im Mittelalter* (Halle, 1925), pp. 93–96.

boys are masked by birds and bishops are lurking under the names of Ovidian heroines, we must be prepared to acknowledge symbolism. Actually, the historical subjects cannot matter much. Do we know, for example, who Lesbia was? She may have been Clodia. Corinna? Everyone agrees that she was a poetic fiction. The masculine-named heroines of the troubadours? A few have been identified, but usually through the totally unreliable biographies that were created out of the poets' fiction. Beatrice? She may have been Beatrice de'Portinari, but Dante never felt the necessity of telling us so, and we cannot be sure. In Alcuin's poems and in these other works, the symbolism is not constructed between a symbol (the bird) and an historical figure (Dodo), but between a symbol and a dramatic, fictional character. In some ways, it might have been better if Dodo had remained forever unknown, since the poems have been appraised in terms of Alcuin's personal history, where they are not so important, and not in terms of a literary tradition, where they are indeed a landmark.

Alcuin's poetry marks the return of the lyric "I." With that personal voice come all the disruptive elements that can create a medium for truly dramatic expression. In the same century Rabanus Maurus, echoing the Psalms, cries out to God: *Respice me miserum!* ("Look at poor me!").[45] The half-crazed monk Gottschalk says: "Alas! what's happened to *me!*" (*Heu, quid evenit mihi!*).[46] The boisterous Irishman Sedulius Scottus confesses: "Asleep I snore, awake I pray to God" (*dormisco stertens, oro Deum vigilans*).[47] Yet although these poets speak from terra firma, their eyes are also firmly fixed on the stars.[48]

45. *An. Hymn. 50,* no. 132, pp. 181–82, 5.
46. *An. Hymn. 50,* no. 170, p. 225, refrain.
47. *The Goliard Poets,* ed. and tr. G. F. Whicher (N.Y., New Directions, 1949), p. 16, 4; hereafter cited as Whicher.
48. Rabanus' *De universo,* for example, insists upon the metaphoric interpretation of nature, despite its obvious appreciation for the visual imagery.

Sedulius' Easter poem written to Tado shows the presence
of two worlds:

Now the various birds delight the air with their songs,
now all night long the nightingale tunes her melody,
now the church choir hymns Zion in its hymns,
singing Hallelujah a hundred times.
Tado, father of your land, may you gain the joy
of a heavenly Easter, the threshold of light: my best!

nunc variae volucres permulcent aethera cantu
temperat et pernox nunc philomela melos,
nunc chorus ecclesiae cantat per cantica Sion,
alleluia suis centuplicatque tonis.
Tado, pater patriae, caelestis gaudia paschae,
percipias meritis limina lucis: ave.[49]

The stress in these lines falls repeatedly on the word *nunc,*
now (Ovid's *etiamnunc*). Sedulius has a scene from the present
world in mind: the nightingales are singing in a tree; Christians are singing in a church.[50] The coupling of images sug-

---

This age marks the beginning of praises to earthly women: e.g., Walafrid
Strabo (*PL 114,* col. 1102):

Qui vos laudat, honore se coronat:
Qui vos laudat; amat, colitque verum,
Qui vos laudat, habebitur benignus;
Qui vos laudat, agit quod est agendum.

See also his praises of Empress Judith (cols. 1095, 1097). This tradition gathers
momentum until in the twelfth century Hildebert addresses Mathilde, queen
of Henry I of England, in language commonly addressed to Mary (*PL 171,*
col. 1443): *Majestate tua stupui, totamque vaganti / Percurrens oculo, sum
ratus esse deam.* Also, comparing her with her mother (ibid., col. 1444): *Est
rosa de radice rosae; de relligione / Relligio; pietas de pietate fluit. / De stella
splendor, de magno nomine majus.*
  49. Whicher, p. 12, 21–26.
  50. The use of bird choruses to imitate societies praising the Lord was
established by Ambrose, *Hexaemeron* 5.12.39 (*PL 14,* col. 223): "*Sed unde mihi
cygnea carmina, quae etiam sub gravi mortis imminentis terrore delectant?
. . . Unde mihi vocem psittaci, dulcedinemque merularum? Utinam saltem*

gests the concord of man and nature. Sedulius does not bother to draw distinctions between spring and Easter; to him, the physical event prefigures the heavenly event (*caelestis paschae*); both have a vital reality. The singing bird and singing Christians exist side by side. The poetic picture is bathed in a quiet, philosophic light. Sedulius does not point up metaphors as Prudentius did; he paints a picture and lets his reader draw his own conclusions. Of course Sedulius leads us toward a heavenly Easter; but his accent is also upon the "now, now, now" of a world in time. The lower-case nightingale is still a Christian bird in this poem, largely through association. But if the distich describing her is lifted from context, she becomes a secular bird of joy.

In an anonymous Anacreontic poem written about the year 900, the hymnologist comes near to doing precisely that.[51] He creates a whole forest of singing birds, blending the happy *lusciola* with the unlikely rooster. All of the birds are singing songs worthy of God (*Cantu deo dignissima*); but the birds, and not God, dominate the poem. Another poem of the same period tells about the joy that fills the hearts of monks when they are visited by an oriole.[52] In an anonymous Alleluia sequence of the tenth century, the poet creates a twofold picture in which the songs of earthly birds are echoed by angelic choirs in the "fields of Paradise" (*prata paradisiaca*).[53] The

---

luscinia canat, quae dormientem de somno excitet! Ea enim avis signare solet diei surgentis exortum, et effusiorem diluculo deferre laetitiam. Tamen si illorum suavitas deest, sunt gementes turtures, et raucae columbae, tum etiam cornix plena voce pluviam vocat. Unde rurale aviarium sermone quo possumus, scientia quam nos rusticani docuerunt, persequamur." The flights of birds were considered sacred: Rabanus (*PL 111*, col. 241): "*Volatus, sanctorum ad Dominum Deum ascensus, vel in Scripturis intellectus*" (citing Ps. 17). Although birds in the Bible were often malignant (Luc. 8:5; Apoc. 19:17–21; Job 28:7), they represented escape (Ps. 54:7–8, 123:7, Job 39:26–27) and reverent worship (Ps. 83:3–4, 103:12–17; Ezech. 17:23; Matth. 10:29, 13:32).

51. *PLAC 4*, pt. 1, ed. P. de Winterfeld, pp. 430–31.
52. *Oxford*, no. 106, p. 147.
53. *An. Hymn. 53*, no. 34, pp. 60 f.

poem is a harmonized bit of dialectic in which neither element is given precedence over the other; if anything, the angelic orders seem to be blessing the kingdom of the birds. Joy (*gaudium*) seems to be possible in either sphere.

When we come to the *Cambridge Songs*, which were collected about the year 1050, we encounter a humanistic viewpoint that was everywhere implied by the very human poetry of the Carolingians. The step from calling a bird "sweet love" or using a bird to symbolize human beauty is not so far from calling a woman "sweet love" and dealing entirely in terms of her beauty. This exciting collection contains prototypes for fabliaux, threnodies (*planctus* in Latin; *planh* in Provençal), and a few love lyrics. Some of the poems written on deaths or coronations of Holy Roman Emperors can be dated as early as the 900s. (The very term *Holy Roman* Empire embodies the dialectic discussed in this section.)

Unfortunately one of the zealous monks in the Monastery of St. Augustine at Canterbury, where the collection was housed after being imported from Germany, obliterated the better part of the poem *Iam, dulcis amica, venito*, which connects so beautifully with the *Iam, dulcis amor* of the Conflict Poem. However the clever reconstruction of Vuolo, based on two additional manuscripts, has restored a great deal of what was lost.[54] Rhythmically, the poem cannot be read either quantitatively or accentually. Raby has suggested that it be read with a "rough equality of syllables."[55] Rhetorically, the poem seems to mark the entrance of something new into western lyrical poetry. The male speaker invites a girl-friend (*amica*) to his house, which abounds with spices, couches, food, and music.[56] The girl is unimpressed by these material con-

54. E. P. Vuolo, "Iam, dulcis amica, venito," *CN*, *10* (1950), 5–25; see also Raby, *Secular Latin*, *1*, 303–04.

55. *Secular Latin*, *1*, 304.

56. For a biblical parallel involving a harlot who wishes to entice a young man from his true *soror*, Wisdom, and *amica*, Prudence, see Prov. 7, esp. 16–18, for similar material elements. Obviously the medieval poem can be moralized

ceits, but tells him that she desires his companionship (*familiaritas*); she explains that she has been wandering in the woods, shunning the vulgar crowd (*vitavi populum multum*).[57] Finally the man launches into a little spring song:

> Now the snow and ice have melted,
> leaves and grass are growing green;
> now the nightingale sings on high,
> love's burning in the cavern of the heart.

> *Iam nix glaciesque liquescit,*
> *folium et herba virescit;*
> *philomela iam cantat in alto:*
> *ardet amor cordis in antro.* (33–36)

The poem ends with the expectation of fulfillment as the man tells the girl to hurry, for he is waiting.

It is a curious poem because the rhetoric is so elusive. If Horace is suggested by the spring invitation and by the avoidance of the *vulgus profanum*, the poem is too simple in its diction and yet also too opulent in its imagery to be Horatian. Raby and others have called attention to the Song of Songs, and this seems to be a more useful source.[58] We might now recall how St. Augustine took what seemed to be lyrics about human love and allegorized them into hymns. But allegory is a dangerous process because it always implies literalization, or what I shall call de-allegorization. If Augustine could raise the Ovidian fires of love (*ignes amoris*) onto the mystical plane (*ignes caritatis*), why could some poetic Prometheus not steal those fires and return them to earth, still preserving some of their religious glow? The *Iam, dulcis amica* seems to break the

---

along the same lines, with the *amica's* rebuff indicating her stern moral fiber; however, the medieval work emphasizes the role of the lover and lacks the in-built lesson. For the figure of the harlot in the garden, Jer. 2:20, 3:6–9.

57. Vuolo, st. 8, 4; cf. the unreconstructed text of W. Bulst, *Carmina Cantabrigiensia* (Heidelberg, 1950), p. 53, st. 6, 3.

58. *Secular Latin, 1*, 303.

chains of religious allegory and return its images to the literal, earthbound realm of lyric expression. Yet because one of the manuscripts containing the poem was a *troparium* for celebrating the mass, Dreves, the editor of the eleventh volume of the *Analecta Hymnica,* printed it as a church hymn (p. 57: *Ad Beatam Mariam*), and Vuolo interpreted the entire poem as a soliloquy of Jesus to the Christian soul! The fate of this little poem therefore parallels that of the Song of Songs. The ambiguity that shrouds both texts merely warns us once again that we must watch Medieval Latin texts very closely, because two strains are at work in the language. Eventually they combined, with interesting results.

Biblical parallels occur in the poem in a striking way. The poet calls his girl-friend *amica* (a very Ovidian name), but also *soror electa* ("my chosen sister," 25). It is inconceivable that Ovid or Catullus would have called a woman he loved his sister. We are drawn first to compare this expression to Christ's "brotherly" love; but before Christ, we find in the Song of Songs 4:9 (*RSV*): "You have ravished my heart, my sister, my bride." Even more arresting is line 4:12: "A garden locked is my sister, my bride." Furthermore, if we compare the narrator's spring song with an ode of Horace, we notice only a slight similarity of surface rhetoric: trees, grass, a nightingale—the simplest images used again and again to describe the spring. If we compare the total expression of the medieval poem with Horace's balanced representation of joy and despair, culminating in a kind of idealized melancholy, the spring song of the *Iam, dulcis amica* seems decidedly one-dimensional. The accent is entirely upon "now" (*iam* occurs twice in four lines). There is no thought of the black fires or Pale Death. We must go to the now-now-now mode of Sedulius Scottus for a similar statement of earthly optimism. In the medieval poem, grass and trees quietly replace the snow and ice without any psychic upheaval; the poet seems to imply: this is nature. And then, wonder of wonders, Philomela, whose tortured history is central to the spring motif, is at last freed from both her pagan agon and her Christian baptism; she is once again a secular bird, and all that she does is sing. Her song is now happy. There is an implicit notion between the 35th and 36th lines of that fragment: the nightingale's song blends into the poet's statement that love is burning in the heart. By coupling human love with the bird's song, the poet implies: it is natural for a bird to warble in the spring; by the same token, it is natural for me to express my love. Both phenomena are part of nature; ergo, they are natural.

Needless to say, we have come a long way from both Augustine and Horace. There is a divinely human simplicity to this poem. If we seek a similar statement, we cannot find it in classical or early Christian literature. We are drawn again to the Song of Songs:

> My beloved speaks and says to me:
> "Arise, my love, my fair one, and come away
> for lo, the winter is past, the rain is over and gone.
> The flowers appear on the earth, the time of singing
> has come, and the voice of the turtledove is heard
> in our land."   (2:10–12)

Here is the invitation to the beloved; here too is the dialogue between the lover and loved one. In Jerome's Latin, here is also the antiphonal structure that defies Classical Latin or accentual Romance scansion. The woman in this portrait, when transferred to the *Cambridge Songs,* is no longer the Christian soul, as generations of Christians had been taught to interpret her; she is just a woman. The man is no longer Christ, the bridegroom; he is just a man. When we descend from the allegorical mists into the clarity of the physical world, we come down with a thud. If the Christians resolved paradox by interpreting everything on a metaphysical plane, the anonymous poet who wrote this poem expelled those mists with the clarity of the spring sun and likewise banished paradox. The ideal spring takes place here and now (*iam*); there is no Boreas lurking in the realm of Zephyr, no fear of time and death to cast

a dark shadow over the Earthly Paradise. Nature's workings
are mechanical: the snow and ice disappear, the leaves and
grass grow green. The statement is as simple as the following:

> Awake, O north wind,
> and come, O south wind!
> Blow upon my garden,
> let its fragrance be wafted abroad.
> Let my beloved come to his garden,
> and eat its choicest fruits.   (4:16)

The north wind, Boreas, does not clash with the south wind
(in Greek terms, the west wind, Zephyr); he merely yields his
ground in the natural procession of events. The poet does not
employ the biblical metaphor of the woman's body as garden;
this transferral remains for the *Carmina Burana:*

> A virgin is an island
> that has a virgin garden.
>
> *Hortum habet insula*
> *virgo virginalem.*[59]

Yet what we are observing here is a phenomenon that has no
precedent except in that book of the Old Testament: a world
view that admits human fulfillment in terms of natural fulfillment without any awareness of paradox. This is precisely
the poem for which we were searching in classical literature,
in vain. Once found, its simplicity may be wondered at.

What energizes the simple organization of the *Iam, dulcis
amica* is precisely the force that moves the Song of Songs: the
portrayal of a moment of impending fulfillment in which that
fulfillment is never quite stated in the poem, although it is

---

59. *Carmina Burana: Lateinische und deutsche Lieder und Gedichte,* ed.
J. A. Schmeller (3d ed. Stuttgart, 1894), no. 78, pp. 165 f., 1–2; hereafter cited
as Schmeller.

everywhere implied. The poem, as reconstructed by Vuolo, ends on a note of urgency:

> Do quickly what you must do,
> In me there's no delay.
>
> *fac cito quod eris factura,*
> *in me non est aliqua mora.* (43–44)

So too the last verse of the Song of Songs begins: "Make haste, my beloved . . ." (8:14). Many Christian hymns hinge upon the mystical union of time and eternity when the world of forever will break through into the world of now. The eyes of the poet who wrote the *Iam, dulcis amica* were not fixed upon any such magic moment of the distant future; he was waiting for the moment after his poem would end. Only the most self-willed allegorizer could make this poem exist *entirely* as a religious parable.

Another strain of emotions is expressed in the Song of Songs: the loss, the languor, the sickness of love unrequited; and it is also expressed in physical terms:

> Sustain me with raisins,
> refresh me with apples;
> for I am sick with love.
> O that his left hand were under my head.
>
> *Fulcite me floribus,*
> *stipate me malis,*
> *quia amore langueo.* (2:5)

One of the most famous *Cambridge Songs, Levis exsurgit Zephirus,* is composed in this vein, although it owes as much to Rome as to Judaea. The poem begins with a spring landscape; Earth is opening up her lap (once again the recurring Vergilian passage from the *Georgics* leaps to mind), reddish spring (Ovid's *ver purpuratum*) walks abroad in the land, sprinkling Earth with flowers. All of these images are clearly classical in origin, and could easily come from Vergil, Ovid, or the *Vigil*. (We must remember that the Codex Thuaneus, in which the *Vigil* was preserved, is dated from the ninth or tenth century.) The poet next describes animals seeking lairs and birds building nests; then he becomes aware of the picture he has created and hears the birds singing; immediately he says:

> Alas! because of such great joys
> I'm swollen with great, great sighs.

> *heü, pro tantis gaudiis*
> *tantis inflor suspiriis.*[60]

It is a somewhat startling transition, but one encountered time after time in the spring poems of classical literature. External nature in its moment of fulfillment (*gaudiis;* the word is now ascribed entirely to the physical world) contrasts with the inner world of the poet.

Then, in the next line, an adjective tells us that a woman is reciting the poem: *Cum mihi sola sedeo* ("When I sit all by myself"). Here the speeches of the woman in the Old Testament seem to have exerted an influence, since few of the spring poems in classical literature, such as Flora's tale in Ovid's *Fasti,* were narrated by a woman. She goes on to say that she grows pale and cannot hear or see anything; then she addresses the spring:

> So you, O beauty of spring,
> hear and consider
> the leaves, the flowers, and grass;
> for my soul is sick and weak.

> *Tu saltim, veris gratia,*
> *exaudi et considera*
> *frondes, flores et gramina;*
> *nam mea languet anima.*   (st. 6)

60. *The Cambridge Songs,* ed. Karl Breul (Cambridge, Eng., 1915), no. 32, p. 64, 15–16; Breul's title, *Verna femine suspiria,* suggests a nonallegorical interpretation.

Christ had said: "Consider the lilies." He asked: if God decked a simple lily in such splendor, what would He not do for a man with a soul? This woman says to nature (she does not mention God): "*You* consider the lilies; *I* am sick at heart." She thus places all tension between the self and nature; she does not consider the supernatural at all. The woman makes no secret about what is troubling her: she is lonely; the harmony of nature has no bearing upon her internal discord. With this poem, we return to the world of the *Vigil,* the arena of "my soul" (*mea anima*). When we read a poem such as this, a thousand years of intervening history seem to crumble. As a poetic expression, it does not approach the complexity of the *Vigil,* which treated love as metaphysical efficient cause, tutelary protector of the state, and supreme fiction. In twenty-four very tight lines, the poet here manages to bring the macrocosm into play with the microcosm, leaving no doubt in the reader's mind as to which the author considered more important. The lyric self is firmly back with all its tragic splendor. To say that the poem is pagan is to belittle both Christianity and antiquity. The poet omits certain values that were very important to his age (the love of God, the Virgin Mary, the Church Militant, and the Celestial Paradise), but he does not discover Venus and the Greco-Roman religion. He merely *re*discovers the tragic nobility of the self, which can recur in any age, and which, by the definitions of lyric poetry formed in the first chapter, seems to be an integral part of the genius of the finest lyrics of any age.

Yet at the same time, this poem admits allegorization just as the Song of Songs does. As a matter of fact, almost anything admits allegorization if one chooses to allegorize. One could, for example, interpret the lonely woman as a desperate soul starved for the love of Christ. Therefore, even though my interpretation of the poem is purely literal, I must acknowledge the possibility of metaphoric raising. The metaphysical view of life constantly renders everything physical ambiguous. This poem omits the metaphysical superstructure of Christianity, but when we pass to the *Carmina Burana,* we will find that layer of superior meanings, overtones in the aesthetic sense, very much in evidence. Yet we shall also find ourselves quite clearly immersed in a tangible world of the flesh.

The Physical Antithesis of the *Carmina Burana*

The collection of poems known today as the *Carmina Burana* was culled from a thirteenth-century manuscript discovered in the early 1800s in the Benediktbeuern monastery in Bavaria. After identifying the authors of a few of the poems from other manuscripts, Raby dated most of the collection in the twelfth century, and some poems even earlier.[61] For the purposes of this study, it is important to know only that these poems were written before or during the flowering of the Provençal tradition.

Let us examine a typical poem selected at random from the edition of Schmeller (p. 184):

Now at last the fields are laughing, 1
now at last young girls are happy,
the face of the earth is laughing,
Summer has now appeared,
it shines happily decked with flowers. 5

The grove is growing green again,
bushes are in leaf,
cruel winter's yielded.
Happy young men,
go rejoice with the flowers: 10
love's luring you now to the girls.

61. *Secular Latin,* 2, 257 (after dating MS in latter part of thirteenth century): "It is true that many of the best of the Latin pieces are of an earlier time. Thus there are poems of Peter of Blois, of Walter of Châtillon . . . of Philip de Grève . . ." (in 1100s).

Therefore, let's fight
together for Venus,
let's avoid all sadness,
we who are tender.   15
Let sight and speech,
Hope and love lead us to our joys.

Iamiam rident* prata,   1
iamiam virgines iocundantur,
terre ridet facies,
estas nunc apparuit,
ornatusque florum lete claruit.   5

Nemus revirescit,
frondent frutices,
hiems seva cessit:
leti iuvenes,
congaudete floribus,   10
amor allicit vos iam virginibus.

Ergo militemus
simul Veneri,
tristia vitemus
nos qui teneri;   15
visus et colloquia,
spes amorque trahant nos ad gaudia.

*Schumann: *virent*

The poem begins with the word *iamiam* (now at last!), a doubly emphatic form of the words *iam* or *nunc* that is similar to
Ovid's *etiamnunc* and the repetitions of *nunc* in Sedulius
Scottus. The word is again emphasized at the beginning of the
second line, where we have the traditional classical picture of
happy girls, laughing fields, and the laughing face of the earth
as the opening of a spring song. Furthermore the poetic technique is similar to that already observed in the *Vigil of Venus*
and the *Latin Anthology:* earth is laughing; the girls are laughing; it is hard to tell them apart because the poet is drawing

few distinctions between nature and humanity. When Summer (one cannot resist capitalization) appears wearing flowers, we are clearly drawn back to the subjective world of the *Vigil*, where the grove was undoing her hair and the Earth had opened her lap to the husband rains. The medieval poet is humanizing nature not through standard Greco-Roman myths but by creating private myths; at the same time he is also "naturizing" humanity through the loose association of the general context and the attribution of natural characteristics to human beings. It is interesting to observe how, in the second strophe, he intensifies this process. For example, in the sixth and seventh lines he describes natural events in natural terms: groves growing green, bushes leafing. The eighth line, however, can be read in two ways: cruel winter (Horace's *acris hiems*) has yielded; or cruel Winter (to match the personified Summer of line 4) has yielded. The second reading is more in accord with what follows.

The poet next exhorts the happy young men, who balance the happy young girls in line 2, to rejoice with (*congaudete*) the flowers. The prepositional prefix *con-* contains a major implication: whatever delights a flower delights a young man. The rhyme scheme then comes to the fore, yoking *floribus* and *virginibus*. Also, there is a curious logical shift: "go rejoice with the flowers: / love's luring you now to the girls." Somehow, the girls have suddenly replaced the flowers; or should we say that, compositionally and conceptually, the boys, the girls, and the flowers are all one?

The last strophe opens with a powerful conjunction: *ergo*. We must not translate this word with some bland term such as: "and so." We are in an age of Aristotelian proof. *Ergo* means "therefore"; some premises have been stated, and a conclusion is being drawn. The poet states his conclusion: "Let's fight together for Venus." But how was this conclusion reached? We are forced to go back to lines 10 and 11 to find the major and minor premises: it is spring; flowers are happy; flowers are reproducing; young men are happy; *ergo*—. The premises are not stated in exact terms; the logic is a little slip-shod, but the meaning is quite clear. The poet is drawing deductions about humanity entirely from the world of nature, just as was done in the *Cambridge Songs*. The poet equates man's life with the flowers and is happy. (Shades of the *Latin Anthology!*)

In the last strophe he constructs a little marching song for Venus Militant. He admits a contradictory premise ("sadness," *tristia*), then expels it with the same dogmatic vigor (but utterly different intent) with which Prudentius expelled the night and human love. When we realize that the opening strophe of the poem is very much like that of Ovid's spring poem in his *Tristia,* we can appreciate the newness of this conception. Finally the poet couples two words of the senses (sight and speech) with two abstractions (hope and love), and brings both mind and matter to a joyous resolution; the poem ends on that note of joy, *gaudia.*

This poem is so simple on the surface that some critics have been tempted to call it childlike.[62] On the other hand, if one compares its rhetoric with Christian hymns and sacred literature, it begins to appear a little diabolical. For example, the poem's structure is based upon the travesty of the word *ergo,* which was an indispensable part of any logician's vocabulary. Would any philosopher from Aristotle to Aquinas agree with the argument suggested by this poem? Of course not. Man is *not* like the flowers; he is not like the birds and the bees. He is rational, and his reason sets him apart from the rest of the physical world. To a rational man, spring is simply a part of the annual round of seasons. The external world may affect man's senses, but the rational man does not live the life of the senses. *Sic* philosophers. The poet's pointed use of the word *ergo* tells us precisely what he thought of them.

Furthermore the word *iamiam,* or the alternate word *nunc* in line 4, is interesting. Albertus Magnus pronounced the final

62. The favorable opinion of Whicher (p. 289): "they possessed a childlike power to free the mind from the dregs of bitterness."

judgment upon such seemingly innocent adverbs when he
called the inferior, fleeting, illusory goods of this world *bona
ut nunc,* "goods for here and now."[63] Similarly, St.
Thomas Aquinas had a restricted use for the word *gaudium:* he used
delectatio as a general word for pleasure, usually that of the
senses, reserving *gaudium* for "intellectual joy" or happiness
deriving from the Perfect Good *(bonum perfectum),* which
is God.[64] The theologians are mentioned in this context merely to show by contrast the continuity of the poem's rhetoric
and its diametric opposition to a systematic Aristotelian vocabulary. The poet's vocabulary is consistent, and it preserves
the illusion of rational presentation, but here it is decidedly
antidogmatic and antimetaphysical.

But if the poet is not a Christian rationalist, he is not a
pagan either, by the standards established in Chapter 1. His
treatment of the external world is far too simplified. There
are no classical spring lyrics that end on a note of unmodified
joy. Joy was first introduced by Christian hymns, in terms of
Easter. Yet in this poem, *gaudium* has been transferred to a
pagan portrait of spring. The laughing fields and personified
Summer are part of a Vergilian-Ovidian heritage. The *Burana*
poem blends the Christian spirit with pagan rhetoric. The
third strophe, for example, mimics the marching rhythms of
a hymn of Prudentius or Venantius Fortunatus: onward Christian soldiers! Yet the rhetorical expression derives from Ovid,
who said: *Militat omnis amans, et habet sua castra Cupido*
("Every lover is a soldier, and Cupid has his own camp,"
Amores 1.9.1). However, Ovid's whimsical metaphor preserved the notion of ceaseless conflict and potential agony:

Love is a kind of warfare; go away, you lazy ones! . . .
Night and winter, long roads and savage griefs
and every kind of toil beset his tender camps.

63. *De principiis motus processivi* 2.2: *Opera omnia, 12,* ed. B. Geyer (1955),
p. 59.
64. *S.T.* 2, pt. 1, 31, 4. For an application to lyric poetry, see J. E. Shaw,
Guido Cavalcanti's Theory of Love (Toronto, 1949), pp. 46 f.

> *Militiae species amor est: discedite, segnes!* . . .
> *nox et hiemps longaeque viae saevique dolores*
> *mollibus his castris et labor omnis inest.*
>
> *(Ars Am.* 2.233–36)

The *Burana* poet is far more self-assured. He preserves the wit of Ovid's "tender camps" (*mollibus castris*) when he says that the soldiers of Venus are "tender" (*teneri*); but he goes on to write a triumphant battle hymn. His hymn to Venus is conceived in the mode and manner of a hymn of the Church Militant.

In the last line of the poem, the poet quietly parodies two of the three prime Christian virtues: hope and love; he omits only faith. Yet we will observe faith entering secular poetry in other Latin lyrics—indeed, a whole body of articles of faith. However here the systematization is not fully developed. In discussing a poem such as *Iamiam rident prata,* it is almost impossible to avoid mentioning rhetorical elements which the poem seems to be parodying or attacking. It is too simple to be classical, too sacrilegious to be Christian. Let us turn to some of the other better-known poems of the collection to see how this one-dimensional statement of earthly joy is developed or contradicted.

THE BETTER-KNOWN SPRING POEMS OF THE *Carmina Burana*

Let us now return to the poem *Omittamus studia,* which was cited earlier in connection with Horace's Spring Ode 4.12.[65] It is interesting to see how the medieval poet wrings new meanings out of stock Horatian material simply by dropping a few very important words. For example, Horace had said,

65. *Carmina Burana,* ed. W. Meyers, A. Hilka, and O. Schumann, 2 vols., 3 pts.: *1,* pt. 2, *Die Liebeslieder* (Heidelberg, Carl Winter, 1941), no. 75, p. 48; this vol. hereafter cited as *CB.*

"It's good to be foolish at the right time" (*Dulce est desipere in loco*, 28). The *Burana* poet says:

> Let's drop our studies,
> it's good to be foolish,
> let's seize the sweet things
> of tender youth!

> *Omittamus studia,*
> *dulce est desipere,*
> *et carpamus dulcia*
> *iuventutis tenere!*   (st. 1, 1–4)

By omitting the words "at the right time" (*in loco;* or "in the right place"), the medieval poet achieves a much broader generalization; by striking out the typical Horatian sense of balance, he arrives at sheer hedonism.

Now let us examine the opening line. The word *studium* is ambiguous in Medieval Latin; it retains the primary classical meaning of "desire" or "pursuit," but it also acquires the modern meaning of "studies." Horace had said: "Let's forget our desire for wealth" (*studium lucri*). The *Burana* poet drops the word "wealth," and also drops the Horatian moral overtone; after all, men ought not to be guided by material instincts. Then, by using the word *studium* with its modern connotation, the poet adopts a patently anti-intellectual attitude. We cannot possibly read the opening line in the Horatian manner as a call away from material pursuits, because the invitation in line 4 is clearly directed toward a material pursuit. Similarly the phrase *carpamus dulcia iuventutis tenere* ("let's seize the sweet things of tender youth") bears a surface relationship to Horace's renowned *carpe diem* ("seize the day!"). Yet, like all the other Horatian echoes, this too is but a one-dimensional call to pleasure, totally removed from Horace's balanced presentation of conflicting motives. The *Burana* poet then states the conflict that troubled Horace:

> The spring of youth is rushing by,
> Our winter's hurrying on . . .
>
> *Ver etatis labitur,*
> *hiems nostra properat . . .*   (st. 2, 1–2)

But the medieval poet leaps to a triumphant conclusion that Horace never seriously entertained:

> Let's imitate the gods!
>
> *Imitemur superos!*   (st. 3, 1)

The cure for mortality is immortality; that makes good sense in Christian, but not Horatian, terms. A Christian was supposed to imitate the perfect life of Christ; the *imitatio Christi* is the road to Heaven. On the other hand, the imitation of Christ is a departure from the earthly conceits that dominate the rhetoric of the poem. The poet is making a classical demand upon reality; when we notice that he says "gods" instead of "God," we begin to get the full force of his joke. The joke depends upon two conflicting tensions: Christian assumption in godhead and classical emphasis upon reality. The poem entertains both modes of expression but cannot be entirely reconciled by either.

The *Burana* poet goes on to invite his friends to a spring dance in the village square. He says that when he sees the young girls dancing:

> They steal me from myself.
>
> *me michi subripiunt.*   (st. 4, 8)

His poem ends on that note of expectant loss of personal identity. We need only compare this statement with a similar line of Catullus to point up a basic difference in the *Burana* attitude toward love. At the height of his passion, Catullus, in an adaptation from Sappho, said that Lesbia stole his senses away (*eripit sensus mihi;* 51.6). Yet he modified the word "me" with the word "poor" (*misero*). The struggle to retain self-identity against the force of mystic inversion in love is a basic tension in classical love poetry. Indeed, the tragic nature of Catullus' love stemmed from the fact that he *could* regain the self, but only with the loss of Lesbia. The soul fights desperately for love; then fights desperately to be free from it; when freedom comes, it is as much a loss as a victory. The classical notion of love is inherently tragic, even when treated satirically or comically, as by Ovid.

The early Christians overruled this frightful paradox by overruling the love of things of this world. By making God, or perfection, the sole proper object of love, they went beyond human corruptibility to eternal value as a means of resolving the all-too-human dilemma. Augustine noted ironically that the ill-fated desire of all earthly lovers was "to make one from the many" (*ex pluribus unum facere; Conf.* 4.8); yet the lasting absorption of the Many in the One is primarily the theme of Christian hymnology and Christian Neoplatonism, where an individual gladly surrenders his identity to "live happily forever after."

The *Burana* poet steps between these two worlds. He transfers mystic rapture back to the human plane, but without any awareness of eventual loss. His dancing girls are goddesses with consubstantiative powers: angels of Venus. The poet blends divine conceits and sensual nymphs in a way that removes him as far from Catullus and Horace as from Augustine and Bonaventure. Yet his poem has a certain magnificence because of its violence; although living in a Christian age, he is less Christian than the pagans.

The poem "Janus Closes Out the Year" (*Ianus annum circinat*) is interesting for its adaptation of Vergil's "Love conquers all—and me, let me yield to love."[66] The *Burana* poet begins by announcing that spring has come; he then employs a two-line refrain in which his first line (*Amor cuncta superat*) is modeled after Vergil's *Omnia vincit amor*. Later in the

66. *CB*, no. 56, p. 1.

poem, he uses a second refrain that is almost identical with
Vergil's lines:

> Love conquers all,
> love governs all.

> *Vincit Amor omnia,*
> *regit Amor omnia.*　　　　　　　　　　　　　(st. 4)

The *Burana* poem ends with the last half of the Vergilian
echo: *nunc tuo iuri cedo* ("now I yield to your laws"). It is a
simple poem with a sing-song chant, and on the surface might
suggest a close understanding of Vergil. Yet the truth is: it is
a travesty of him. In Chapter 1, there was a brief discussion of
Eclogue 10, in which the line is spoken by Gallus, who is then
urged by Vergil to rise up and put love aside. The lyric voice
of the *Burana* poem identifies itself with Gallus, and totally
excludes the voice of Vergil. In short, it reduces a very complex poem stated in two dimensions to one. The surface rhetoric has a Vergilian gloss; but beneath that gloss is an interpretation of love that Vergil, creator of the great romantic
passion of Dido that haunted the Middle Ages from Augustine
to Dante, never dreamed of uttering. Vergil's attitude toward
love and the self is always tempered by his awareness of human
destiny and the demands of society. The *Burana* poet ignores
or is ignorant of these latter factors in the equation, and ultimately ignores or is ignorant of Vergil.

Even when the *Burana* poets present love from an unfulfilled or tragic viewpoint, they do so with a cry of vengeance.
In "The Time Is Pleasant" (*Tempus est iocundum*), the pagan metaphor of man's life depicted in terms of the rose is
revived:[67]

> O! o! I'm all in flower!

> *o! o! totus floreo!*　　　　　　　　　　　　　(st. 1)

---

67. *CB*, no. 179, pp. 298–99; cf. Schmeller, no. 140, p. 211.

The poet calls his sweetheart "flower of girls" (*flos puellarum*) and "rose of roses" (st. 3). Rhetorically speaking, the effect is confusing: the first expression recalls Tiberianus or Florus, but has none of their brooding melancholy. The second expression recalls the Hebraic-Christian convention of compounding abstractions (light of lights, king of kings) already cited in the hymns of Ambrose. Yet the transferral of this technique from the Christian God to a medieval woman is striking. The poet is enjoying the best of two worlds: he compares his girl to a flower, thus suggesting the naturalness of his love and the vividness of her beauty; but he makes her the paragon of flowers, thus suggesting that she exceeds the bounds of nature and partakes of a consummate beauty.

The removal of this poem from the classical world is stamped by the appearance of the happy nightingale singing about earthly love:

> The nightingale sings
> so sweetly
> and I hear her melodies;
> inwardly I burn.
>
> *Cantat philomena*
> *sic dulciter,*
> *et modulans auditur;*
> *intus caleo.* (st. 2)

Yet it is not the classical Philomela who is singing; it is now just a common, lower-case nightingale. Her song excites a single response from the poet: the sudden inflammation of love. This is the new service that "Philomena" has acquired: she returns from Christian assumption as an earthly idealized bird of joy. Once again the recurrent chop-logic of medieval love poetry asserts itself: the bird's singing has a direct correspondence with the poet's state of mind; the poet suggests that there is only one possible response after hearing a nightingale sing: the hearer burns with love. Later the poet orders the poor secularized creature to shut up: *Sile, philomena!* He wants to continue his song without interruption. We are certainly far removed from the *Vigil,* where the poet wondered if he could continue living after hearing the poignant call of the bird. The *Burana* poet next draws a very telling parallel:

> *Tempore brumali*
> *vir patiens,*
> *animo vernali*
> *lasciviens.* (st. 7)

"In the winter, a man is patient; in the spring, he's full of lust." It's now spring; *ergo* farewell, winter; farewell, Christian patience; farewell, paradox.

The last strophe depends a great deal upon the rhyme scheme:

> Come, my little lady,
> and satisfy me!
> come, O come, my lovely!
> for I'm now dying!
>
> *Veni, domicella,*
> *cum gaudio!*
> *veni, veni, pulchra!**
> *iam pereo!* (st. 8)

*Schmeller *bella*

These lines are so lightly and wittily stated that we might ignore the fact that they are a parody of mystical death-in-life. In fact, this poem seems to show the excessive exhibitionism that C. S. Lewis would like to attribute to Catullus.[68] Catullus very seldom surrendered to love in the unreflecting manner of this lyric. To Catullus, death was an unmitigated catastrophe; love was half better. To the *Burana* poet, love is all good;

68. *Allegory of Love,* p. 5: "If Catullus and Propertius vary the strain with cries of rage and misery, this is not so much because they are romantics, as because they are exhibitionists."

and even the love-death, parodied as it is in this instance, has an unqualified splendor. The martyrs of Venus in the *Burana* are related rhetorically to Ovid, who cried out in helpless rage:

Why do you strike down me, a soldier who never
deserted your standards; why am I wounded in my own camp?

quid me, qui miles numquam tua signa reliqui,
laedis, et in castris vulneror ipse meis?   (*Amores* 2.9.3–4)

But they show a closer spiritual affinity to those unflinching Christian martyrs who accepted their deaths for a glory yet to come.

The blending of Christian and classical rhetoric is most startling in a poem called "In the Sweet Springtime" (*Veris dulcis in tempore*). Their contrast can be seen in two adjoining strophes:

> Look, the lilies are in flower!
> And the ranks of virgins offer
> Songs to the highest of the gods.
> Sweet love!

> If I could hold what I catch
> in a grove beneath the leaves,
> I'd kiss her with happiness.
> Sweet love!

> *Ecce florescunt lilia,*
> *et virginum dant agmina*
> *summo* deorum carmina.*
> *Dulcis amor!*

> *Si tenerem quam capio†*
> *in nemore sub folio,*
> *oscularer cum gaudio.*
> *Dulcis amor!*[69]

*MS *summa*   †Schumann *cupio*

69. Schmeller, no. 121, p. 195, sts. 3–4; cf. *CB*, no. 85, p. 72 for variants.

The first strophe bears the mark of Christian Easter hymns, where the lily replaced the hyacinth and narcissus as a traditional spring flower. The lily connotes purity and virginity. It is coupled here with a chorus of virgins, who seem to continue on a human plane the metaphoric connotation of the flower. The technique in these two lines suggests Prudentius. Next we learn that the virgins are singing songs to "the highest of the gods." This statement, of course, jars the Christian context; we expect *summo deo* (the highest God) instead of the plural expression. Furthermore, the word for songs (*carmina*) is often, though not always, a secular word; we might have expected the more appropriate Christian word *hymnos* (hymns). Yet the scene still holds until we enter the second strophe. There we are suddenly thrown into a grove or forest, such as that encountered in the *Vigil*. The quietness of the preceding strophe is shattered with the words "catch" and "kiss." The scene becomes purely secular; the virgins are not saintlike creatures, but just young girls; the lily is now just another spring flower; the highest of the gods is not Christ, the god of Christian love (*charitas*), but Cupid or Amor, the god of material love (*amor*). Yet what prevented us from drawing these conclusions immediately was the poet's clever handling of such very ambiguous but highly charged words as "love" and "virgin." The *dulcis amor* that serves as a refrain seemed in the first strophe to be part of the virgins' song to God. It loses its ambiguity in the second strophe. Yet what makes the poem dramatically effective is the manner in which the rhetoric hovers between two worlds before the sudden resolution in the final words: "Sweet love!"

The history of the word *virgo* itself discloses a tradition of poetic change. In Classical Latin, the word was ambiguous; it could mean "virgin" or, more often, simply "young girl." A great deal of classical spring literature was constructed around the rape of the virgin: Proserpina, Flora, Philomela. The defilement of purity seems to be an integral part of the spring archetype. Yet classical authors consistently related these tales of rape with a mixture of horror and fascination that was but one facet of the essentially tragic juxtapositions that characterized most of their spring poems.

The Christians transformed the word *virgo* into its idealized meaning by making it a fixed epithet of the One Virgin, Mary. Their lifting of the word onto a metaphysical plane is but another example of the way in which they transformed spring into Easter and lyric poems into hymns. I have not traced the *Ave, Maria* poems in this study, because they are removed from the central theme of spring. Now, however, they must be mentioned, for the transformation (or should we say the reduction?) of the word *Virgo* to *virgo* parallels the late medieval creation of a new pagan spring that emerges from the clarity of a Christian Easter. The *Burana* virgins singing to the highest of the gods have the aura of Mary about them; that is what makes their projected rape a kind of double travesty. In the twelfth century, the Latin word *virgo* had such a strong Christian connotation that it acquired only that connotation in its Romance developments: Italian, *vergine;* French, *vierge;* Old Provençal, *vergena.* Yet in this poem, and in other poems of the *Burana,* the poets use the word with its purely secular meaning, although they draw on its metaphysical overtone. They endow the virgins or young girls of this world with the splendor of the Heavenly Virgin. In this poem about a proposed seduction, the achievement is sublime travesty. Other poets, however, employ the technique more cleverly and more seriously.

We can best show the ambiguity of this word by citing three random samples of secular and religious poetry drawn from the medieval time span. In evaluating these selections, the reader should ask himself: is this poem written to a real virgin (or young woman) or to the Virgin Mary:

> 1. Hail, most beautiful,
>   most precious gem,
>   hail, beauty of virgins,

> virgin glorious,
> hail, light of lights,
> hail, rose of the world.

2. Hail, star of the sea . . .
   outstanding virgin,
   gentle before all.

3. Beautiful virgin,
   standing still with sighs,
   your mind is full of love . . .
   O generous goddess . . .
   O muse not to be spurned.

1. *Ave, formosissima,*
   gemma pretiosa,
   ave, decus virginum,
   virgo gloriosa,
   ave, lumen luminum,
   ave, mundi rosa.[70]

2. *Ave, maris stella . . .*
   Virgo singularis,
   inter omnes mitis.[71]

3. *virgo speciosa.*
   sistens in suspirio
   mens est amorosa . . .
   diva generosa . . .
   musa non exosa.[72]

1. This selection is purely secular; it comes from a Latin prototype for the *Roman de la rose* entitled *Si linguis angelicis.* The lines are addressed to a girl whom the protagonist meets in a forest, and whom he subsequently seduces. The poet not only parodies the entire *Ave* tradition in passage to this seduc-

70. *CB*, no. 77, p. 53, st. 8.
71. *An. Hymn.* 2, no. 29, pp. 39–40, 1, 17–18.
72. *Oxford*, no. 290, pp. 442–48, 1–4.

tion, but also tramples over Venantius Fortunatus' famous hymn *Pange, lingua, gloriosi* by saying *Pange lingua igitur* ("And so my tongue tell forth") as a prelude to the narrative. 2. The virgin in the second poem is the Virgin Mary. This hymn comes from an unknown hand and may have been written in the 800s. It has no secular connotation whatsoever, and is distinguished for its sobriety and refinement. 3. The virgin of this specimen is again the Virgin Mary, but she is addressed with rhetoric that is far closer to the first sample than the second. These lines were written by Richard Rolle of Hampole (d. 1349), a mystic who applied sensual images to a religious subject.

These three specimens embody a long history of rhetorical interdependence. The Virgin Mary of the second specimen seems to have inspired the parody of the first; yet the secular virgin of the first specimen led eventually to the very human Virgin of the third. The religious and secular strains intertwine; it is sometimes impossible to separate them.

For the purpose of this study, it is important to point out that the virgins of the *Burana* are neither the Virgin Mary nor the virgins of classical antiquity. The *Burana* poem just examined is a travesty of the good taste and complex presentation of the classical world; it is also a sacrilegious bringing-down-to-earth of the religious world. Yet the possibilities that the *Carmina Burana* present are enormous. With taste and refinement, the de-allegorization process could open up a whole new world. If, in debasing the mystical realm, poets insisted on preserving some of the idealism of the metaphysical sphere in the physical, the result would not only be more compelling but also perhaps more in accordance with the actual human condition. In other words, the *Carmina Burana* analyzed up to this point are far too simple. They merely reverse the mystical coin and end up with a human counterfeit. The fields of Paradise, when transferred to earth, become a glorified garden of lust; when divine virgins walk in the earthly meadows, they are merely objects for rape. The Easter hymns had stated a metaphysical thesis; these lyric poems state a physical antithesis. But after the world has known the Crucifixion and the Virgin, you cannot return to the ethos of Catullus' crucifixion in love and Ovid's virgins so smoothly. The descent from the world of spirit (*nous*) to the world of flesh (*hyle*) is a long, long fall in which the intermediate realm of reason-*ratio-Logos* is lost. For example, the famous hymn *Dies irae* contains the line: *Gere curam mei finis*[73] (Take care about my end). The *Confession of Golias* contains the seminal line: *curam gero cutis*[74] (I care about my skin). Isn't there some pathway between mystic immersion in the One and sensual immersion in the Many? The *Carmina Burana* themselves contain a two-line poem that poses the problem:

Always, in all that is, it's good to have a mean,
for without measure the court of the king will not stand.

Semper ad omne quod est mensuram ponere prodest,
Nam sine mensura non stabit regia cura.[75]

I have translated *cura* (care, administration) as if it were *curia* (court), because the notions and etymologies are related. Thus we are searching for something upon which a court (symbolizing the Earthly Paradise or order realized in terms of human perfection) can be built.

We must now turn aside from the better-known *Burana* selections which appear in the collections of Waddell, Whicher, and Raby, and approach those contained in the much criticized but complete nineteenth-century edition of the manuscript by J. A. Schmeller and the much protracted edition of Hilka, Meyer, and Schumann.[76] The edition of Schmeller, despite its conjectures and lack of correlation with related manuscripts, presents the total picture, for it contains

---

73. *An. Hymn. 54,* no. 178, pp. 269 f., st. 17.
74. Schmeller, no. 172, p. 68, st. 5, 8.
75. Schmeller, no. 82a, p. 169.
76. See Bibliog. for details; also above, nn. 43, 47, 59, 65.

saints' lives, satires, and two nativity plays blended with the very earthy spring songs just examined.[77] There too we find Latin poems that would seem to satisfy a need for courtly refinement or, as the *Burana* define it, the quest for a synthesis or mean.

THE LESSER-KNOWN POEMS OF THE *Carmina Burana*

In a very unusual poem, Ovid's god of love, Amor, appears to a poet in a vision and pronounces much the same sort of critical judgment upon the *Burana* concept of love as I have pronounced upon the poetry:

> The art of love's
> No longer taught
> As handed down by Ovid:
> Gradually, it's been perverted.

> *Artes amatorie*
> *iam non instruuntur*
> *a Nasone tradite,*
> *passim pervertuntur.*
> (Schmeller, no. 156, pp. 220–22, st. 7, 1–4)

Amor then goes on to attribute to Ovid extraordinary powers that no modern critic would ever dream of assigning to that connoisseur of love:

77. B. Bischoff is continuing the still incomplete *CB*, which is excellent for textual comparisons beyond the Burana MS but, perhaps because of the succession of editors, lacks a critical attitude toward the text (note asterisked comparisons in quoted matter). Schmeller frequently took indefensible liberties to create rhymes and preserve rhythmic patterns (sometimes of his own making), but he at least attempted to create poems. Many of his emendations (e.g., no. 156, pp. 220–22, st. 11) were adopted by Otto Schumann in *CB*. I have used both editions, depending on the conditions of the specific poems: e.g., most of the lines discussed in Schmeller, no. 36, pp. 121–24 are excluded from the main text by Schumann; but they are very important lines and, even if interpolated, were written by somebody of the age.

> By my arts, Ovid
> was happily instructed
> in the pleasures of the world,
> and brought up on my laws
> he tried to call the world
> back from its errors (sins) . . .
> he taught men to love with wisdom.

> *Naso meis artibus*
> *feliciter instructus*
> *mundique voluptatibus*
> *et regulis subductus*
> *ab errore studuit*
> *mundum revocare . . .*
> *docuit sapienter amare.* (st. 8, 1–7)

The poem sounds very funny to the modern reader accustomed to the wit and satire of Ovid's "art" of love. But the *Burana* poem is presented as one of those curious visionary poems of the twelfth century which demand serious consideration. We sense in the expression "tried to call the world back from its errors (sins)" a kind of parody in which Ovid's doctrine of secular love rivals Christ's doctrine of brotherly love, and in which the Roman love god Amor speaks with the full seriousness and authority of God, the loving Creator. Yet, on the other hand, we are dealing with an age that was capable of moralizing Ovid; in this poem, are we witnessing a similar process: the raising of Ovid to a transcendental level? It is difficult to say, because the poem never really commits itself. It walks the tightrope between comic parody and absolute dogmatic sincerity without totally yielding to either tone. We may laugh at the notion of Ovid as "divinely" ordained minister of love; but at the same time, is the notion of human love as a reflection of some divine agency laughable? Similarly, we may ridicule the fact that Ovid taught men to love "wisely" (*sapienter*)—a more appropriate word would be "cleverly";

but is the notion of human love totally removed from the sphere of wisdom (*sapientia*)? This little poem, under the guise of a rather playful surface, poses some very serious questions that will occupy the realm of poetry for several hundred years.

It is to be noted here that the poetry uses Ovid and Ovidian trappings without really perpetuating Ovid at all. At the same time, it is far removed from St. Augustine, who said: "The friendship of this world is a fornication from Thee" (*Conf.* 1.13). Similarly, by its insistence upon idealism in the physical world, the work removes itself from the context of the poems we have just examined; it insists upon taste and wisdom as facets of earthly love; it equates refined earthly love with salvation, and base love (*turpiter* occurs in the seventh strophe) with sin (*errore*). This is neither Ovid understood nor Ovid misunderstood; it is Ovid being reinterpreted in a Christian age. The poem is not entirely metaphysical; it insists on the pleasures of this world (*voluptatibus mundi*). On the other hand, it is not entirely material; it insists on wisdom as the source and ethos of love. It is a cross between both worlds, and it wavers conceptually between the two just as it wavers tonally between comedy and seriousness.

The poet goes on to suggest a whole metaphysical framework constructed around this earthly love. He speaks of Ovidian love as a supernatural religion (*Veneris mysteria;* st. 9, 1) and the lover as a silent initiate in those mystical rites (*iubet sua sacra taceri;* st. 9, 7). Then, in a remarkable closing stanza, the god of love calls Ovid the father of all virtuous love, all just rewards for the lover, and all the lovers' laws; here, in brief, are the external trappings of what nineteenth-century scholars called courtly love:

> The secret affairs of Venus
> must be carried on with virtue;
> must be purchased with highest merit
> and the very finest manners;

but now they're for sale in the market
and reduced to a bargain price:
my laws must be redeemed by the people
to pay for such great wrongs.

> *Res archana Veneris*
> *virtutibus habenda,*
> *optimisque meritis*
> *et moribus emenda,*
> *prostat in prostibulo,*
> *redigitur in pactum:*
> *tanta meum populo*
> *ius est ad damna redactum.*

Despite its obviously comic tone (since love is spoken of as a business, a *negotium*), the poem adopts a patently moral point of view. It makes a distinction between refined love (what the troubadours call *fin'amors*) and false or base love (*fals'amors*). Unger's study of Ovid has shown us the direct Ovidian parallels for such expressions; indeed, Fränkel has emphasized the way Ovid's love, satiric though it be, is a critique of both the gross, materialistic life of upper-class Roman capitalism and the pompous Olympic machinery upon which Augustus was erecting his thousand-year Reich.[78] Yet we would be wrong to see just Ovid in these lines. The Christian overtones are unavoidable: buying back (*re*-demption); love travestied by wrongs (*damna*, damnation); love as a necessary adjunct of virtue. Through Christ's love, He redeemed the world from error; Christ paid back to the Father the debt of mankind created by the wrongs of Adam. Through Christian love, man

---

78. Hermann Unger, *De ovidiana in Carminibus Buranis* (Strassburg, 1914); Fränkel, p. 189: "Roman erotic poetry cannot be properly understood unless we realize its very iniquitous position. A triple handicap was imposed on it: the disparagement of poetry; the disparagement of love; and third, the prohibition against concerning itself with the affection between a man and a woman who hoped to be married. . . . Nevertheless, Roman love-poetry survived and throve . . . for two reasons. First, erotic poetry was the one form for the expression of sensibility . . . and second, amor vincit omnia."

follows the image of Christ, imitates his perfect virtue, and thereby re-deems himself. The rhetoric works both ways: it draws from the best elements of both worlds and refuses to be an irreconcilable partner of either. For example, it suggests all the happiness that comes as a natural reward of Christian love, yet, at the same time, promises all the earthly satisfaction that derives from an Ovidian context. If we examine just the first two lines of this final strophe, we can see the blending of these two strains. For example, the secret or hidden love of Venus is clearly pagan (*Ars Am.* 2.607); there is nothing secret about Christian charity: it is open, frank, and freely expressed. Yet the notion that charity is bound up with virtue is eminently Christian; however, it is not at all Ovidian, for Ovid advocated deceit, trickery, or any other ruse for gaining the loved one. The methodology here shrouds the very vital Ovidian world of the senses with Christian idealism. It is something new, although it derives from two very ancient traditions.

The poem is a hybrid dogma work; it establishes the framework for idealized earthly love, but does not show the expression of that love in act, as accident. Yet it is obvious from the way this little artificial metaphysical world is constructed that it will offer tremendous possibilities for paradox, wit, and ambiguity. If Ovid is the new Bible and Amor is the new God, the lover will most probably be cast in the image of suffering Christ, with the loved one as the Virgin Mary; the *virgo* of this poetry will no longer be a purely earthbound nymph contrasted with heavenly saints, but a kind of intermediary agent, a fusion of the two, who can rise into the mists of mystic idealism or descend into the bright reality of the flesh. Once the lyric "I" is loosed in this brave new world, he will indeed be capable of extended flights (and falls) of the imagination. His field of paradox will be extended from a Christian-like macrocosm to an Ovidian microcosm; the tensions deriving from the self will have a conscious or unconscious metaphysical overtone.

The spirit of the Christian Ovid can be observed in a very

fine poem called *Axe Phebus aureo* ("Phoebus in His Golden Car," Schmeller, no. 44, p. 134). At first glance, various stanzas of this poem appear to be directly Ovidian. For example, the first four lines of the fifth stanza are an almost direct paraphrase of the Ovidian paradox of "pursuing what flees and fleeing what pursues," which was cited in Chapter 1:

> The girl who desires me
> I run from;
> the girl who runs from me
> I chase;
> the more I renounce what I ought to do
> the more I'm drawn to what I shouldn't;
> the more the unpleasant's allowed,
> the more the unlawful's pleasant.

> *Que cupit*
> *hanc fugio,*
> *que fugit,*
> *hanc cupio;*
> *plus renuo debitum,*
> *plus feror in vetitum,*
> *plus licet* illibitum,*
> *plus libet† illicitum.*

*MS *libet*   †MS *licet*

But although the opening lines of the stanza are Ovidian, the last four lines introduce moral tonalities that are singularly un-Ovidian. Ovid never questioned the basic premise of the desirability of love's pleasure; any love (adulterous, homosexual) was a good—if attained; the tension lay all in the attaining and holding. This poet, however, has a guilt complex. He thinks about certain loves that are "unlawful" and about "things I shouldn't do." Ovid pictured love as war, and any object or any ploy was fair game. The Christian love-soldier is caught in the typical Christian battle of the soul, the *psy-*

chomachia waged between Virtue and Vice. Therefore, the
conflicting elements in the last part of the strophe are closer
to the Augustinian statement of paradox: "one is ashamed of
not being shameless" (*pudet non esse impudentem; Conf.* 2.9).
Morality is being employed in what Augustine would ultimately consider an amoral sphere. Yet the poet insists on talking about his love in Christian terms.

For example, the last strophe of the poem tells us that the
lover has been betrayed. He launches out and attacks love in
the same way Augustine in the later phases of his life attacked
it, using such words as poison (*venena*), fraud (*fraude*), deceit
(*dolo*), frenzy (*furoris*), wrath (*ire*), and malice (*livoris*). Yet
he does not do what Augustine would advise: move on to more
enduring things. Instead, he revels in his agony, raising it to
the height of passion:

> And so my tears are many,
> and so my tears are flowing.
> My face is all pale;
> it is because I'm betrayed in love.
>
> *Hinc mihi fletus abundat,*
> *hinc fletus inundat.*
> *Est mihi pallor in ore,*
> *est, quia fallor amore.* (st. 6, 13–16)

At this point Catullus might have imagined his first acid epigram about the loved one. This poet, however, is so proud
of his passion that he seems to exult in his suffering. His betrayal is raised to the level of that most famous of all betrayals
through Judas. Despite the nasty things that he says about
love, there is no question left about its importance. The depth
of loss in a betrayal can be measured in terms of the idealism
that was once attached to the thing lost.

Actually, this poem is a complex of paradoxes. It is a spring
poem, and opens on a note of joy as Phoebus rides his golden

car across the heavens. Next we have a picture of a budding forest and singing birds. Out of these birds, Philomena comes into focus, and she is once again singing an ambiguous song (*querule*). We recognize, in terms of the rhetorical tradition being traced, the classical nightingale. Soon the scene shifts from external nature to the inner world of the poet:

> And now Dione
> in jest and agony
> lightens and crucifies
> the hearts of her worshipers.
>
> *Iamque Dione*
> *iocis, agone*
> *relevat, cruciat,*
> *corda suorum.*　　　　　　　　　　　(st. 2, 5–8)

We seem to have returned to the *Vigil* and the classical spring song. Yet in a Christian age, the expression "I am crucified" has to suggest much, much more than it did to Catullus. The poet knows that Christ died through His love of the world in order to redeem it; the poet, on the other hand, is undergoing a similar death entirely within the world and for it. In one sense, it is absolute presumption to express a totally human passion in terms of Christ's passion. The rhyming of the Christian word *agone* (agony; it is Greek, and comes from the New Testament) with *Dione* might seem to be the kind of parody we observed earlier; and yet the poem continues in the serious vein of conflict and subsequent loss. At the same time that it contains an Augustinian renunciation of love, it contains a statement of love's grandeur and its dire necessity; for, as the poet tells us:

> And so she steals me
> from my sleep,
> and makes me keep
> my vigil of love.

> Me quoque subtrahit
> illa sopori,
> invigilareque
> cogit amori. (st. 3, 1–4)

With the mention of the love-vigil, we are thrown back into the shadow-world of the *Vigil of Venus*, where idealism was possible, but reality was not excluded; where the two competing tensions were voiced, but not resolved. We have entered an area of expression where the soul is not sullied to pleasure body, as in the other *Burana;* nor is the body bruised to pleasure soul. Both exist in an abiding tension that will admit either harmony (comedy, the expectant happy ending) or discord (tragedy, loss and return to the self).

The poem "Summer's Now Gone into Exile" (*Estas in exilium / iam peregrinatur;* Schmeller, no. 42, pp. 131–32) shows the secular adaptation of Paulinus of Nola's mystical inversion of the seasons. It is now possible for a man who loves a woman to say, "Spring exists all year round":

> But whoever nourishes love, that's warmth,
> no bitterness of cold can weaken.

> *Sed amorem,*
> *qui calorem*
> *nutrit, nulla vis*
> *frigoris,*
> *valet attenuare.* (st. 2, 1–5)

Then, with the fierce determination of a martyr, the poet exclaims:

> Bitterly I'm crucified. I die
> by the wound that gives me glory.

> *Amare crucior, morior*
> *vulnere, quo glorior.* (st. 2, 9–10)

Glory in death: this is the new Christian dimension that is utterly lacking in Ovid, Catullus, and Sappho, where death is always a disaster. We must go to Prudentius' hymns to the saints or to the *Acta Martyrorum* for this tonality. Suddenly, however, the wings of the poet droop. He thinks about a remedy for his love-sickness: a kiss to repair the wound created in his heart by the shaft of love. In Christian hymns, the loving Christ is the only remedy for the sickly soul:

> Christian medicine,
> save the healthy, heal the sick.

> *Medicina christiana,*
> *salva sanos, aegros sana.*
>
> (*Oxford,* no. 147, p. 207, 64–65)

or, as Reginald of Canterbury (d. c. 1110) wrote of St. Malchus' words to his guardian angel, an intermediary agent functioning in the religious sphere as the woman increasingly functions in the secular sphere:

> You, who are my doctor, my hope, the cure for my wounds,
> wounds which, unless cured, will cause my mind to perish.

> *qui medicus meus es, mea spes, mea vulnera cura,*
> *vulnera, mens quibus est, nisi cures me, peritura.*
>
> (*Oxford,* no. 145, p. 202, 22–23)

The difference between the guardian angel's benefaction and the lady's kiss shows us that we are once again in the realm of the sensible. That realm becomes even more vivid as the *Burana* poet describes the lady's sweet laughter and budding lips. Then, as the thought of a kiss becomes an obsession, he says that one touch will make him "deny that I was ever a mortal" (*ut me mortalem negem aliquando,* st. 3, 9). The confirmation of immortality by the loved one (Christ) upon the lovers (Christian souls or Church) is, of course, a basic tenet of Christianity. In secular terminology, it can be traced all the way back to Sappho:

That man seems to me like the gods,
or even more, who just sits near
you.[79]

It is an old hyperbolic conceit about the mystical powers of
love, but, stated in an age when the finest minds in Europe
were making discursive affirmations on a mystical plane, it
has a curiously jarring ring. Or does it? Perhaps it is simply a
logical earthward extension of the metaphysical sphere in
which the love of Christ had marked the end of old mortality.
   The poem ends on a note of high idealism. The poet turns
the lady's physical features into abstractions, thereby employing a process advocated centuries earlier by Plato: from earthly images of goodness and truth and beauty, we form abstractions that mirror the one Goodness, the one Truth, the one
Beauty, which are but facets ultimately of the One, which is
the real object of the purest contemplation.[80] The poet never
reaches the One; his flight does not extend to the Dantesque
stratosphere; however, he is well off the ground when he has
bypassed the lady's mouth, eyes, nose, and snow-white body,
and says:

   I laugh when I see so much elegance,
   such courtliness, such gentleness,
   such sweetness.

   rideo, cum video
   cuncta tam elegantia,
   tam regia, tam suavia, tam dulcia.   (st. 4, 6–8)

Thus the woman is raised to the level of *ideas*, according to
the Platonic and Neoplatonic systems, the intermediary agents
functioning between idealism and reality. But where is the
poet? He is left laughing in his contemplation of such beauty.
One is tempted to think, perhaps wrongly, of the endless

---

79. Frag. 31.1–3 (Lobel-Page); cf. Plato, *Symp.* 207D: "human nature strives
ever to be immortal" (through love).
   80. *Symp.* 210; with respect to love, the vision of beauty predominates.

smiles (Latin *su*bridere; Italian *sor*ridere) in Dante's Paradise. Yet the temptation is not totally misguided, for Dante will eventually carry everything implied in this poem back to the metaphysical plane by making that very important equation of the earthly woman Beatrice with Reginald of Canterbury's guardian angel. But that is the end of the process (and a glorious end at that); this poem is merely a beginning.

If we translate the last two lines into Provençal, we have one of those abstract categories that we encounter so often with the troubadours, whose ladies always represent *beutat, cortezia, plazer (suaveza), doussor.* Since Provençal descends from Latin, the words have almost identical connotations. For the moment, we must emphasize in the Latin poem the blending of sensual images with idealized abstractions, the passing from a crucifixion to an ambiguous laugh, the alternation of grief and joy: in short, a kind of resolution of paradox that hovers around the elusive laughter. Is it the chortle of a lecher or the smile of a contemplator? Neither, exactly, but perhaps a combination of both. The poet stands on a kind of mean between sensual desire and philosophical contemplation. The poem, which expresses that complicated frame of mind, employs grave imagery in an atmosphere of metaphysical wit.

Another poem, "I'm Torn by the Fierce Force of Love" (*Dira vi amoris teror;* Schmeller, no. 158, pp. 223–24), alternates Ovidian trappings with the language of hymns. The poet tells us first that he is carried along in Venus' chariot and is burned by a terrible fire. Then he cries out: "Blessed one, take away my crucifixion" (*Deme, pia, cruciatus;* st. 1, 4). Next he compares his lady to a spark of flame that rushes upon the standards (*vexilla*) of his heart; he also calls her the seal (*sigillo*) of his mind. When symbols such as standards crop up in troubadour poetry, they are usually related to circumambient cultural history, as signs of feudal hierarchy. However, here the Latin word *vexilla* does not necessarily have an historic-social connotation at all. For example, the most famous use of the word occurs in Venantius Fortunatus' *Vexil-*

la regis prodeunt. Therefore, in interpreting the word *vexilla*, we may just as easily visualize Christian standards as Franco-Germanic standards. Furthermore, since Ovid himself had adapted the Roman standards and the whole military vocabulary for use in his love lyrics, there is a secular amatory precedent for such terms. The rhetoric in a poem like this is very shifty. If, on the one hand, it suggests twelfth-century France, it might just as easily suggest first-century Rome. Even when these words are transferred to Provençal (*vexillum* or *signum* can be translated as *gonfano*, based on Germanic *gunthfano*), they may still be the standards claimed on the one hand by Ovid and on the other by Venantius Fortunatus.

The poet continues by calling his lady "outstanding" (*singularem*) and "chaste" (*pudicam*); he says that his lady's love presses him onward (*urget me*) and binds him to her (*illi ligor*). Then he launches into a very delicate lyric outburst:

> Virgin lily,
> lend me your aid;
> a man sent into exile
> calls on you for counsel.

> *Virginale lilium,*
> *tuum presta subsidium;*
> *missus in exilium*
> *querit a te consilium.* (st. 5)

The term "virgin lily" has no precedent in pagan love poetry; it derives solely from hymns to the Virgin Mary.[81] Similarly,

---

81. For a striking identification of the lily and rose with Mary, see Walafrid Strabo, *PL 114*, cols. 1126, 1128–30; also *Oxford*, no. 101, p. 140, 4, for generic statement: *virginum liliis candida*. In and after the twelfth century the tradition flourishes: Hugh of St. Victor, *Sermo* 65 (*PL 177*, cols. 1102–05) and Hildebert (*PL 171*, cols. 1285–86; col. 1238, where the "golden rose" Christ triumphs over the ephemeral earthly rose; col. 1382, referring to Christ; col. 1444, applying the image to Queen Mathilde). The flowers were first applied to Christ: Rabanus Maurus (*PL 111*, col. 509): "*Flos enim Christum mystice*

135

the call for assistance and counsel is cast in the quiet frame of a prayer. The "exile" should not be interpreted in a purely literal way. In medieval symbolism, the earthly life was often referred to as a pilgrimage or exile in which earth was but a way-station and heaven was the real home and final destination. The lady is thus both "in another land" and in heaven, at home. This poem may have a direct bearing upon Jaufré Rudel's far-off lady, who may be the princess of Tripoli or queen of another world.

Then we revert to the Ovidian arena, where the prayer is repeated in a different tone:

> My heart doesn't know what to do;
> it's dying; it's carried by your love;
> it will be killed by the shaft of Venus
> unless you help it.

> *Nescit quid agat, moritur,*
> *amore tui vehitur,*
> *telo necatur Veneris,*
> *sibi ni subveneris.* (st. 6)

These lines, through their sly suggestion of a kiss as a cure, reduce the woman at once to an earthly status. But the poet swings upward again, insisting that his lady is the paragon of chastity (*castitas*), that she has a beautiful face, and that she is clothed in the garb of wisdom (*veste sophie*). The "garb of wisdom" suggests Boethian allegory, but the beautiful face remains tactile. We may be a little surprised to find a beautiful face peeping out between a Christian virtue and a Neoplatonic term (Greek *sophia;* but the word was given common coinage by Christian Neoplatonists such as Scotus Erigena); however, the tendency to move toward idealized abstraction culminates

---

significat qui in Cantico canticorum dicit: Ego flos campi." Scriptural bases for the lily include Os. 14:6 and Matth. 6:28. The rose, though mentioned in the Bible (e.g. Sap. 2:8, where it is associated with lechery), is primarily classical in origin with respect to secular lyrics.

in the final strophe, where the poet returns to the language and mode of prayer:

> I hymn to you alone,
> please don't despise me;
> I pray you'll let me worship you
> as my splendid star of heaven.

> *Psallo tibi soli,**
> *despicere me noli,**
> *per me precor velis coli,*
> *lucens ut stella poli.* (st. 8)

*Words rearranged by Schmeller to create a rhyme; cf. *CB*, no. 107, p. 177.

Mary, star of the sea (*Ave, maris stella*)—this is the traditional symbolism to be found in hymns to the Virgin.[82] It took many centuries for a Christian woman to be compared to a star, but when it happens, the comparison seems inevitable. Most of the words in this final strophe are religious: "pray" (*precor*), "worship" (*coli*), "hymn" (*psallo*). *Psallo* (originally, "play the zither; sing") is a Greek word that was absorbed into Classical Latin; but it achieved its fullest use in Christian hymnology, where its connotation approaches the English cognate "psalm."

This poem presents as startling a fusion of religious and secular diction as one can find in any medieval verse. The lady is lifted into the heavens and treated as a source of perfection, a link with an ideal world, but she is also treated as a tangible creature whose kiss can calm the poet's frenzy. We may forget that frenzy in the closing prayer, but the two conflicting strains are very much a part of the poem; the prayer merely casts the "fierce love" of the opening lines into a new perspective. The struggle toward that prayer is a very civilized, and very complex, form of expression. It is perhaps worth noting that Helen Waddell compared this poem to Jaufré Rudel's "When Days Are Long in May," concluding that the

82. E.g., *An. Hymn.* 2, no. 4, p. 49, and no. 186, p. 170; see also Hildebert, *PL 171*, col. 1286.

Latin poem is sensual and that "its end is possession."[83] But
if the poem expresses the direst emotional urges, it also tells
how they are fought and finally transcended; might we even
say "Christianized"? When the woman is compared to a star,
she is as remote, yet as vital, as the God implored by St.
Augustine.

Actually, the bridge from the more obscure *Carmina Burana* to the troubadour poems becomes clearer as one reads on
in the Latin poetry. For example, the favorite troubadour
metaphor for expressing the conflicting emotions of the lover
is that of a ship tossed at sea. The metaphor is not a medieval
invention; it is derived from Ovid; it was negated by Christians, whose love was firm and abiding; it was then restated
by an anonymous poet in Latin:[84]

> I'm like a waving branch
> upon a tree,
> a light little ship
> upon the sea,
> that has no anchor to sustain it.

> *Sicut in arbore*
> *frons tremula,*
> *navicula*
> *levis in equore,*
> *dum caret anchore subsidio.*
>
> (Schmeller, no. 159, p. 224, st. 3, 1–5)

It is conspicuous in the poetry of Bernart de Ventadorn.

Perhaps the most extraordinary of all the *Carmina Burana*
is a long, 31-strophic poem (Schmeller, no. 36, pp. 121–24;
cf. *CB,* no. 61, pp. 14–19) in which the lady becomes the source
of masculine perfection; she is even addressed as "my leader"
or "my duke" (*mea dux;* st. 29, 4); yet at the same time, she

---

83. *Wandering Scholars,* p. 227.
84. See Appendix, VI; also, Prudentius, *Cath.* 5.85–88; cf. Paulinus of Nola,
Carmen 13.14–17: *CSEL 30,* pp. 44–45.

is called the perfect virgin or young woman (*virgo perfecta;* st. 12, 2). The poet attributes miraculous powers to her: she can dispel sadness, grief, and fear (st. 5, 4–6); she is the source of clarity, charity, and generosity (st. 6, 1–3). Yet, despite these parallels with the Virgin Mary, the poet also talks about her in terms of Helen of Troy, the Muses, the decrees of Solomon, handsome Absalom, and Venus—in short, the whole Greco-Roman-Judaic-Christian tradition. If ever a poem showed the fusion (at times, the confusion) of a thousand years of tradition, this is it. Yet it is a clever poem, and manipulates all these diverse strains until they culminate in a prayer to the virgin (or young woman) to answer her worshiper's plea. A single set of lines will illustrate the poet's interweaving of tones:

> yet nobility still clings to that for which
> my humility has been so militant.
>
> *sed hesitat adhuc nobilitas*
> *cui mea dudum militat humilitas*   (st. 17, 3–4)

Ovid had spoken of militant love—ironically. It remained for a Christian age to create the paradox of militant humility. Ovid paid for his individualism with exile; the *Burana* poets seem to have been more clever; they avoided excommunication, as well as fame, by anonymity.

SUMMARY AND A LOOK AHEAD

In tracing the spring motif from Christian hymns to the later *Carmina Burana*, we have reached the point where a spring song becomes a love lyric (in Romance terminology, a *canzone* or *canso*, from Latin *cantio*). The Carolingian poets reintroduced the nature lyric to western literature. The later poets of the twelfth century seem to have carried the growing awareness of natural beauty to its culmination; their tone is one of Christian joy, but their rhetoric is, as Curtius suggested, clearly classical.[85] The common poetic transition from the broad world of nature to the interior world of the soul or self is one that we observed again and again in Latin literature, especially in Horace. However, the body of the later Latin love poem owes more to Ovid than to any other classical poet. During the Middle Ages, the name Ovid crops up everywhere, from the treatise of Andreas Capellanus to Chaucer's *Legend of Good Women*. The poetry itself, by the very nature of its fusion, is neither entirely pagan nor entirely Christian, although it utilizes both sources. In this sense, the rhetorical, it is a synthesis, or ultimately something new.

We might at this point summarize the basic techniques already touched upon, using the symbol of "the standards of the king":

I. Classical love poetry (personal mysticism deriving from cultus worship but largely the product of the subjective imagination):

Poetic rhetoric: signa imperatoris Amoris (standards of love-god)

Physical world: signa imperatoris (standards of Emperor Caesar)

II. Christian mysticism expressed in allegory or metaphor, but firmly attached to dogma and belief:

Metaphysical: vexilla Regis (standards of King Jesus, the Lord)

Physical: vexilla regis (standards of a king, a lord)

III. Late medieval Christian secular poetry:

	The Lady	The Virgin	The Standards of Christ
Christian Metaphysics	(Domina)	(Virgo)	(Vexilla Regis)
Poetic rhetoric	Poet's lady (domina)	His virgin? girl? (virgo)	Amor's standards (vexilla regis)
Physical world, twelfth century	Any mistress (domina)	Any young girl (virgo)	The king's standards (vexilla regis)

85. Curtius, p. 184: "The descriptions of landscape in medieval Latin poetry are to be understood in the light of a continuous literary tradition." With these words, all ethnic and climatological theories vanish.

I: Classical love poetry. This is the romantic-subjective world of Ovid; its symbols are drawn from the real world and transferred to the cult of Cupid; but Cupid or Amor or Eros was a god attended by poets far more than by priests or prophets. The superior element in this world, poetic rhetoric, is imaginary and illusory, not anchored by dogma, faith, or a church. Yet it is a fascinating world of make-believe, of private and personal mysticism. If this idealism usually evaporates, and the poet is left without Corinna and Lesbia, it is perhaps only because the lower element, the sensible world, had a very vital reality to most Greeks and Romans. Plato, however, is an outstanding exception; his numinal-phenomenal vision of reality prefigures the mystical framework of the second part of the diagram. Augustine freely confessed that Neoplatonic philosophers started him on the road toward Christianity because in their works "God and His word are implied in every way" (Conf. 8.2). In the Ovidian ethos, we can label the bottom line "the self" and the top line "immersion in something other than the self," because these poetic fantasy worlds prefigure vital mysticism

II: Christian mysticism. This is the spiritual world of Prudentius, Ambrose, and Augustine. It is a world of mysticism triumphant if we emphasize the top line; if we emphasize the bottom line, it is the debased world of the more popular Carmina Burana. They are both facets of the same Weltanschauung. The Christian God of love has a Church and articles of faith and dogma to sustain his reality. Theologically, the Celestial Lord is given full precedence over the Earthly Lord, even when the latter is a Charlemagne. The middle ground does not really exist in such an ethos; there is no mean. One tends to assert either metaphysical or physical values. However, strong correspondences connect the two spheres. Mystical expression is based upon the physical, through the process of allegory or symbolic raising, such as we observed in the hymns of Venantius Fortunatus and Prudentius. Eventually, however, the process is reversed, and physical values are idealized through what I have called de-allegorization. Yet the superior elements in this world still infuse and define the inferior; when the inferior are given priority, they sound like parodies to the modern reader.

III: Secular medieval. This is the twelfth-century world of the more refined *Burana*. The poets achieve a kind of mean by refusing to give either world absolute priority, and by suggesting that both have certain values. Metaphysics is not disregarded; neither, however, is human beauty. Poetically, the poets are reassessing reality in a way that mirrors the work of Albertus Magnus, Aquinas, Roger Bacon, and other Aristotelian philosophers and theologians; they do not necessarily question faith, although at times they may; but they reinterpret and apply human values on a much broader basis than Augustine was willing to grant dogmatically, although the human side of Augustine is abundantly revealed through the *Confessions* and his Platonic dialogues. The later poets ask themselves, in one of the two inscriptions cited for this chapter: "If God bound the spheres with love, can human love be a crime?"[86] This is a very Platonic question: isn't there some place for Alcibiades in the realm of Eros? Plato ultimately said no; or did he?

The Middle Ages had a very keen sense of metaphysical wit. One facet of this wit is revealed by the way the poets elude classification. They do not openly state that their *virgo* is the Virgin Mary; on the other hand, they will not allow their particular lady (who is *singularis,* one from the many) to descend to the level of generic mistresses. She is one from the many, but she is not the One who transcends the Many, simply because she is human and is always defined as such. No matter how far this poetry diverges into mystical expression, it is never totally removed from a kiss or sensual communication. These human elements are what ultimately destroy any heavy-handed religious allegory that would reduce the poetry to

86. Schmeller, no. 84a, p. 171.

expression of an ascetic religion such as Catharism. A century after the *Burana* were written, Dante took Beatrice out of the subjective imagination and placed her firmly among the divine ideas or angelic orders. Yet even in his day and in philosophically inclined Italy, the less daring Guido Guinizelli apologized for mistaking his lady for an angel. In the troubadour tradition, many of the poorer poets could not embody physical reality with rhetorical reality, and their ladies often seem to evaporate into clouds of abstractions; yet this circumstance would seem to be more the result of defective poetry than any vital or convincing metaphysic. It is interesting to note that the great hymnologists of the later Middle Ages (*Stabat mater; Dulcis Jesu memoria;* Richard Rolle; finally, the great mystic poets of Spain, St. John of the Cross and St. Teresa of Avila) seem to reverse the whole process by addressing divinities in very human and sensual terms: kissing Jesus, sighing for Mary, etc. Yet it is impossible to say that this dramatic mystical expression was influenced by the secular; in the twelfth century, both strains were active. Drinking songs, hymns to Christian saints, religious plays, and love songs exist side by side in the *Carmina Burana.* The manuscript makes no distinction between secular and religious poetry such as modern anthologists tend to do; yet the fact that it was hidden away in a monastery might indicate that somebody did.

The collection is as rich in the variety of secular poetry as it is in genres. Little single-strophic German songs and macaronic French-Latin songs are tucked in the middle of the most polished Latin stanzas. One of the most famous German poems says simply: "If I owned the world from the sea to the Rhine, I'd give it all away if I could hold the Queen of England in my arms."[87] This is the type of poetry that nineteenth-century scholars associated with a folkloristic tradition.[88] Insofar as

87. Schmeller, no. 108a, p. 185.
88. E.g., Gaston Paris, review, *JS* (1891), 685 f. For a modern critique, see Dmitri Scheludko, "Zur Geschichte des Natureinganges bei den Trobadors," *ZFSL,* 60 (1937), 258: "*das Volkslied . . . keine Eigentümlichkeiten hat*"

it exists merely in terms of surface expression, the poem could conceivably have been written by an untutored hand or come from the people. Yet most of the German poems are clearly imitations of the Latin.

For example, a rather intricate ten-strophic Latin poem is followed by a single-strophic German poem that picks up a Germanic refrain that had crept into the ninth strophe of the larger piece, where it replaced a Latin refrain:

LATIN
(Schmeller, no. 125, st. 9)

Vérum iúbet díligi	A
si quis est in illa,	B
nec in se vult corripi	A
vel unguis pusilla,	B
que vix potest corrigi	A
ut Tyndaris Sibylla.	B
Lodircundeie lodircundeie.	

GERMAN
(Schmeller, no. 125a)

Eine wúnnechlíche stát	A
het er mir bescheiden;	B
da diu blumen unde gras	A?
stunden grune baide,	B?
dar chom ih, als er mih pat;	A
da geschach mir leide	B?
Lodircundeie lodircundeie.	

There seems to be little doubt that the Latin, in its diction, allusions, rhyme, and rhythm, has influenced and takes precedence over the vernacular.

When the German poems of the *Burana* do rise to an ac-

---

and "Beiträge . . . : Volksliedertheorie," *ZFSL*, 52 (1929), 1–38, 201–66. Also, P. S. Allen, *Medieval Latin Lyrics* (Chicago, 1931), p. 202: "The old dance songs are too narrow a foundation for the mighty edifice of troubadour poetry."

complished level of expression, they reveal the so-called
Frauendienst or courtly-love tradition, just as some of the
Carmina Burana do:

> I praise my beloved lady
> before all good women,
> I will always be there to serve her,
> by her side I'll stay.
> She is like a mirror,
> a magnet for every virtue.

> *Ich lob die lieben frovven min*
> *vor allen guten vviben,*
> *mit dienst wil ich ir stete sin,*
> *und immer stete beliben.*
> *Si ist als ein spiegelglas,*
> *si ist gantzer tugende ein adamas.*
>
> (Schmeller, no. 94a, p. 174, st. 1, 1–6)

Since we cannot accurately date many of the individual
pieces of the *Burana* (although the foregoing discussion may
imply that the refined poetry was written after the cruder
pieces), we cannot relate their growth to the growth of vernacular poetry in authoritative historical terms. Raby dates
most of the Latin poems in the twelfth century; that is also
the period of troubadour florescence. It is my personal opinion
that vernacular and Latin poetry grew contemporaneously,
with the Latin striking the first real, but crude, notes of the
literary renaissance, then finally yielding to the vernacular in
its full flowering. Raby placed the *Burana* in a religious atmosphere: "The composers of these pieces were not wandering
clerks; the songs required elaborate musical accompaniments
and highly trained singers such as could be found only in
cathedrals and perhaps in monasteries."[89] They could also be

89. *Oxford,* p. xv; criticizing Waddell's separation of secular and religious
spheres.

found in the castles of wealthy nobles, where the troubadours lived.

The tone of the Latin poems hovers near religious expression, either in terms of parody or metaphysical overtone. These overtones continue into Provençal, which is a linguistic development of Vulgar Latin. Parody, however, is either masked or gives way to open, forceful satire, such as could best be written under secular patronage. In the long run, we must deduce something from the fate of the *Carmina Burana,* which were hidden for centuries in a monastery, whereas the Provençal poetry circulated freely and has come down to us in numerous songbooks. The one tradition was doomed to extinction; the other managed to elude it until the protectors of the poets were crushed in the Albigensian Crusade. History tells us something about the ends of traditions, even if it is vague about their beginnings and ambience.

The theory that medieval poetry emerges as a synthesis of Christian mysticism and classical rhetoric is supported by the eminent musicologist J. A. Westrup:

> Two early melodies survive the obstacle of notation. One is a setting of Horace, *Odes,* iv.11, 'Est mihi nonum,' where the tune is recognizable as that of the hymn 'Ut queant laxis.' The other is a love-song addressed to a boy, 'O admirabile Veneris idolum,' which . . . [appears] on the same page as the pilgrim song 'O Roma nobilis.'[90]

How did a man in the Middle Ages feel when he heard Horace sung to the tune of a well-known hymn? We cannot be sure. Perhaps the word "parody" as a description of de-allegorization is a modern subjective judgment. The descent to the physical world may have seemed to the poets a purely natural

90. "Medieval Song," *Early Medieval Music up to 1300, 2: New Oxford History of Music,* ed. Dom Anselm Hughes (2d ed. Oxford, Clarendon Press, 1955), p. 220.

step. However, poets do not compose society. Letters written by Peter of Blois and Abelard in their old age reveal a strong contempt for erotic verse; yet both Peter and Abelard wrote love songs in their youth.[91] The dialectic between romantic youth and ascetic old age is germane to most great lyric poetry. This dialectic can exist in a single individual.

Westrup goes on to say: "No valid distinction can be made between the religious and secular Latin songs of this period; the same types of melody, the same forms occur in both. There is also a close connexion with songs in the vernacular."[92] Finally, in discussing the emergence of vernacular music (as I have broached the problem of vernacular poetry), Westrup dismisses any exotic hypothesis: "So far as the music is concerned, the argument in favor of Arab influence lacks foundation, since we have no specimens of Arab music; it is also unconvincing in face of the obvious influence of Gregorian chant and popular song."[93] In transferring his remarks from music to poetic rhetoric, I would substitute "hymns" for "Gregorian chant" and "pagan rhetoric" for "popular songs," since there is very little literature that can be said to come from "the people."

Westrup also notes that the opening bar of the troubadour poet Bernart de Ventadorn's most celebrated poem "When I See the Lark Moving" is based upon the *Kyrie eleison* from the *Cum jubilo* Mass.[94] He adds: "The melody was also used

91. My attention was called to these points by Brinkmann, *Liebesdichtung*, pp. 30–31 (Peter), 27–28 (Abelard).

92. Westrup, p. 222.

93. Westrup, p. 225.

94. Westrup, p. 237. This theory is now supported by most musicologists; see Beck, Becker, Chailley, Gennrich, Spanke in Bibliog. The literary correspondence has been stated in various ways by Scheludko, Brinkmann, Errante, and Zorzi (see Bibliog.). The inquiries coincide with the musical-literary MSS of St. Martial, in the domain of Duke William; cf. Hans Spanke, "Untersuchungen über die Ursprünge des Minnesangs: Marcabrustudien," *AGWG*, III Folge, *24* (1940) and Guido Errante, *Lirica romanza del primo secolo* (N.Y., 1943); *Marcabru e le fonti sacre dell'antica lirica romanza* (Florence, 1948).

for other texts, including the equally famous argument between the heart and the eye, 'Quisquis cordis et oculi Non sentit in se jurgia,' by Philippe, the Chancellor of Paris." The musical settings for Latin hymns, Latin love songs, and vernacular lyrics are all related. Let us now turn to Bernart de Ventadorn to see what part he plays in the unfolding poetic tradition.

Peter, a man who loves is mad,
for the liars among the women
have ruined joy and worth and merit.

Peire, qui ama, desena,
car las trichairitz entre lor
an tout joi e pretz e valor.

BERNART DE VENTADORN

3 The New Poetic Synthesis:
Bernart de Ventadorn and the Classical Provençal Troubadours

WHEN I SEE THE LARK MOVING

I.

When I see the lark moving   1
His wings with joy toward the light,
Then forget and let himself fall
From the sweetness that enters his heart,
O! what great envy I feel   5
Toward whomever I see who's glad!
I wonder why my heart
Doesn't melt right away from desire.

II.

Alas! how much I thought I knew
About love, and how little I know!   10
For I can't keep myself from loving
Her who'll give me nothing in return.
She's stolen my heart and all of me
And all herself and all the world;
And after she robbed me, left me nothing   15
Except desire and a longing heart.

III.

Yes, I lost all power over myself,
I wasn't mine from the moment on
When she let me look into her eyes,
Into a mirror I like so well.   20

Mirror, since I first saw myself in you,
Deep sighs have murdered me,
And I lost myself the way
Handsome Narcissus lost himself in the pool.

IV.

About women I feel great despair.   25
Never again will I trust them.
And although I used to protect them,
From now on, I'm defecting,
Since I see not a one will help me
Against her who destroys and upsets me.   30
I despair of them all, distrust them all,
For I know very well that they're all like that!

V.

And so My Lady's acting like a "woman"
(And I blame her for it!),
For she doesn't want what a man ought to want   35
And whatever a man forbids, she does.
I've fallen into very foul grace.
I've carried on like the fool on the bridge,
And I don't know why it's happened:
Did I climb too high on the hill?   40

VI.

All grace is lost—it's true—
(And I never even tasted it!)
Since she who ought to have it most
Has none; where will I find it?
O! how bad it seems (if you see her)   45
That she who owns this longing slave
Who'll never have anything good without her
Lets me die, won't lend me her aid.

VII.

Since prayers, thanks, and the rights I own
Can't help me gain Milordess,   50

And she doesn't care a bit
That I love her, I'll never tell her of it.
No, I'll leave her. I'll give her up.
She's murdered me. As a corpse I speak.
I'm going away since she won't retain me   55
Downcast, to exile, I don't know where.

VIII (TORNADA).

Tristan, you'll get nothing more from me.
I'm going away, downcast, I don't know where.
I'm through with songs. I'm giving them up.
I'm hiding myself from love and joy.   60

CAN VEI LA LAUZETA MOVER

I.

Can vei la lauzeta mover   1
de joi sas alas contral rai,
que s'oblid'e.s laissa chazer
per la doussor c'al cor li vai,
ai! tan grans enveya m'en ve   5
de cui qu'eu veya jauzion,
meravilhas ai, car desse
lo cor de dezirer no.m fon.

II.

Ai, las! tan cuidava saber
d'amor, e tan petit en sai!   10
car eu d'amar no.m posc tener
celeis don ja pro non aurai.
tout m'a mo cor, e tout m'a me,
e se mezeis e tot lo mon;
e can se.m tolc, no.m laisset re   15
mas dezirer e cor volon.

III.

Anc non agui de me poder
ni no fui meus de l'or'en sai

que.m laisset en sos olhs vezer
en un miralh que mout me plai.   20
miralhs, pus me mirei en te,
m'an mort li sospir de preon,
c'aissi.m perdei com perdet se
lo bels Narcisus en la fon.

IV.

De las domnas me dezesper;   25
ja mais en lor no.m fiarai;
c'aissi com las solh chaptener,
enaissi las deschaptenrai.
pois vei c'una pro no m'en te
vas leis que.m destrui e.m cofon,   30
totas las dopt'e las mescre,
car be sai c'atretals se son.

V.

D'aisso.s fa be femna parer
ma domna, per qu'e.lh o retrai,
car no vol so c'om deu voler,   35
e so c'om li deveda, fai.
chazutz sui en mala merce,
et ai be faih co.l fols en pon;
e no sai per que m'esdeve,
mas car trop puyei contra mon.   40

VI.

Merces es perduda, per ver,
(et eu non o saubi anc mai),
car cilh qui plus en degr'aver,
no.n a ges, et on la querrai?
a! can mal sembla, qui la ve,   45
qued aquest chaitiu deziron
que ja ses leis non aura be,
laisse morir, que no l'aon!

VII.

Pus ab midons no.m pot valer
precs ni merces ni.l dreihz qu'eu ai,   50
ni a leis no ven a plazer
qu'eu l'am, ja mais no.lh o dirai.
aissi.m part de leis e.m recre;
mort m'a, e per mort li respon,
e vau m'en, pus ilh no.m rete,   55
chaitius, en issilh, no sai on.

VIII (TORNADA).

Tristans, ges no.n auretz de me,
qu'eu m'en vau, chaitius, no sai on.
de chantar me gic e.m recre,
*e de joi e d'amor m'escon.**   60

*Reprinted with permission from *Bernart von Ventadorn: Seine Lieder,* ed. Carl Appel (Halle, Max Niemeyer, 1915), pp. 250–54; hereafter cited as *Bernart: SL.*

Bernart begins his poem with the image of a lark flying upward toward the sun, but the bird never reaches the source of light; it "forgets itself" (*s'oblid'*) and lets itself fall back to earth, overcome by the ecstasy of that flight toward the unreachable. Yet it is the sheer excitement of the quest for a far-off goal that inspires the animal with joy. Then the image of the lark is suddenly replaced by the voice of the poet. While the bird still seems to be winging its way back to earth, Bernart, who remains on the ground, contrasts his envy with the lark's joy. Does the poet envy only the bird? No; he tells us that he envies everything that's glad. This contrast of joy and happiness might seem very striking to a person reading the poem for the first time *in vacuo,* although few critics seem to pay much attention to this shift. Yet in terms of the tradition thus far traced, Bernart's lark belongs to the same sorrow-creating species as the swallow of the *Vigil;* it has a dire effect on human beings, but is itself a symbol of natural joy (the word *joi* in line

2 is a Poitevin-North French development of Latin *gaudium,* which occurs along with the more regular Provençal *gaug).* The lark is the only feature of the ideal landscape that Bernart employs in this poem. He compresses an entire tradition into a single, vivid image, but uses the idealized portrait to establish a contrast, just as we have observed many times before. The opening bar of the music that accompanies this poem is based on the *Cum jubilo Kyrie eleison;* after this point, the music too departs from religious tonalities into something totally personal.

The figure of the lark has long been considered one of Bernart's most original contributions to poetry. It is surely that, although it does bear a certain similarity to a figure created in the *Vestiunt silve* of the *Cambridge Songs,* which were written at least a century before Bernart ever put pen to paper:

> The eagle flies to the stars; the lark
> sings in the winds, loosing tunes,
> bending back with a different song
> till it touches the earth.

> *Ad astra volat aquila; in auris*
> *alauda canit, modulos resolvit*
> *de sursum vergit dissimili modo*
> *dum terram tangit.*[1]

The upward-downward flight of the bird, coupled with the eagle's flight to the stars, had already suggested to the Latin poet the grandeur of unfulfilled fulfillment. The Latin poet links the lark and the eagle with a convention of birds who are pursuing their natural instincts. Then he contrasts them with the busy bee, which he interprets as a symbol of chastity (*tipum*

---

1. *Cambridge Songs* (ed. Breul), no. 30, p. 63, st. 4; a much less congruous reading in Strecker, *Die Camb. Lieder* (Berlin, 1926), p. 64, st. 4, based on MS *V* (usually superior to *C*).

castitatis). The Latin poet further says that the bee resembles the Virgin Mary. His poem ends in a tension between instinct and virtue, and although some critics, such as Whicher, see in the poem a triumph of virtue, I see only a contrast without the statement of a preference.

Bernart did not necessarily know this poem; in fact, if he used it, he enlarged its terms, because it is he, the poet, who sings a "different song"—and not the lark. Bernart's lark sings the idealized song of fulfilled nature; Bernart's different song is the rest of the poem. The poet's plight is sketched in at the end of the first strophe, where the suggestion that his heart might melt *(fon)* with desire again recalls the image of the sun, which would have melted the bird if it had reached its destination. The poet's situation is doubly difficult: he is incapable of a grand flight to the sun (traditionally, the symbol of perfection, from Cleanthes' Hymn to Zeus through Christian Neoplatonists), yet even in his earthbound state he suffers an agony that is not unlike the love-death of Semele, who was melted by the love of Zeus.

The second strophe begins with one of the most memorable generalizations in Provençal literature: there is really very little wisdom to be gained from loving. We should recall that, so far, Bernart has not really mentioned the fact that he *is* in love. The first strophe ends with the word "desire," but the desire there might be Bernart's envious wish to imitate the bird or anything else that is full of gladness. The woman is first introduced in lines 11 and 12 through the implied metaphor of the magnet, which in turn can be related back to the sun and the lark: the poet cannot hold himself back from loving her any more than the bird can resist his ill-fated flights; furthermore, the woman is as remote and aloof from the poet as the sun is removed from the bird. We should note the double nature of these metaphors connecting the woman to the sun: if she is bright and attractive and exerts an irresistible power over the poet, she is also unreachable and cold. The images suggest a Neoplatonic structure (indeed, Guido Guinizelli will codify them into doctrine), but here they are still free-moving and decidedly double-edged.[2]

The last half of the second stanza shifts from image to abstract statement. The woman retains some of the idealism of the first stanza because she is tacitly compared to a divine force: she has stolen the poet's heart, his self, her self, and the whole world. It is a charmingly hyperbolic catalogue of possessions, since the "whole world" seems to include the other features. Similarly, although it is a basic conceit of love poetry that the loved one robs the lover of his identity, the statement that the woman "has stolen herself" seems either tautological or nonsensical.[3] Actually Bernart is stressing the lady's self-possession, as opposed to his own loss of identity. Yet he clearly contradicts himself in lines 15 and 16 when he says that his lady has left him nothing but desire and a willing heart. Who owns the heart: the lady or the poet? The jumbled logic of these lines is a fitting expression of the confusion (the word *cofon* occurs in line 30) that is very much a part of the poet's state of mind.

Bernart continues to stress his loss of identity in the third strophe: "I wasn't mine from the moment on" (18). At this point we might wonder if the dominant theme of the poem is submission to a cruel mistress or goddess (the Provençal word *domna* is as ambiguous as Latin *domina*) who owns the world. Yet the poet's self crops up again. In line 15, he again blames the lady for robbing him; *tolc* and *tout* are strong words, based on Latin *tollere*, "to snatch." Yet just when the notion of the lady as thief begins to take root, he goes on to praise the very eyes that he was condemning, by likening them to a mirror. This is a very complicated image, for if one looks into a mirror,

---

2. *Al cor gentil*, st. 5.

3. For 13–14, cf. editions of F. J. M. Raynouard, *Choix des poésies originales des troubadours* (6 vols. Paris, 1816–61), *3*, 68 (3d vol. hereafter cited as Raynouard): *Quar tolt m'a'l cor, e tolt m'a me, / E si mezeis, e tot lo mon;* and Karl Bartsch, *Chrestomathie provençale* (6th ed. rev. E. Koschwitz, Marburg, 1904), col. 68, 31–32 (hereafter cited as Bartsch): *tout m'a mon cor e tout m'a se / e mi mezeis e tot lo mon.* Both readings are also redundant.

he sees himself, and not his lady. In later lyric poetry, the eyes are traditionally "windows of the soul"; for example, Beatrice's eyes in the *Paradiso* are mirrors of an inner truth that fortifies the pilgrim Dante.[4] Yet this lady's eyes in no way fortify Bernart; for although they fascinate him, they also murder him; although they draw him toward her, they also threaten him with immersion or drowning; the poet himself makes the allusion to Ovid's Narcissus. Yet this allusion is not necessarily Ovidian. Narcissus was drawn to the love-death entirely in terms of the self; Bernart hovers near it, partially in terms of another. It has been suggested that Bernart took the mirror image from romantic epics of the period, preserving its positive qualities.[5] Yet that comparison is more applicable to Dante, who perfected all such secular expressions in his religious epic. If the lady's eyes show Bernart how ignoble he is in comparison with her full beauty, then her eyes are the agents of destruction as well as enlightenment, and they thus deserve Bernart's reproach as well as his praise.

In the fourth strophe Bernart begins to play up his reproaches and to play down his praise. He condemns not only his lady, but makes the leap from the individual to the species when he says that *all* women are potentially the enemies of love. Now this statement is surely not what we might have expected. Yet, in pursuing images and feelings, the third stanza leads quite naturally into the fourth, just as the third evolves from the second (in Appel's version).[6] The fourth strophe has been criticized frequently for being a tissue of antifeministic clichés that have no part in a courtly-love lyric; yet as the foregoing analysis of images and thoughts shows, the antifeministic tone is a recurrent element in the poem. It is

4. *Par.*, XV.32–36, XVII.112–17, XVIII.13–18, XXII.154, XXIII.1–15. The last echo of blind secular love occurs in XXV.136–39.
5. Jackson, p. 249.
6. *Bernart: SL* is the definitive edition; however, the later *Ausgewählte Lieder*, ed. Appel (Halle, 1926) incorporates the critical comments of Schultz-Gora and Lewent (see Bibliog.).

the idealized concept "courtly love" that creates the problem, not the poem itself or the notion of paradox as a basic element of lyric poetry. The fifth stanza continues to trace the downward course of the lady. In fact, all the images in the poem and the personae are moving down or out. The lady, and she was always called by the grand name *domna* in Provençal, becomes in lines 33 and 34 a mere "woman" (*femna*, from Latin *femina*). The gap between the modern North French word for woman (*femme*) and the Italian (*donna*) is enormous; Provençal preserved both words in the twelfth century, but with different connotations. Stripped of her mystical veils and worldwide possessions, Bernart's lady then becomes just one of the opposite sex. The way in which Bernart shifts from the One Lady to the Many Women is interesting. This process of dissociation leads quite naturally to an Ovidian battle of the sexes. The word *om* in lines 35 and 36 should not be translated "one." It is derived from Latin *homo* (not *unus*), and can be used with the indefinite meaning (like French *l'homme*), but the word here means "man," and is contrasted with the preceding *femna*, woman. Here the notion of woman is one that is connected with forbidden things and opposition to man's rules. The comparison with Eve is unmistakable; in fact, the telling word is *deveda* (forbidden, from Latin *vetare*); in both Provençal and Christian religious literature this word is consistently applied to events surrounding the archetypal bad woman.[7] The mind that conceives an all-powerful mistress of the world (the Virgin Mary, the Great Lady or Domina) also conceives the all-conniving mistress within the world. Helen of Troy or Penelope, Eve or Mary—which truly embodies the spirit of woman? None? Either? Both? Religion can resolve the paradox through mysticism; secular terminology can only perpetuate it in the debased atmosphere of romantic mystery. It is important to

---

7. Bartsch, col. 21, 13–15: *Eva mot foleet,* | *quar d'equeu frut manjet* | *que Deus li devedet;* cf. *Oxford,* no. 256, p. 386, 4–6, where Mary says: *fructus quem virgo peperi* | *nil debet Adae veteri* | *fructum gustanti vetitum.*

notice here, however, that the refractory mistress (at least she is that in the fifth stanza, though she will always change) seems to have destroyed the ideal image that opened the poem in much the same way that Eve destroyed the Garden of Eden. Since both the classical and secular Christian landscapes exist within the memory of religious archetypes, it seems natural for the secular spring song to be primarily tragic or unfulfilled in its outcome.

The Eve comparison continues into line 37, where the woman is linked to the poet's having fallen into "foul grace" (*mala merce*). *Merce* is a highly ambiguous word in Provençal. In some respects, it resembles the modern French *merci* ("thanks"); in others, it is like Classical Latin *mercedem* ("reward for service"); and of course it acquires the modern English meaning "mercy" through Christian hymns. I have translated it here as "mercy" because the contrast of woman as black angel and good angel seems to reach a climax in this stanza. At the same time, I am aware that the word could be translated "reward," and thus connote a social, rather than religious, milieu. This level is reached, however, in the following stanza, where the process of "coming down to earth" is completed; I translate the *merces* of line 50 as "thanks."

Lines 38 to 40 seem to introduce the rhetoric of popular speech to the poem. Bernart says that he has carried on "like the fool (*fols* can also mean 'madman') on the bridge." What exactly does this mean? The figure has the ring of a dead metaphor, but it may derive from a simile in Ovid.[8] Whatever the source, Bernart's meaning comes through: a fool on a bridge is thirsty and wants a drink of water; but although there is water everywhere, there is not a drop to drink; the fool rushes madly from side to side, trying desperately to satisfy his thirst; but he is unwilling to surrender his secure footing because he is afraid of drowning. The simile seems to carry a

8. Perhaps adapted from *Am.* 3.4.17–18, which links forbidden water with a sick man: *sic interdictis inminet aeger aquis;* or *Ars Am.* 2.605–06, which mentions Tantalus.

slight reminiscence of the Tantalus myth: grasping after fruit and water that forever elude the tortured one. The notion of water as an attraction, with an accompanying fear of drowning, relates beautifully to the Narcissus allusion in the third strophe. Elements of wildness, folly, thirst, and fear (balanced by a burning desire to satisfy a basic need) are interwoven in these lines. Then Bernart seems to condemn himself for his folly and to probe for a rational explanation of it. When we recall some of the illogical statements in the second stanza (which are not to be confused with the symbolic and emotional ordering of the poem, which is based upon rhyme, meter, and a continuity of sensations), we can see that we are dealing with a clear-cut case of Platonic love-madness (*mania*).[9] It has its blessings, but it also has many woes.

How does Bernart account for this excess of passion? He suggests, but does not definitely say, that he climbed too high on the hill, a statement which also carries the ring of popular speech. Needless to say, the notion of climbing too high on a hill is an earthly metaphor pertaining to the movement of human beings that parallels the celestial flight of the lark. However, the lark was formed by nature to fly high; its excursions into the unknown are natural. Bernart here suggests that it is unnatural for a man to behave in a way that is not suited to humanity; he suggests a mean of conduct and expression. It is very curious to note this Horatian ring in what is basically an un-Horatian context. Up to this point, most of the poem has been stated in terms of hyperboles ("she's stolen my heart and all of me," etc.). Yet Bernart never allows us to stay long in any sphere: the humanistic, the semidivine, the realistic-social, the mystical. And we must note here, because it will be contradicted in the last stanza, that Bernart himself is willing to take all the blame for not getting what he wants from his lady, because he was a passionate slave to love and did not be-

9. *Symp.* 178 f., 186 f.; see Dodds, pp. 64–82.

have right. Some critics interpret "climbing too high" as social climbing or loving a lady beyond one's station, but this is a forced interpretation, conjectured on the basis of external conditions and in no sense validated by the poem itself. The sixth strophe echoes the notion of lost grace that was stated in the fifth strophe; it is the last tribute to the lady as goddess, yet even this tribute is mixed. In line 41, the poet denies his loved one the basic attribute of a goddess: the ability to bestow mercy. Yet in line 45, she still seems to have that power if she cares to use it. If the poem were a religious allegory, lines 41 to 44 would make no sense. How could one deny that a divinity, whether the Virgin Mary or Venus or some dark-matter principle of mystical cults, was capable of bestowing mercy upon her servant or slave? Yet if we refuse to acknowledge the mystical overtone of the language, and if we translate *merces* as "reward" (thereby restricting the poem to a feudal, hierarchical level of meaning), lines 45 to 58 make no sense. What earthly lord has the power to save his serf or slave from death—except in romantic, debased-mystical fiction? Only a divine lord is capable of such an act, and only the language of the hymns presents these notions in coherent terms; it is from this level of meanings that the poem is still drawing its primary inspiration. In this very same stanza, the poet tries to reduce the lady to nothing (he had previously tried to make her "a plain woman"); yet he is incapable of effecting this annihilation, because he still sees certain attributes that consciously or unconsciously suggest the relationship between a superior being (a great lady) and a poor earthly being (the poet himself). Bernart never lets us judge his woman exactly, though he is constantly assessing her, and in the widest possible terms: as robber, as goddess, as murderer, as magnet, as mistress, as deceiver.

The word *saubi*, for example, couples a sensual notion with the mystical idea of grace in line 41. In Classical Latin, the root *sapere* primarily means "to savor or taste," but may also mean "to know"; in modern Italian, however, the primary meaning is reversed. In Old Provençal, the word retains the older sensual meaning, as translated here, but it can also assume the more modern meaning related to cognition, as translated in line 9. It is always hard to select the proper translation for this word. In lines 9 and 10, Bernart told us that he had learned nothing about love; here he seems to be stressing the physical side that he has never savored. Physical enjoyment is merely implied in this poem; yet in his other poems, Bernart is not at all as coy as some critics would have us believe.

Another slippery word occurs in line 46: *chaitiu*, from Latin *captivus* ("captive or slave"). The word also had the meaning "wretched or miserable" and finally descended to the depths implied in the English word "caitiff" and modern Italian *cattivo*, "bad." I have translated it here as "slave" because of the modifier "longing" (*deziron*), and because in this stanza we are leaving the airy kingdom of the lark, where the relationship was that of a cult-worshiper and his divinity, and are firmly settled in the earthly kingdom, where the relationship is that of a serf and his master. However both levels exist throughout the poem, and neither can be seized for a full interpretation. The phrase could be translated more blandly as "miserable poor fellow."

In the last stanza the lady becomes a lord (*domina* to *dominum; domna* to *midons*). It is almost a commonplace to say that the Romans often admired women to the extent that they were men (Livia, Messalina, Agrippina, etc.). I am not sure that this commonplace is correct with respect to ancient history, and I fear that a similar cultural generalization could be drawn from this common Provençal rhetorical practice. Can the shift of genders be explained purely in terms of rhetorical realism? The lady or *domina* makes sense on the mystico-religious level because of Christian service to the Virgin Mary; but when the literal side of the rhetoric drawn from the world of external reality (but still largely conventional, since it can all be found in Ovid) is asserted, the woman as earthly mistress does not make sense, precisely because only a few women such as Countess Matilda of Italy had the power to make the conceit convincing. Thus, the poet's lady must be endowed with the habit of the king and duke to preserve her authority in the earthly sphere. It is sadly ironic that, despite the tomes written about courtly love and the adoration of women in twelfth-century France, history furnishes no convincing proofs to support the cultural generalizations based on poetic fiction. Possibly the conceit is merely witty.

The lady-lord, after undergoing her change of sex, behaves very much like a tyrannical divinity: she strips her man of his prowess and reduces him to the level of serfdom. Yet she herself has fallen from a goddess to a lord, and that is quite a fall too. The mode of address to the earthly ruler (I use the term Milordess merely to preserve the basic wit of the situation that my interpretation has been underplaying) employs some of the very same terms that we encounter in the religious sphere: "prayers" (or entreaties; *precs*) and "thanks" (*merces* is here given the social interpretation). Only the word *dreihz* ("rights" from Latin *directos*) clearly signifies the earthly kingdom, because the acolyte does not address a Bill of Rights to a goddess.

Then, accusing his loved one of indifference, the poet vows silence; silence is a threat to any divinity, for as Augustine said: *vae tacentibus!* Bernart affects aloofness, thereby seeking to repay his lady in her own coin. He threatens a self-imposed exile (she certainly does not impose it upon him). He accuses her again of having murdered him (somehow, she has acquired all the guilt that he was so anxious to assume in line 40). Then he paints a self-pitying picture of himself wandering disconsolately (here I translate *chaitiu* as *"down*cast") into exile, although he is not sure quite where.

The last four lines of the poem constitute the tornada (or "turning") and have a musical value as a last reprise. Rhetorically, they repeat (often but not always) sentiments contained in the last stanza. Here the tornada is particularly effective as a last call to the lady to show a little mercy. The name Tristan could refer to the *joglar* (the *jocularis* or "funny man" who sings the poem as a kind of musical epistle); or it could be the lady herself, since the masculine form of the name continues the convention of *midons*.[10] In the tornada, the vow of separation and the rejection of love and joy form a contrast with the joyous flight of the bird. The downward flight of the lark finds its last echo in the exiled flight of the poet.

We must now say something about the poem's form, the structure of its sounds. During the present century, several scholars such as Burdach, Singer, and Nykl have attempted to relate the Provençal stanzas and rhyme schemes to Arabic *muwaššahs, zejels,* and Mozarabic *jarchas,* without ever really supplying poems that show convincing similarities.[11] Working on the theory that what is indigenous may have more value

10. In Raynouard, p. 49, 61–64, the name seems to be that of a lady or friend: *Ma chanso apren a dire, / Alegret, a'N Dalferan; / Porta la n'a mon Tristan / Que sab ben gabar e rire.*

11. Konrad Burdach, *Vorspiel* (2 vols. Halle, 1925–26), *1,* pt. 1, 253–333. Samuel Singer, *Arabische und europäische Poesie im Mittelalter, APAW, 13* (1918). The sensual quality can be seen in a typical Arabic nature poem: *Hispano-Arabic Poetry,* tr. A. R. Nykl (Baltimore, 1946), p. 128; the spring topos is nowhere as consistently handled as in the Christian European tradition. Proponents of the Arabic theory, which was advanced as early as the nineteenth century, have never been able to meet the objections of August Wilhelm Schlegel, "Observations sur la langue et la littérature provençales," in *Essais littéraires et historiques* (Bonn, 1842), 211–340 (essay published Paris, 1818, p. 67): "*dans tout ce que j'ai lu sur ce sujet, je n'ai pas vu l'ombre d'une preuve; et il en faudrait de fort bonnes pour me persuader que l'inspiration d'une poésie toute fondée sur l'adoration des femmes et sur la plus grande liberté dans leur existence sociale, ait été prise chez un peuple où les femmes étaient des esclaves soigneusement enfermées; et que les chevaliers chrétiens aient été chercher des maîtres parmi les infidèles qu'ils combattaient à outrance.*" To which might be added the difficulty of abstracting idealized heterosexual love from poems often more fiercely homosexual than the speeches of the *Symp.* For another disposal, see Errante, *La Lirica romanza,* pp. 269–82.

For the sparser and even less likely *jarchas* (which created a flurry of excitement upon their discovery) see Leo Spitzer, "The Mozarabic Lyric and Theodor Frings' Theories," *CL, 4* (1952), 1–22; for the spring motif, 7: "Easter comes and comes without him. / How my heart burns bright for him!" These

than what is exotic, let us follow Westrup's suggestion and examine Philip the Chancellor's "Dialogue between the Heart and the Eye," which can easily be related to the medieval Latin tradition:

Cor síc affátur óculúm:
Te peccati principium,
Te fomitem, te stimulum,
Te voco mortis nuntium;
Tu, domus meae janitor,
Hosti non claudis ostium,
Familiaris proditor
Admittis adversarium.
(*An. Hymn. 21*, no. 168, pp. 114–15, st. 2)

Anc nón aguí de mé podér
ni no fui meus de l'or'en sai
que.m laisset en sos olhs vezer
en un miralh que mout me plai.
miralhs, pus me mirei en te,
m'an mort li suspir de preon,
c'aissi.m perdei com perdet se
lo bels Narcisus en la fon.
(*Can vei la lauzeta*, st. 3)

The poems are identical in their stanzaic patterns. The rhythms are the same: octosyllabic accentual, which, as Raby notes,[12] is a quite logical development of quantitative iambic dimeter, the dominant meter of early Church hymnology, al-

---

slender verses are as much a part of the Hebrew-Semitic tradition as the troubadours are of the Roman Christian; they may reflect contemporaneous developments, but are totally different in tone, imagery, diction, and structure. See Cantera, Garcia, Stern, and Zumthor in Bibliog. for variant readings. N.B.: Spitzer's essay was later omitted from his *Romanische Literaturstudien: 1936–56* (Tübingen, 1959).

12. *Secular Latin, 1*, 304: "the quantitative iambic dimeter seems to have changed itself by an easy and, as it were, painless process into rhythmical form."

ready seen in the hymns of Prudentius and Ambrose. The rhyme patterns are almost identical, except that the Latin poem, which employs feminine rhymes, carries the B-rhyme throughout the stanza, whereas Bernart substitutes two new sounds. We must remember that Latin, with its case endings, was far richer in rhymes than even the very rich vulgar languages (Italian, of course, being a major exception, since its conservative nature caused a retention of final syllables). Therefore it would be easy for Chancellor Philip to rhyme *ingenium* and *pretium*, for example; but when these words appear in the popular speech of southern France as *genh* and *pretz*, a close assonance is lost, and the troubadours are too much the craftsmen to pretend that similar sounds are exact rhymes. However, given the added handicap, the great troubadour virtuoso Arnaut Daniel can match or outdo any poet writing in Latin at the same period.

Philip's poem was probably written later than Bernart's, for the Chancellor died in 1236, but few would claim that Bernart's poetic techniques influenced Philip, since the Latin poem can be compared to accentual, rhymed Latin poetry existing long before Bernart (c. 1150–80). Indeed, in the *Vigil*, a premedieval or early medieval production, we could observe the presence of accentual and quantitative rhythms, as well as an abundance of internal rhymes and even occasional end-rhymes. Scholars such as Lote have traced these developments, showing how vernacular poetry, when it finally appeared, merely joined the mainstream of Latin poetic evolution.[13] It is difficult in this period to distinguish between ictus and stress, stanza and strophe, because the basic poetic elements of composition are constantly changing, just as the popular speech is evolving out of the Latin matrix.

Yet although Bernart and Philip are brothers with respect to form, they are absolutely antithetical with respect to meaning.

13. Georges Lote, *Histoire du vers français: le moyen âge* (3 vols. Paris, 1949–56); cf. William Beare, *Latin Verse and European Song: A Study in Accent and Rhythm* (London, 1957).

In fact, we can take the two poems (curiously enough, sung to the same music) and erect a dialogue between them. Philip's poem is a debate (in Latin terminology, a *conflictus* or *contentio;* in Provençal, a *tenso*) between the Eye and the Heart, in which each physical member blames the other for the sin of love. The argument is settled by Reason, who, in effect, blames them both. An interesting image occurs in the third stanza, in which the Heart says: "Can't you be called the window by which death enters the soul?" (We are reminded of Bernart's ambivalent attitude toward the eyes of his lady, and his words, "As a dead man I speak.") The Eye says: "Since I'm a glassy window and I announce what I see, why do you blame me for it?" (38–40). The Eye thus falls back on the arguments for instinct and natural behavior. Reason, however, will not accept these rationalizations; it declares that love is a sensual act and therefore a sin; both organs deserve the blame, and the debate is closed. The Chancellor of Paris presents the accepted clerical view of romantic love as disaster; writing in the elevated Latin style, he leaves no doubt about how he would construe Bernart's clever rationalizations and conceits. When Bernart asks the key question in the sixth stanza—since my lady doesn't show me mercy, where will I find it?—Philip would answer: in God. As a theologian and poet of morality, the Chancellor was not deceived by poetic fantasy.

When we return to Bernart's poem, we cannot ignore its popular qualities. Compared to the grave, humorless style of Philip, the Provençal poem has a gay, semiserious air. In one sense the classification of troubadour poetry as aristocratic court poetry has obscured the universal appeal of the verse. Not all of the writers or singers were aristocrats; neither, necessarily, was the audience, although men of money were required to provide patronage for the poets. The term "courtly love" poetry was given wide coinage by nineteenth-century scholars such as Diez, Paris, and Jeanroy, who contrasted it with "popular" poetry, a small collection of albas, pastourelles, and dance songs that were believed to have provided an origin for all vernacular expression.[14] The studies of Faral and Scheludko have pointed up the aristocratic qualities in both the alba and pastourelle, so that now an even slimmer corpus of poetry could possibly be attributed to that amorphous creative agent known as "the people."[15] Auerbach carried the argument further by suggesting that the hermetically contained, hierarchical nature of medieval secular society did not admit the cleft between the people and the nobility that the nineteenth-century romantics had imagined.[16] The cleft, when any existed, appeared between secular society and the clergy, the nobles and the Church. The Albigensian Crusade, which crushed poetry, heresy, and South French political power, was waged between the Provençal people, led by their nobility (save for those who defected to Simon de Montfort), against North French nobles and Pope Innocent III.[17] The argument between Philip and Bernart indicates a certain gap in attitudes toward the things of this world, just as Philip's polished Latin is removed from Bernart's language of the streets. Yet the voice of Philip is also present in vernacular poetry, just as the voice of Bernart could be heard in the more polished *Carmina Burana*. Medieval literature is striking for its continuity, even in contrasting spheres.

The voice of Philip, for example, can be heard in the anti-

14. Friedrich Diez, *Die Leben und Werke der Troubadours*, ed. K. Bartsch (2d ed. Leipzig, 1882); Gaston Paris, *La Littérature française au moyen âge* (6th ed. Paris, 1922), p. 199 et passim; Alfred Jeanroy, *Les Origines de la poésie lyrique en France au moyen âge* (3d ed. Paris, 1925), p. xvi: "On est ordinairement d'accord pour appeler courtoise *la poésie des Provençaux et celle qui en fut imitée: ce terme est excellent. En effet, elle fut exclusivement composée pour le divertissement des cours.*"

15. Edmond Faral, "La Pastourelle," *Romania, 49* (1923), 204–59. Dmitri Scheludko, "Beiträge . . . Die Volksliedertheorie," *ZFSL, 52* (1929), 1–38, 201–66. Scheludko relates secular and religious music.

16. Review, *RP, 4* (1950–51), 65–67; about folk theory (66): "irrefutable as it is unprovable, since one cannot show the folk genius actually at work."

17. Clearly summarized in H. J. Chaytor, *The Troubadours* (Cambridge, Eng., 1912), pp. 76 ff. Contemporary history: *La Chanson de la croisade contre les Albigeois*, ed. Paul Meyer (2 vols. Paris, 1875–79).

feministic fourth stanza of Bernart's poem. In fact, if we try to summarize the basic tone of the Provençal work, we face a dilemma because of the numerous contrasting elements and contradictions of thought. If Bernart treats his lady as Celestial Mistress and then Earthly Master, he also casts her in the light of devilish Eve. We may think of her in terms of the sun or an irresistible magnet, but she is also a pool in which a man can drown. Is she the Great Lady, a lady, or a mere woman? Bernart would seem to suggest that she is all of these things, and therefore ultimately none by itself; it is impossible to label her nature or his attitude toward it, because the subject of this poem is nothing less than the paradoxical nature of woman. It is only this mysterious part of her that is ultimately idealized; the poet would like to, and indeed tries to, tear away her veils and possess her physically, or else reduce her to a mere generic status, but he is incapable of doing these things. Provençal poetry is always, in its florescence, a prelude to the act of love in which the woman as untouchable divinity is contrasted with the woman as an object to be enjoyed; between these two extremes the poet tries to forge a document of his emotions, yet his expressions run the gamut from mystical adoration to absolute rejection, from deification to dismissal. In one sense, the opening image of the lark (which contrasts with, as much as it establishes, the basic tone of the poem) prefigures at the start the sadly contradictory fact of human love for human beings, in which the real situation somehow never lives up to the vitality of dreams. The poem itself is a dream-revery hovering between idealism and realism; it is an illusion, and Bernart seems to be keenly aware of this. Why else would he compare himself to a madman or a fool? Perhaps the most important lines of the poem are:

> Alas! how much I thought I knew
> About love, and how little I know!

Yet there is an insistence at the end of the poem that this kind of illusion is as valid as any other.

Bernart uses the full-blown spring motif in some of his other poems; we shall turn to the most important of these to see if the conflicting attitudes of *Can vei la lauzeta mover* are exceptional in his work or part of his basic attitude toward that perplexing force called love.

Bernart portrays a conventional spring landscape in his poem *Can l'erba fresch':*

> When fresh grass and leaves appear
> And the flower buds in the meadow
> And the nightingale loud and clear
> Raises his voice, moves his song,
> I rejoice in him, I rejoice in the flower,
> I rejoice in myself, and more in Milord;
> On every side I'm enclosed and bound with joy,
> A joy that overcomes any other joy known.

> *Can l'erba fresch'e.lh folha par*
> *e la flors boton'el verjan,*
> *e.l rossinhols autet e clar*
> *leva sa votz e mou so chan,*
> *joi ai de lui, e joi de la flor*
> *e joi de me e de midons major;*
> *daus totas partz sui de joi claus e sens,*
> *mas sel es jois que totz autres jois vens.*[18]

The obsession with joy in these opening lines recalls the repetitions of *gaudium* in the less mature *Burana*, where the appearance of spring often aroused the single response of gladness. We might note too the linking of the secularized nightingale to this joyous landscape. Bernart avoids the word *filomena*, which existed in literary Provençal. He uses the new Romance word for the creature: *(il)lum lusciniolum*, the neutral Latin word for the bird, yields *rossinhols*, by a typical Provençal dissimilation of liquids. Similarly, he does not link the flower to

18. *Bernart: SL,* no. 39, pp. 220–23, 1–8.

any mythic connotation, such as a lily or narcissus would have done. And so his scene, despite its clarity of images, has a certain perpetually abstract air to it; it could describe the coming of spring in Rome, Seville, or Athens, as well as in Ventadour. The landscape itself is traditional, but the poetry sounds fresh and excited. Since the word "joy" is repeated six times in the last four lines, we might be tempted to call the poetic technique naive. Yet we cannot ignore certain devilish, though not necessarily Satanic, elements in this little portrait that qualify this naiveté. For example, the statement that joy in the spring and in Milord overcomes any other joy means, with reference to the *Burana,* that it overcomes the joy of Easter and My Lord. This little parody is more forcefully implied in another poem where Bernart uses the stronger word *pascor.*

And so we have a traditional spring opening, with the poet and the lady linked in joy to the nightingale and the flower, the same tacit coupling observed in the *Burana.* Will the scene continue in this one-dimensional way? No. The next strophe begins:

> Alas! how I'm dying of worry!
> for so often I stand in thought
> that thieves could carry me away
> and I wouldn't know what happened.
> By God, Love! you know I'm your prey!

> *Ai las! com mor de cossirar!*
> *que manhtas vetz en cossir tan:*
> *lairo m'en poirian portar,*
> *que re no sabria que.s fan.*
> *per Deu, Amors! be.m trobas vensedor.*   (9–13)

The first thing one observes about these lines is their sudden switch of tone, from joy to worry. Then, if he examines them more closely, he can detect the same subtle parody that was noticed in the first strophe. For example, the notion of a man so deeply wrapped in thought that he is unaware of reality is

173

an ideal of contemplation, in which the mind and the object are one. Yet the contemplator is surely not thinking about a woman; he is at one with God, and he also knows peace. Bernart avoids the scholastic, bookish word *contemplatio*. He uses the vaguer *cossirar*, from Latin *considerare*, which originally meant "to contemplate the stars, ponder," but finally simply "to worry." The Latin word is not necessarily an important Scholastic term of cognition. In the terminology of Richard of St. Victor, the three phases of knowing in their ascending order are: cogitation, the mind flitting aimlessly around an object— the lowest form, and the one used by Andreas Capellanus to define love in the opening sentence of his Christian *Ars Amoris;* meditation, the mind fixed steadily upon an object; and contemplation, the union of mind and object in which, as Blake said, "we become the thing we contemplate."[19] Now it is fairly obvious that Bernart is playing games with us; he is pretending that his cogitations, which contain the taint of the emotions, are contemplations. Neither Plato nor Richard of St. Victor would take this stanza seriously for a moment. The lines are ironic, and the irony arises from transferring the attributes of a higher function to a lower one. Indeed, this ele-

---

19. *De amore (Trattato d'Amore)*, ed. S. Battaglia (Rome, 1902), 1.1: *"Amor est passio quaedam innata procedens ex visione et immoderata cogitatione formae alterius sexus, ob quam aliquis super omnia cupit alterius potiri amplexibus."* Battaglia's judgment is excellent (p. v): *"La definizione . . . non oltrepassa la sfera dell'egoismo e della sensualità . . . senza nessun presagio di volersi elevare verso la vita dell'intelletto."* For a consideration of the treatise's wit, see D. W. Robertson, Jr., *A Preface to Chaucer* (Princeton, 1962), pp. 391–448.

Cf. Richard of St. Victor, *De praep. animi ad contemp. (Benj. Min.)* (*PL 196*, cols. 1–64); note the use of *consideratio* (col. 13): *"ex tali consideratione, quidquid mens illicitum suggerit";* also col. 14: *"illecebrosae cogitationes";* col. 5: *"De vitio imaginationis et sensualitatis";* ibid.: *"dum psallimus vel oramus, phantasias cogitationum vel quaslibet imagines rerum ab oculis cordis amovere volumus, nec valemus";* for the image of the fool on the bridge inverted (col. 5): *"quantumque bibat, semper ad bibendum inhiat."* Of course Andreas in his third chapter accords entirely with Richard, who speaks about contemplation (col. 51), praise or *laus* (col. 21), and joy or *gaudium* (cols. 25–26) entirely in terms of God.

ment of wit is implied in Bernart's so-called idealization of the woman as goddess; it does not explain all the humor in Bernart's poetry, but it is a basic factor.

We cannot be sure how Bernart's audience reacted to line 13. Did they cringe when they heard the Christian God of Love coupled with Ovid's love-god Amor? We should note that it *is* a love god, personified, in the flesh, although elsewhere he is a mere abstraction. It would seem that the classical phrase "by Jupiter" was totally colloquial; but the Romans did not have a commandment against taking the name of their lord in vain. Neither did they have a commandment against adultery. In Bernart's poetry, one is not quite aware that the Christians had any such commandments either. The notion of the lover as prey (*praeda*) to Love is, of course, an essential part of the Ovidian sensibility.[20]

In the third strophe, Bernart surprises us somewhat by saying that he has not even told his lady about his love for her. Yet every time he looks at her, he can scarcely hold himself back from running toward her. (We might recall what Chancellor Philip had to say about the eyes.) Bernart frankly confesses that he is afraid of her (*si no fos per paor*, 22). These lines could cast the lady in either the role of the Celestial Lady or Earthly Lord; we are not sure which. But suddenly Bernart casts off all his metaphors, and we realize that he is talking about a tangible flesh-and-blood lady:

> For never did I see a body so beautifully shaped and colored, and yet so miserably slow to the task (need) of love!

> *c'anc no vi cors melhs talhatz ni depens*
> *ad ops d'amar sia tan greus ni lens.* (23–24)

Lines such as these are a little painful to critics who tell us that Provençal women are always abstract shadows and never seem to have any corporal unity.[21] Here the corporal reality

---

20. *Am.* 2.17.5–6; 2.9.29 f., etc.
21. Jeanroy, *La Poésie lyrique*, 2, 106.

seems to emerge quite naturally out of the basically unreal psychic situation. How can the poor lady be expected to give Bernart her love when he hasn't even told her that he *is* in love? We must not expect consistency from a lover, however well he may rationalize at times. Furthermore, these two lines give us about as clear a picture of the beloved as we usually get in any love poetry, whether written by Catullus, who described Lesbia largely in oblique terminology, Marvell, or E. E. Cummings.[22] The greatest lyric poets seldom employ the exhaustive descriptive techniques of a nineteenth-century novelist. Perhaps a few quick strokes are all that are needed.

Yet after moving very near to the loved one as physical object, Bernart retreats to a world of abstract service. Lines 25 to 32 describe his promise to serve and worship his lady; these lines, if taken on the social level with the woman as duke or *dux,* have parallels in Ovid; if interpreted on the religious level, they imitate Christian worship.[23] Such lines are often lifted from context to prove the ethereal, remote medieval-hierarchical nature of troubadour poetry, despite the witty context and Ovidian parallels; but this stanza, even if it were meant to be taken seriously and applied to twelfth-century culture, yields to a wildly sensual stanza in lines 33 to 40:

> If I knew how to bewitch people,
> I'd turn my enemies into babies,
> So that no one could ever find us out
> Or say anything toward our loss.
> Then I know I could see my beauty,
> Her lovely eyes, her lively color;
> And I'd kiss her mouth in every way
> So the marks would last a month!

22. E.g., Catullus, no. 43. When poets do indulge in naturalistic detail, the features are also often traditional; the Arabs seem to have inherited the "blonde" ideal in their poetry from another race.

23. For the supposed "social" elements, see Wilibald Schrötter, *Ovid und die Troubadours* (Halle, 1908), pp. 79–102.

S'eu sabes la gen enchantar,
mei enemic foran efan,
que ja us no saubra triar
ni dir re que.ns tornes a dan.
adoncs sai eu que vira la gensor
e sos bels olhs e sa frescha color,
e baizera.lh la bocha en totz sens,
si que d'un mes i paregra lo sens.

Such discourteous, uncourtly sentiments are often Ovidian-classical mosaics, as Scheludko has shown.[24] The fact that they are not the description of an actual event, but a wish, does not lessen their intensity, although it may perpetuate the notion of troubadour poetry as revery or dream composed of many varied elements.

The next stanza softens the sensuality, but does not dull it. The marks become a sweet kiss, and the notion of love as an emotion bound to youth and time moves compellingly to the forefront in a manner that recalls both Marvell and Ovid:[25]

O how I'd like to find her alone,
sleeping (or just pretending),
so that I could steal a sweet kiss
(since I'm not worth asking her for it).
By God, lady, we're achieving little in love!
Time's going by; we're losing the very best part!
We'll have to resort to secret signs:
Since boldness isn't helping, maybe trickery will!

Be la volgra sola trobar,
que dormis, o.n fezes semblan,
per qu'e.lh embles un doutz baizar,
pus no valh tan qu'eu lo.lh deman.

24. "Ovid und die Troubadours," *ZRP*, 54 (1934), 129–74.
25. For the stolen kiss motif, see *Ars Am.* 2.617 f.; the passage of time, 3.59–72; cf. Scheludko, "Ovid," p. 152.

> *per Deu, domna, pauc esplecham d'amor!*
> *vai s'en lo tems, e perdem lo melhor!*
> *parlar degram ab cubertz entresens,*
> *e, pus no.ns val arditz, valgues nos gens!*   (41–48)

This stanza would have delighted Philip the Chancellor; he could have pointed to it and said: you see, the lust finally creeps through the rhetorical conceits; the trickery is acknowledged by the poet himself; *this* is what the poetry's really about. Yet Philip is just one voice in a dialogue; Bernart himself becomes Philip in his antifeministic phases. It is interesting to observe the way that the "hidden signs" (*cubertz entresens*) in this passage supply us with the rationale for the "hidden name" (*senhal*) of troubadour ladies; furthermore, the Ovidian context clearly shows that the motivation for calling the woman by a secret name is highly practical in a love affair in which not a word is ever mentioned about marriage. Ovid spoke of the "mystique of love," and his "secret name" Corinna is both practical and pseudo-mystical; Bernart's masculine "Tristan" is a more witty development of the same principle. Curiously enough, Ovid seems to have been more faithful or, since we are talking in rhetorical terms, more consistent, because he wrote love poems almost exclusively for Corinna. Bernart wrote them not only to Tristan, but also to Aziman, Bel Vezer, and Bel Conort.

As a direct corollary with the passage of time, the last stanza offers a word of warning for women who keep their lovers waiting too long. Bernart surrenders to the lady and promises not to betray her:

> Good lady, if you'd only deign to love me,
> I'd never try to lie to you.

> *bona domna, ab sol c'amar mi dens,*
> *ja per mentir eu no serai atens.*   (55–56)

Then in the tornada Bernart tells the joglar to sing his song to the lady because he does not have the courage to face her.

When we realize that this love poem is an epistolary song, the contradiction of Bernart's not having told the lady that he loves her dissolves; for this poem, when sung in its entirety, will do precisely that. Scheludko's attempt to relate Provençal poetry to the epistolary handbooks of the day, and ultimately to Ovid's *Heroides*, is illuminating, although, of course, no one would state that the rules that govern letters also govern poetry.[26]

Bernart's poem is too tasteful to be classified as erotic, too frank to be esoteric. Bernart never allows us to pigeonhole his emotions; indeed, he seems incapable of allowing us to do this, simply because he is not rational in his attitude toward the thing he loves, although his poetry creates the illusion of rational presentation because it is clearly stated. His use of the spring opening is misleading, because it would seem to follow the tradition of the *Burana;* but it is actually used as a contrasting element, just as it was in *Can vei la lauzeta mover.* The linking of that landscape with the time element that is the dominant theme of the poem merely stresses again the terrestrial nature of the conception. If the spring portrait is ideal, it is only half related to the psychic state that is responsible for the rest of the poem.

Another lyric, *Lo gens tems de pascor,* shows a much subtler blending of the hymn and the *Burana* state of mind. The word *pascor* is an ambiguous word in Old Provençal. It is derived from the Late Latin-Semitic word *Pascha* (Easter) and was, as we have seen, the dominant word in Christian spring hymnology. Yet through repeated secular usage, the word lost its essentially religious connotation and came to mean simply "spring," an alternate word for *temps novel.* The ambiguity of the word in Old Provençal does not extend to modern Italian, for example, where one says *Pasqua* if he means "Easter" and *primavera* if he means "spring" (in French, *Pâques* and *printemps*). Yet in Old Provençal, the connotations

26. "Beiträge . . . ," *AR, 15* (1931), 137–206.

are intermixed, and a totally different word such as "rebirth"
may capture both the religious and secular overtones:

> The beautiful time of rebirth
> brings us leaves
> with fresh greenness
> and flowers of varied hues,
> and therefore (ergo) all lovers
> are gay and singing—
> except for me; I wail and weep
> without a taste of joy.

> *Lo gens tems de pascor*
> *ab la frescha verdor*
> *nos adui folh'e flor*
> *de diversa color,*
> *per que tuih amador*
> *son gai e chantador*
> *mas eu, que planh e plor,*
> *cui jois non a sabor.*[27]

Here Bernart's handling of the spring motif approaches the
melancholy of *Levis exsurgit Zephirus;* and in these lines we
can also see the same tacit coupling of man's life with the life
of nature. Bernart's use of the conjunction *per que* is also
roughly equivalent to the startling use of *ergo* in the *Burana.*
Yet the change from Latin to a Romance language softens the
parody value, and endows the secular portrait with a dignity
all its own.

If we expect this poem to develop into a melancholy Latin
lament over the passing of time, we find that we are only half
right. Bernart tells us that he has not tasted (again the word
sabor reflects the primary Latin connotation of *sapere*) joy because his lady-lord and Love have betrayed him: two traitors
(*dui traidor*, 11). Needless to say, Philip the Chancellor would
assent to all the statements made thus far in the poem. Bernart

27. *Bernart: SL,* no. 28, pp. 165–69, 1–8.

goes on to build up his own case and tear down the case of the loved one and Love. He claims that he has loved with honor and nobility; surely he does not deserve all this pain and grief. We might note that a passive acceptance of suffering, the willful martyrdom to Amor, is not necessarily an integral element of this poetry. We might also notice that Bernart does a great deal more talking about himself than about his lady; and he, not she, is the subject of any idealized pattern created to this point. The ego assertion and exploration of the poet's psyche are very important in Bernart's poetry; they create, in fact, the field in which the poetry operates. The lady is an eternally variable quality wavering in that field between the poles of virtuous abstraction and naked sensuality. However much she may maltreat her lover, becoming masculine even in her name, she may pay dearly for not cooperating by being reduced to the (obviously low) status of woman. This is what Bernart does to her in the next lines, which grow out of his struggle for self-identity; he links his one lady to the many; then he rejects the lot:

> For I don't go around changing
> The way those ladies do.

> *qu'eu no.m vau ges chamjan*
> *si com las domnas fan.*   (23–24)

Abruptly he shifts his tone. (If this is a love poem, he has shown very little tenderness.) He gives us a brief history of the affair, saying "we met when we were both children" (25), and every year since then "my joy has doubled" (a very curious statement in relation to what was said earlier). At any rate, his setting of love in youth is particularly striking, and in some ways recalls the opening chapters of Dante's *Vita Nuova*. In terms of Provençal literature, we must stress the fact that "spring" is called *temps novel,* the "new" time or "young" time. Here we see the repetition of the classical Ovidian poetic ideogram in which youth, springtime, and romantic love were inextricably linked (*Ars Am.* 3.59–72). The notion of romantic love as young love is an implicit feature of erotic poetry; the denial of it, as was already suggested, may be voiced by maturity (and marriage), morality, and old age. At any rate, thoughts about the past lead Bernart to thoughts about his miserable present state, and ultimately to thoughts about the future:

> And when she's old, let her ask me
> To want her then.
>
> *cant er velha, .m deman*
> *que l'aya bo talan.* (31–32)

Horace's *carpe diem* and Ovid's warning to the lady leap immediately to mind.

The awareness of the brevity of life then evokes another of those erotic passages that Bernart handles with excellent taste:

> O, and life—what's it worth to me
> if daily I don't see
> my fine natural joy
> in her bed, beneath the window—
> her body white just like
> the snow at Christmas-time,
> so the two of us together
> can measure each other's sides?!
>
> *Las! e viure que.m val,*
> *s'eu no vei a jornal*
> *mo fi joi natural*
> *en leih, sotz fenestral*
> *cors blanc tot atretal*
> *com la neus a nadal,*
> *si c'amdui cominal*
> *mezuressem egal?!* (33–40)

Perhaps the most striking word in this portrait is *natural*. It is a very tricky word, since some lexicographers and editors would like to define it as "excellent" or "perfect"; yet the etymology (from Latin *naturalis*) indicates that the word may mean simply "natural," as in Augustine's significant phrase *amor naturalis*, which describes secular love. The definition "excellent" springs from a preconceived notion that is not substantiated by the poem itself. Why then does Bernart bother to call his "fine love" natural? Is this another echo of the *Burana's* use of *ergo*, the insistence upon the naturalness of human love? Does it also tie in with the *nature* opening of the poem and make explicit what was implied in that portrait? I suspect so; at least I can see no other reason for its use. It would be unfair to the gifted Bernart to say that he used the word for the rhyme scheme. Furthermore, the description of the lady's body in terms of snow continues this naturizing technique; of course, in the discussion of Ovid's portrait of Narcissus we observed a traditional source for the image. Yet the presence of the words *a nadal* (at Christmas-time) adds an extra touch of joy stolen from the religious realm that matches the joy of Easter (*pascor*) suggested at the beginning. Is this sublime travesty? Gentle parody? It is difficult to assess. There is very little of the direct parody of hymns in Bernart's poetry, such as we observed in the cruder *Burana;* however, the more polished *Burana* showed a similarly deft manipulation of secular and religious terms. In the main, Bernart is too good-humored to be either a Satanic inverter or an embittered heretic; his original interweaving of rhetoric is what one might expect from the term "secular Christian" poetry.

The words "fine joy," here referring to the woman herself, or the variant "fine love" are often taken as a key phrase to describe the "idealized" love of the troubadours. Recently a critic connected the Provençal word *fi(n)s* with Latin *fidem* (faith), reading loyalty, service, and honor into the word's etymology, taking the phrase to describe the poetry, and ultimately forcing the poetry into doctrine.[28] No doubt the ser-

28. Maurice Valency, *In Praise of Love* (N.Y., Macmillan, 1958), p. 142: "The adjective *fin, fis,* from Latin *fides,* had the sense of faithful, honest, sincere, true. The expression *fin amor . . .* honest love, pure love, perfect love, or,

vice elements are there, just as they are in Ovid. The questions that we have been asking in this study are: how are they to be read—seriously or comically? In a purely social way or in a mystical-service way, or both? Insofar as the etymology of the word *fi(n)s* is concerned, the traditional derivation from Latin *finitum* is still the most plausible, since a Latin dental never yields a Provençal nasal, and the nasal occurs in the feminine forms of the word: e.g., *fin'amors*. The word means "finished, polished, refined"; then by extension, "precious, valuable"; and finally, "lasting, abiding." Its occurrence in this erotic stanza shows the essentially antidoctrinaire possibilities of the word, and I have translated it "fine"—although the word "pretty" or even the catchall "wonderful" might do it justice here.

Finally, in the last stanzas of the poem, Bernart begins the idealization process that somehow got sidetracked in the fifth stanza. He insists that he is a "true lover" *(drut leyal)*, though I would hestitate to define that term from the preceding parts of the poem. He demands a kiss as reward for his service, affirms the beauty of his lady's eyes, thus softening the charge he made in the second stanza, and begs the woman not to be proud. Since the kiss wish follows the passionate scene imagined in the fifth stanza, the ending sounds a bit anticlimactic. Yet the notion of a kiss as a preface to something else seems to be a tacit understanding in Bernart's poetry. Andreas Capellanus affirms it in the early chapters of his pseudo-Ovidian treatise in his remarks on "mixed" love, and William of Aquitaine, the first troubadour, leaves no doubt that the notion of women as objects to be enjoyed (as well as adored) was very much a part of the literary convention in its florescence.[29] Bernart has exquisite poetic taste. He never overplays

---

after Gaston Paris, courtly love, is very well translated as true love." Another adjective, *fis-fia,* "loyal" (from *fidus-fida*) exists, but is not etymologically related to the term *fin'amors.*

29. The stages of "mixed" love as set down in the *De amore* 1.6a (p. 38) are: the granting of hope, a kiss, an embrace, complete possession. This

the sensual or the idealized; nor does he omit either element. The later troubadours, who may have confused social manners with poetic mannerism, tend to omit this interplay. Since most of these poets (e.g., Bonifaci Calvo, N'At de Mons, Aimeric de Belenoi, Bertolome Zorzi) do not attempt the Christian Neoplatonic framework of the Italian *dolce stil nuovo,* their poetry is singularly lifeless, although their etiquette may have been excellent. However, since no reliable history of social behavior exists for this period, and we are not privileged to deduce such matters from poetic fiction, this supposition is very much open to question.

Bernart shows perhaps the first signs of the *dolce stil nuovo.* There is a hint of Dante in these opening lines of another poem:

> When the cold (sweet?) breeze blows
> out of your land,
> it seems to me I feel
> a wind from Paradise
> because of my love for the beauty
> toward whom I bow my head.

> *Can la frej'* aura venta*
> *deves vostre päis,*
> *vejaire m'es qu'eu senta*
> *un ven de paradis*
> *per amor de la genta*
> *vas cui eu sui aclis.*[30]

*Raynouard, *doss'* (sweet)

If the woman's country is likened to Paradise, then the woman

---

sensual hierarchy is implied in Bernart's poetry, where the end is seen through a visualized dream. If "perfect love" without sexual culmination were actually practiced, there would seem to be little need for the thorough renunciation of human love at the end of the treatise.

30. *Bernart: SL,* no. 37, pp. 212–15, 1–6; cf. Raynouard, p. 84; Bartsch, col. 63.

is tacitly likened to an angel or even the Virgin. Yet the proposition is stated in very equivocal terms: "it seems to me." The picture of the poet walking with bent head seems to enforce the religious analogy rather than weaken it. The spring topos is very neatly handled here, for the Earthly Paradise is clearly contrasted with the Celestial. It is also worth noting that the poet describes the occurrence of spring as a physical fact; the heavenly wind and Paradise itself are mentioned hypothetically (but not, of course, ironically). Thus, if I may filch De Rougemont's definition of materialism: the lower order is always affirmed.[31] However, it is precisely this affirmation of physical events and reality that casts into doubt De Rougemont's thesis that the poetry is heretical, mystical propaganda. The lady may be likened to an abstract principle of beauty or she may also be discussed in terms of a devil, but Bernart's mode of expression leaves no doubt that he is talking about a lady at the literal level of meaning.

In this poem, Bernart goes on to beg his lady's pardon for having mentioned that foul lovers get better rewards than good ones get; then, in the very next stanza, he seems to berate all women for granting the unjust gifts that he just denied. In the fourth stanza, he begs her to relent; in the fifth he says: "good-fated lovers know peace and joy / and ill-fated lovers know misery" (49–50). Finally the logic of the poem reaches the height of grandeur (and absurdity) in the sixth strophe and the tornada:

> I'm the kind of man who never scorns
> Any good that God makes for him . . .
> Every Christian soul
> Would like to have the kind of joy
> I've had and have;
> It's the only thing to brag about.

31. De Rougemont, rev. ed., p. 59, where the notion is applied to modern thought.

And if she makes me sure of this
Another time I'll trust her;
If not—I won't believe
That she's a Christian.

Cel sui que no soana
lo be que Deus li fai . . .
tot'arma crestiana
volgra, agues tal jai
com eu agui et ai,
car sol d'aitan se vana.

Si d'aisso m'essertana
d'autra vetz la.n creirai;
o si que no, ja mai
no creirai crestiana. (51–52, 57–64)

Bernart has been called the Racine of the troubadours for the clarity of his expression; as far as grammar is concerned, this reputation is well merited. But let us examine his logic, which seems simple on the surface but is actually quite complex. In lines 51 and 52, there is an embryonic deduction that proceeds from the following terms: God is good; everything God makes is good, God made my lady; ergo, my lady is good. This very same argument applied to human love occurs in the second Latin inscription for Chapter 2. After a break, the argument continues: my lady brings me joy (*gaudium*); joy or bliss is the desire of every Christian; ergo, every Christian would like to have my lady. This is a boast, a *vanto,* and the poet tells us frankly that he is bragging. The word derives from Latin *vanitas,* and if we recall the Book of Ecclesiastes, we can guess what the Church thought about the boast and the logic behind it.

The worst parody of syllogistic form occurs in the tornada, and depends upon the ambiguous word "joy" in the preceding stanza. In effect, it proceeds this way: Every true Christian believes in love and joy; if my lady believes in love and joy, then she's a true Christian; and if she doesn't believe in them, she's not. What on earth are we to conclude from this argument? It hinges upon Bernart's definitions of love and joy. If he is referring to Augustine's *amor Dei* and the *gaudium* of the Easter hymns, then this is quite an acceptable (though almost tautological) deduction. Needless to say, Bernart is thinking only about his own love and his own joy; God never enters this poem, except through the simile with Paradise. The wit, as I suggested before, rises from the application of material conceits to a metaphysical structure. Is Bernart logical? He probably studied logic in the school at Ventadour that he refers to in another poem, because it was a basic part of the trivium. Yet the havoc he wreaks with it is comparable to the *Burana's* profligate use of the Scholastic's *ergo*. Logic is as dangerous a tool as allegory, for logic cannot fully escape the vague definition of basic terms. Has any love poet ever been logical? I doubt it. If we think of Catullus' "Let's live, Lesbia —let's make love," it is obvious that the conclusion is stated in the first line, and the premises (the sun sets but rises the following day; when we go down, we do not rise; time is passing—or, as Bernart said, *vai s'en lo tems*) are stated later. The whole concept of logic with relationship to lyric poetry does not seem to be a very fruitful one.

The poles of contrast that furnish the dynamics and wit of Bernart's poetry can be illustrated by the opening and closing lines of his "My Heart's So Full of Joy" (*Tant ai mo cor ple de joya*). The title is the opening line of the poem, but the tornada says:

> Messenger, go and run
> and tell my most beautiful one
> the pain and grief
> I've suffered—and the martyrdom.

> *Messatgiers, vai e cor,*
> *e di.m a la gensor*
> *la pena e la dolor*
> *que.n trac, e l.martire.*[32]

32. *Bernart: SL,* no. 44, pp. 260–63, 73–76.

I have translated *martire* (suffering) as "martyrdom," not only because it is etymologically related, but also because it illustrates Auerbach's thesis that the language of romantic passion and the great Christian Passion are intertwined. Yet in terms of the ideas thus far developed, I am primarily interested in the expression of the individual poem, and how one goes from joy to grief in 76 lines.

Returning to the first strophe, we observe the mystical inversion of the seasons that was first apparent in hymnology and then in the *Burana:*

> My heart's so full of joy
>   everything loses its nature for me.
> White, red, and yellow flowers
>   are what the chill means to me,
> For with the wind and the rain
>   my happiness grows . . .
> And so the ice seems a flower to me
>   and the snow is green.
>
> I could go outside without my clothes,
>   Naked in my shirt,
> Because my true love keeps me safe
>   From the icy blasts.
> But a man's a fool to lose measure . . .
> And so I've taken care of myself . . .
>
> *Tant ai mo cor ple de joya,*
>   *tot me desnatura.*
> *flor blancha, vermelh'e groya*
>   *me par la frejura,*
> *c'ab lo ven et ab la ploya*
>   *me creis l'aventura . . .*
> *per que.l gels me sembla flor*
>   *e la neus verdura.*

> *Anar posc ses vestidura,*
> *nutz en ma chamiza,*
> *car fin'amors m'asegura*
> *de la freja biza.*
> *mas es fols qui.s desmezura ...*
> *per qu'eu ai pres de me cura ...* (1–6, 11–17, 19)

The first stanza is the kind of poetry that occurs again and again with such authors as Paulinus of Nola. Yet after stating his complete disregard for natural phenomena, Bernart suddenly introduces the concept of measure, proportion, balance. In my discussion of the *Burana,* I pointed out the fact that rhetorical balance was the quality finally lacking in that verse in its cruder and more obvious forms; yet the *Burana* themselves posed this very question, and offered samples of poetry that can rightfully be compared with Bernart's work. Rhetorically speaking, Bernart's poem is the expression of measure.

Philosophically, the mean with relation to love can be stated in these terms: is there some love between the attraction of brutes and the love of God that is worthy of consideration? Poetically, it can be stated this way: can one sing about a human being in a way that includes the reality of his or her existence, yet somehow embraces the eternal world of beauty and truth that lies within the boundaries of the human imagination? Perhaps the first question is also poetic, because philosophers do not seem to be much concerned with it. The best lyric poets, however, are very much concerned with the relation of ideals to reality (the Beautiful as it relates to Lesbia or Tristan); and here, perhaps, is where they part company with philosophers. We do not find Beatrice in the *Summa Theologica;* Alcibiades wanders away drunken from the Symposium. Sappho, Catullus, Bernart, and Villon envision the goddess as flesh, and therein lies the ironic crux of the matter.

Here Bernart is applying the moral concept of "measure" to his conduct, in the old Horatian manner. He is looking for a golden mean to preserve himself from his excesses. Quite consciously he compares his emotional state to madness. If classical poetry is often subjected to interpretation in terms of Aristotelian balance, then I see no reason why the same terms cannot be applied to Bernart. Yet the notion of a mean is as old as the Temple at Delphi. The mad lover knows he is mad (Anacreon's *mainomai*), but what can he do about it? The lines are sadly funny. The poet knows that he's unnatural, and *not* in a truly mystical way.

Bernart comes down from his grand flight gradually. He tells us in the third strophe that his soul goes where his beloved is, but his body is stationary. He next discusses his love affair in terms of faith, hope, and love, the three prime Christian virtues. Then in line 39, the midpoint of the poem, he descends into the Ovidian arena, telling us that he is swayed like a ship at sea (*com la naus en l'onda*); he catalogues the traditional Ovidian ailments: tossing and turning at night; worrying, suffering, grief (41–48).[33] Then, in a superb strophe that articulates the bird-wish of the poet of the *Vigil*, he says:

> O God! why am I not a swallow
> so I could fly through the air
> and go in the depths of night
> into her chamber?

> *Ai Deus! car no sui ironda,*
> *que voles per l'aire*
> *e vengues de noih prionda*
> *lai dins so repaire?* (49–52)

This fantasy yields in turn to a portrayal of the suffering lover as Christian worshiper; but his lament to the Virgin is stated in physical terms:

> Lady, for your love
> I join my hands and worship!
> O sweet body with lively hue,
> You make me suffer great woe.

33. For a catalogue of the symptoms, see Schrötter, pp. 62–79.

domna, per vostr'amor
jonh las mas et ador!
gens cors ab frescha color,
gran mal me faitz traire!   (57–60)

The last strophe and tornada describe that woe. Far from rev-
eling in it, Bernart sends his messenger to the lady-doctor for
a cure; and thus the poem ends on a sly note of expected
"health."

There has always been a temptation in Provençal scholarship to ignore the wit in Bernart's poetry; to interpret it with
absolute seriousness and then attempt to relate it to contemporary culture. I seriously doubt that Bernart literally enacted
the varied gestures of this poem any more than Ovid did his.
Did Ovid's poetic mannerism not have *some* social basis in
contemporary manners? Was adultery in ancient Rome, which
had no commandment against the practice but censured it,
worse than adultery in old Provence? Ultimately these questions are irrelevant. Ovid's wit and satire are obvious, often
oppressively so; Bernart's humor is subtler. Yet Ovid did
evolve a whole mystique of love that has influenced poetry for
centuries: a world of private, poetic illusion. In Bernart's day,
a vital mysticism existed, and the physical-metaphysical spheres
infused each other in a natural way; if Bernart never adopted
either the purely mystical or the social-realistic mode of expression, but wavered between the two, his symbolism is as
original and illusory as Ovid's. We should not think of Bernart as Christian or non-Christian, but as a poet who used the
symbols that were at hand. At the same time, we should not
condemn poor Ovid for not living in a Christian age. Both
poets were romantics without being full-fledged mystics. Their
favorite subjects were woman and love—to which, perhaps
fortunately, they did not give the world any definitive answers.

Bernart is considered the master of the troubadour love
song. He lived in the latter part of the twelfth century, and

thus played a vital role in the classical period of troubadour verse. The poems analyzed up to this point are his most famous works; in fact, *Can vei la lauzeta* is often taken as the credo of the courtly-love tradition. There is no point in analyzing the entire corpus of Bernart's poetry; if his most famous poems show religious overtones clashing with sensual elements, his less famous works are even more contradictory. His anti-feministic phases will be mentioned again later. We might now take a look at some of the earlier Provençal poems with nature settings to see if Bernart's deft handling of natural and supernatural tropes has a precedent.

THE ALBA AND THE FALLACY OF GENERIC CLASSIFICATION

One of the first creations in Provençal literature is the alba or dawn-poem, the earliest of which is a macaronic, half-Latin, half-Provençal work that exists in a highly corrupt state; it has been dated as early as the 800s, the great century of the Carolingian Revival:

Phoebus' light has not yet risen;
Aurora brings faint light to Earth;
The watchman cries to the lazy, "Rise!"
Dawn through the wet sea draws on the sun (?)
Then the vigil passes (?) watch the shadows brighten (?)

Behold! the treachery of the enemy
Spreads to ensnare the weak unwary
Whom the watchman urges, shouting "Rise!"
Dawn through the wet sea . . .

The northwind's loosened from the north.
The polestars bury (establish?) their rays;
Out of the northeast comes the Bear.
Dawn through the wet sea . . .

Phebi claro nondum orto iubare;
Fert aurora lumen terris tenue.
Spiculator pigris clamat surgite
L'alba par umet mar atra sol
Poy pasa vigil miraclar tenebras.

En incautos (h)ostium insidie
Torpentesque gliscunt intercipere;
Quos suadet preco clamat surgere
L'alba par . . .

Ab arcturo disgregatur aquilo;
Poli suos condunt astra radios,
Orienti tenditur septentrio;
L'alba par! . . .[34]

The insurmountable problems of the text have created two
very different interpretations. Some critics consider it a secular
love poem, a precursor of the Provençal alba; others consider
it a hymn. Georg Schläger, who made a detailed study of the
tagelied, has accounted for the Latin rhetoric with samples
drawn from Ovid's albas and from Scriptural and patristic
literature.[35] He also compared the poem to another Latin
work of the period, the vigilant soldiers' song at the gates of
Modena,[36] and noted that the alba is ambiguous. Words such
as Phoebus and Aurora seem to be out of place in a Christian
hymn, although even in classical times the gods were merely
metaphors for the sun and dawn. Yet aside from some other
Ovidian elements, the poem shows marked Christian overtones. A watchman (*spiculator, preco*) has replaced Prudentius'

34. Emended from Johannes Schmidt, "Die älteste Alba," *ZDP, 12* (1881),
333–41. Cf. Paul Zumthor, "Au Berceau du lyrisme européen," *Cahiers du Sud,*
40, pt. 326 (1954), 30.

35. *Studien über das Tagelied* (Jena, 1895). For a religious poem cast in the
alba form, in which the poet cries to the hearer, "*O car amic!*", see Raynouard,
2, 111–16.

36. *PLAC 3,* pp. 703–05; allusions to Trojan War combined with Christian
soldiers' vigil.

rooster, but his warning to the lazy and the unwary is the same: "Rise up! The dawn is coming! The adulterous night is being driven away!" The very confusing final strophe shows definite parallels with the Apocalypse and Jeremiah, and may signify the mystical breakthrough of Judgment Day that seemed imminent in Prudentius' "Hymn at Cock-crow."[37] The figure of the watchman is interesting from a critical point of view, because proponents of the Arabic-origin theory attempted to relate the later Provençal watchman (*gaita, gacha*, from Germanic *wahta*, akin to English "watch") to the Arabic *raqīb*.[38] However, this essentially religious alba shows that he has replaced Ovid's guardian (*custos*) and Prudentius' rooster entirely within the bounds of an evolving Latin rhetoric. The Provençal alba therefore begins with a half-Latin hymn that seems capable of many further developments.

The next surviving alba is clearly secular, but also anonymous and difficult to date; it is usually ascribed to the twelfth century:

> In a meadow, under the hawthorn leaves,
> A lady draws her lover to her side
> Until the watchman shouts that he's seen the dawn:
> O God! O God! how swift it comes—the dawn!

> *En un vergier sotz folha d'albespi*
> *tenc la dompna son amic costa si,*
> *tro la gaita crida que l'alba vi.*
> *Oi Deus, oi Deus, de l'alba! Tan tost ve!*[39]

---

37. Apoc. 21:13, 22:5, 16:3, 3:2–3; also, Jer. 1:14: *Ab aquilone pandetur malum super omnes habitatores terrae;* 4:5, 6:17: *Et constitui super vos speculatores. Audite vocem tubae;* 13:20: *Levate oculos vestros, et videte qui venitis ab aquilone.*
38. *A Book Containing the Risāla,* tr. A. R. Nykl (Paris, 1931), pp. 73–76. Nykl said later in *Hispano-Arabic Poetry*, p. 395: "In view of the *custos*, the flint-hearted eunuch whom Ovid often tries to bribe in *Amores*, there is no necessity to derive the *gardador* . . . directly from *raqīb*." Nykl would have done better to relate Arabic poetry to Ovid.
39. Bartsch, cols. 107–10, st. 1.

This alba shares one thing with both Ovid and Prudentius: a pressing, dramatic concern for the passage of time. Ovid had shouted: "run slowly, you horses of the night"; and his Latin appears as one of the last outcries of that arch-humanist, Faustus, in Marlowe's play. This lady does not address the dawn or a god representing that natural function, but God himself, who controls his agent, Nature. We are in a Christian age, but Ovid's will to impose his adulterous desires upon the workings of nature finds an echo in the lady's words:

> "I wish God would never let the night fail,
> And my lover was never parted far from me,
> And the watchman never saw the morning dawn!
> O God! O God! how swift it comes—the dawn!" (st.2)

The lady goes on to tell her young lover not to worry about the *gilos*, the jealous one. In Ovidian terms, the envious one is Aurora or Nature, which opposes him in his albas, and a husband in his lyrics. The lady calls her young lover to play a *joc novel*, which may be translated a "new game," a "spring game," or a "game for the young"; the ambiguity of the word *novel* forces us to think of spring, youth, and love together. On the purely literal level, we see Ovid throughout this poem; the lady who narrates it glorifies adultery and places her own personal desires over the God-ordained rules of nature with the kind of zest that is absolutely antithetical to Prudentius' condemnation of the *nox adultera*, adulterous night. Her concern with time is like Ovid's—and she is tragically doomed to loss.

On the other hand, the poem also owes something to Prudentius and the hymnologists. For example, the stanzaic patterns, the refrain, and the rhymes are very much like the crude forms found in the macaronic alba, which developed from the Ambrosian hymns. Even more important perhaps is the frightening assurance with which the lady places physical entities over metaphysical truths. The medieval sinner bears the same kind of courage and certainty as the saint. The lady acknowledges the presence of God and order, and she knows perfectly well that the night will not last, yet she insists on leading her man down into that garden where birds are singing and games are played; it is the Earthly Garden of Paradise: from the Church's point of view, the garden of sin and lust; from the lady's point of view, the only garden of reality. There are really two values operating in this poem, where there was only one in Ovid. Ovid demands the immediate and real, and acknowledges only a natural working that is interfering with his personal designs; his albas are finally witty because *he* is unnatural, and he knows it. The late-medieval alba is witty only because of the way it inverts traditional Christian symbols and elicits absolute sympathy for the sinner. The urgency of the flesh is taken for granted in Ovid, as a purely "natural" thing, something to be regulated according to the hours and seasons as a part of life. This is not the case at all in the albas of Provence, where higher truths are constantly calling lower ones into question. You cannot in the twelfth century employ images that have acquired sacred values (the name of God, the ideal garden, the dawn star "Christ") without being sacrilegious; however, the alba just considered is not sacrilegious after the manner of the cruder *Burana*. The lady insists upon the urgency of her pursuits, and the whole poem, with its idealized setting, exists to create a natural atmosphere for what the poem insists upon as a natural act. It seems to me that Prudentius is hovering in those shadows, or perhaps is standing next to the watchman. And it seems to me that the "jealous one" in the poem is not only the lady's husband but perhaps the "jealous God" (*Deus zelotes*) of the Old Testament.[40] The word *gilos* is Greek in origin, and enters the Romance vocabulary largely through Jerome's Latin Bible. Can

---

40. Classical Greek *zelotes* (rival, emulator), based on *zelos* (strong passion, often jealousy), was applied to God in Jerome's translation: e.g., Exod. 20:5: *ego sum Dominus Deus tuus fortis, zelotes.* The word was applied righteously to deceived husbands in Num. 5:13 f. It acquired a thoroughly pejorative meaning in Romance descendants: *jaloux, geloso, gilos,* etc.

we then call this poem a secular alba? Perhaps: if we are thinking of the values that are asserted, and the meanings that are ascribed directly to the images. Yet, at the same time, it would be pointless to ignore the metaphysical meanings which hover over the poem's surface.

The next great alba in Provençal literature was written by Guiraut de Bornelh, a contemporary of Bernart. His alba begins with what is ostensibly an ode to the sun,[41] but the natural image also clearly represents the Son Jesus:

> Glorious King, true light and clarity,
> Powerful God, Lord, if it pleases you,
> Be a faithful aide to my companion;
> For I haven't seen him since the night came on,
> And soon will come the dawn!

> *Reis glorios, verais lums e clartatz,*
> *Deus poderos, Senher, si a vos platz,*
> *Al meu companh siatz fizels aiuda;*
> *Qu'eu no lo vi, pos la nochs fo venguda,*
> *Et ades sera l'alba!*[42]

In fact, the two spheres are so closely linked that the opening quickly becomes a prayer. The voice speaking is that of a friend of an adulterer who has assumed the task of being a friendly watchman for the lovers. (The fact that the watchman is now friendly informs us of the strongly positive values that secular love, which is the basic theme of the poem, has now acquired.) He implores Christ's help in this love-vigil without any apparent feeling of conflict, as if it were perfectly natural for the Christian God of Love to assume the practical functions of pagan Amor. In fact, he mentions that he has prayed

41. Thus interpreted by Jackson, p. 251.
42. *Guiraut de Bornelh,* ed. Adolf Kolsen (2 vols. Halle, Max Niemeyer, 1910), *1,* no. 54, 342–47, st. 1; cf. Jeanroy, *Origines,* pp. 80–81 for a French tr. with seventh stanza (from Bartsch).

to Christ to help his companion avoid the lady's jealous husband:

> Beautiful companion, after I parted from you,
> I did not sleep; I did not move from kneeling;
> Instead, I prayed to God, son of St. Mary,
> To send you back to me, through loyal companionship,
> And soon will come the dawn! (st. 5)

It is extraordinary to observe how the friendly vigilant casts himself in the role of a worshipful Christian attendant of the dawn, after the mode of Prudentius, while he is actually maintaining a frustrated Ovidian night watch. He offers a kind of Christian-Platonic companionship (*paria; amicitia*) in the midst of the perilous service of *amor*. Guiraut thus effects a brilliant fusion of Christian and non-Christian symbols, mixing the morning star Christ-Venus with the jealous lord of the lady and the night-singing, day-seeking bird of romance. The romantic world, under his touch, blossoms within a distinctly religious framework, and the painfully repeated refrain "And soon will come the dawn!" constantly reminds us of the presence of a moral order in the universe which cannot be totally ignored. In the last analysis, Guiraut's alba is moral, for, although it supplies us with a sympathetic portrait of an adulterous love affair, the watchman's voice, like that of Vergil speaking to his love-consumed friend Gallus, maintains the other pole of thought by which love, despite its charms, is clearly condemned. The watchman's last outcry about the coming of the dawn sounds like a last judgment being pronounced on the lovers' souls:

> Beautiful companion, outside there on the terrace
> You begged me not to be sleepy-eyed;
> Instead, to keep awake through night to day.
> Now you don't care for my fellowship or song,
> And soon will come the dawn! (st. 6)

Bel companho, la foras als peiros
Me preiavatz qu'eu no fos dormilhos,
Enans velhes tota noch tro al dia.
Era no.us platz mos chans ni ma paria
Et ades sera l'alba!

In some editions, though not the definitive one of Adolf Kolsen, the lover inside the palace answers in an interpolated seventh strophe, insisting that his love is the only thing that matters; he thus condemns his own soul to any hell that awaits him, while at the very same time he quite literally tells the lady's jealous "lord" (husband; but one cannot quite forget the *Senher* or Lord of the first stanza) to go to Hell. Actually, the lover's reply, which heightens the structure of the dialogue, is not essential, and is even inimical to the poem's subtle tones, for his reply is fully evident in the interior dialectic of the poem: his friend's lonely vigil implies the lover's sensual satisfaction.

We could very easily call this alba a religious alba, because, although the theme of the poem is not basically the love of God, this sphere of reference pervades the surface rhetoric. In fact, one could easily allegorize the entire work by converting the lovers into figures of the Christian soul betrayed by a love of the shadowy things of this world and unwilling to espouse the resplendent Bridegroom Christ. The watchman could then be converted into a voice for traditional morality, despite his earlier compliance. However, although this procedure is standard with scholars of the period, most modern critics are content merely to point out the interlocking spheres without forcing them into a strict, and awkward, juncture. Some things are better left implied.

Unfortunately, the fate of the alba after Guiraut is as sad as the fate of the love song after Bernart. The two spheres became separated, and the poetry suffered. Folquet of Marseille, who began his life as a secular troubadour and ended it as the almost demonic Bishop of Toulouse, playing a key role in the

Albigensian Crusade, wrote an alba that is quite clearly religious:

> True God, in your name and in the name of St. Mary,
> I shall awake (*esvelherai*), since the morning star
> Comes from Jerusalem to teach me what to say.[43]

Folquet banishes ambiguity by reducing the symbol of the morning star to a fixed metaphor: the star equals Christ, a traditional equation. There is little point in calling his poem a religious alba, because the dawn situation is really only a part of the opening and the refrain. His alba is a hymn.

On the other hand, the very slick troubadour Raimbaut de Vaqueiras (c. 1155–1205) wrote an alba that is quite clearly secular. His poem is really more interesting for its technical virtuosity than for its images or meanings, a sure sign of a waning tradition:

> Lady, goodbye; for I can't stay;
> Despite myself, I have to go;
> How I hate to see the dawn,
> Harsh to us, lightly rise.
>   The dawn would like
> To trick us, yes, the dawn, the dawn.
>
> *Domn' adeu! que non puis mais estar;*
> *Malgrat meu, me.n coven ad annar;*
> *Mas tan greu m'es de l'albe*
> *Que tan leu la vei levar.*
>   *Enganar*
> *Nos vol l'albe, l'albe, oc l'albe.*[44]

I have noted the internal rhymes, which are quite extraordinary; yet I can find very little to say about the poetry itself.

43. *Anthology of the Provençal Troubadours*, ed. R. T. Hill and T. G. Bergin (3d ed. New Haven, 1957), no. 71, pp. 104–05, 1–3; hereafter cited as Hill–Bergin.
44. Hill–Bergin, no. 86, p. 127, 19–24.

Because of its labored politeness in what is basically an impolite situation, it does not even rise to the level of contrast presented by the cruder *Carmina Burana*.

We now face the very difficult question: what is an alba? If we give the traditional answer, a poem about the dawn, that is so vague in relation to the examples cited that it is ultimately meaningless. For we have just considered secular albas, religious albas, and secular-religious albas. The rhetorical elements in the two greatest (the anonymous *Oi Deus!* and Guiraut's poem) are so finely interwoven that they cannot be separated. Georg Schläger concluded, not a little ironically, that the one way to classify a poem as an alba was to find the word "alba" inside the poem.[45] It is obvious that the generic name really tells us nothing except that the poem concerns a dawn setting and some kind of love: the love of God or the love of a woman. The greatest albas, of which there are only two specimens, show the same kind of ingenious rhetorical blending of seemingly contradictory images and words that we have observed in the love poems of Bernart. These love poems also bear a generic name in Provençal scholarship: *canso,* from Latin *cantio,* or *vers,* from Latin *versus,* as the earliest poems were called. Let us turn to the four great predecessors of Bernart to see how the love song, with its nature opening, began. As we move from the alba with its dawn landscape to the canso with its spring landscape, we must remember that Easter hymns, which are also dawn hymns, first forced us to consider the similarity of these landscapes. When we recall that the albas we have just considered dealt with the problem of love (*amor Dei* and *amor mundi*), we find that the transition from a dawn poem to a love poem is not really a transition at all.

---

45. P. 25: *"Das band, welches alle diese gedichte zusammenhält, ist rein äusserlicher, zufälliger art, ohne jeden genetischen zusammenhang mit der situation: das strophenweis wiederkehrende wort* alba *an signifikanter stelle."*

THE FIRST PROVENÇAL POETS: A VARIETY OF ATTITUDES

Provençal literature begins with religious literature. The earliest surviving pieces of prose include a translation of the Book of St. John and moral sermons, one in praise of the Virgin Mary.[46] Poetry was also present from the start: a rhymed translation of Boethius, a confession to God, a lament (*planch;* Latin, *planctus*) for St. Stephen, a Latin-Provençal hymn for Christmas glorifying the *virgo Maria* (sung to the tune of the Latin hymn *In hoc anni circulo*), and a prayer to the Virgin entitled *Versus sancte Marie*.[47] The Latin name for a poem (*versus*) was apparently taken over intact by the first secular poets, who referred to their works as *vers*.

The hymn to the Virgin is not as rich in symbols as the Latin hymns of the period. Furthermore, it devotes almost half of its lines to Adam and Eve, the eating of the forbidden fruit, and the destruction of the Earthly Paradise. This obsession with Eve is not surprising, because the notions of Mary as the second Eve or redeemer of Eve, and Christ as the second Adam are medieval commonplaces from Augustine to Chaucer. In the medieval view, Eve does not cancel out Mary's goodness; nor does Mary cancel out the reality of an Eve. Unfortunately, since Mary clearly symbolized the ideal woman, Eve tended all too frequently to become associated with the real woman. Many scholars would like to give the Church credit for sanctifying the sacrament of marriage, for raising the position of woman by admitting her to sainthood and by creating the concept of feminine purity through the living model of the nun. These points are justifiable. Yet, on the other hand, it would be hard to ignore a very vigorous anti-feministic tradition that is observable in almost all the early

46. Bartsch, *St. Jean: Chap. 13–17*, cols. 9–18; *Deux Sermons*, cols. 27–30.
47. Bartsch, *Boèce*, cols. 1–8; *Confession*, cols. 21–24; *Planch de Sant Esteve*, cols. 23–26; *Noël*, cols. 19–20; *Versus sancte Marie*, cols. 19–22.

Church Fathers from St. Jerome and Tertullian to the very
liberal Scotus Erigena.[48] The good and bad elements which
compose the dialectic in Chaucer's portrait of the Wife of
Bath were not created *in vacuo*. Both traditions were alive, and
both were stated in hyperbolic terms: woman as savior and
woman as agent of the devil. Both tonalities were pointed out
in the poems of Bernart de Ventadorn.

We can say that Provençal poetry begins with woman conceived in ideal religious terms through the figure of Mary; yet
the fact that Eve occupies about 30 lines of a 48-line poem is
also an interesting bit of information. The Earthly Garden is
merely suggested through the mention of fruit, the serpent,
and the two archetypal figures of humanity. The poem swings
up beautifully at the end into the metaphysical realm, the
Celestial Paradise that infuses the lower, "realistic" elements:

> The Life that murdered Death
> gave us Paradise;
> and may God give us truly
> glory equally!

> *Vida, qui mort aucis,*
> *nos donet paradis;*
> *gloria aisamen*
> *nos do Deus veramen!*   (17–20)

The first secular poet whose work survives is Duke William
IX of Aquitaine, seventh Count of Poitou, who owned more
land than the King of France. We might have expected Duke
William to formulate a courtly attitude toward women, but,
alas, that fractious noble did no such thing. The Italian critic
Pio Rajna has called William "two-faced" (*bifronte*).[49] That
term may be enlightening if it implies poetic paradox and not

---

48. The locus classicus: Jerome, *Adversus Jovinianum* (*PL* 23, cols. 211 ff.);
also, Tertullian, *Ad uxorem* (*PL 1*, cols. 1273 ff.), *De cultu foeminarum* (ibid.,
cols. 1303 ff.); Erigena (*PL 122*, cols. 532 ff.). Cf. Plato, *Tim.* 42, 91.

49. "Guglielmo conte di Poitiers, trovatore bifronte," *Mélanges Jeanroy*
(Paris, 1928), pp. 349–60.

an assessment of the Duke's character, for if ever a man embodied the spirit of the Earthly Lord (*seigner*), it was William. Since many of the histories of southern France were composed by Benedictine monks or men with ecclesiastical frames of mind, they describe the period with the same ironic bitterness that we find in Tacitus' accounts of the Caesars. In fact, Odericus Vitalis' famous portrait of William reads like Tacitus' portrait of Petronius: a man who wanted to turn the night into day.[50] In terms of the symbolism of the alba, William's behavior is perfectly consistent with that of a man who represents the World (and not the Church, which excommunicated him), temporal power, and the reality of the earthly estate. In my discussion of Bernart's poetry I avoided the term "courtly love" because that secular term is incapable of describing the interwoven rhetoric of the poems, and because it has a dangerous tendency to lead critics from a discussion of poetry to a discussion of courts.[51] The term itself derives from the age of

50. *Historia ecclesiastica*, ed. A. le Prévost (5 vols. Paris, 1838–55), *4*, 118; see Karl Vossler, "Die Kunst des ältesten Trobadors," *Miscellanea Attilio Hortis* (2 vols. Trieste, 1910), *1*, 419–40.

51. The term "courtly love" is a nineteenth-century invention, given broad coinage by Gaston Paris, "Lancelot du Lac: Le Conte de la Charrette," *Romania*, *12* (1883), 459–534. The notion of courts of love originated from the fiction of Andreas Capellanus and the sixteenth-century prevarications of Jehan de Nostredame, *Vies des plus célèbres et anciens poètes provençaux*, ed. C. Chabaneau, introd. J. Anglade (Paris, 1913). Chabaneau and Anglade disproved all of Nostredame's theories. The troubadours themselves distinguished between refined love and false love, which, given the context of Christianity, seems to be but a secular imitation of the true and false love of God. Yet, pressing even more deeply, one must acknowledge the presence of the lyric ego; every troubadour usually claims to be a "true" lover, while attacking his friends and the rest of society; the poet stands alone, as did Catullus when he said:

> No woman can ever say she's truly been loved
> As much as you, my Lesbia, have been loved by me;
> No faith (*fides*) was ever offered in any pact (*foedere*)
> Like the faith that I once offered you. (87)

Probably every lover imagines that his own love is pure, and that others love like beasts.

The fourteenth-century rhetoricians who wrote the *Leys d'Amors* spoke of a

Ivanhoe, the *Idylls of the King,* Victorian etiquette, and what Auerbach has called, with reference to A. W. Schlegel, Herder, Jakob Grimm, and Uhland, "the late romantic, sentimental, and idyllic style of German scholarship" in the late nineteenth century.[52] With William, the first poet, a man who owned the largest and most brilliant court in southern France (centered at Poitiers and Limoges, where the Monastery of St. Martial has preserved many musical manuscripts of the period), we find that the term has no application at all. Indeed, poor Duke William has always been troublesome to critics who attempt to create a romantic, idealized picture of the age, based primarily upon the romance of the poetry.[53]

The truth of the matter is that William is sometimes obscene the way Ovid is sometimes obscene. There is no point in constructing a dictionary of erotica to offset a theory of idealized cultural history, because the dictionary would be excessive too. The fabliau that William wrote (once again we see a supposedly "popular" form emanating from a court, a movement which ought to suggest the notion that "popular" poetry is secular poetry) does not concern the spring motif and hence will go unanalyzed. Yet in opposition to this poem, we must mention the fact that William wrote what is basically a hymn upon his death (some critics say "before his departure

---

"Gay Science" (which preserves an element of metaphysical wit), but the love of God dominates their rhetorical handbook and poetry. It remained for the Renaissance scholars, with their antipathy toward medievalism, and nineteenth-century romantics to cut off the poetry from the total sphere of culture, earlier traditions, and to literalize and apply poetic rhetoric in a way that has never been applied to other periods. For a history of the evolution of the structure, with its many contradictions and unanswered questions, see Käte Axhausen, *Die Theorien über den Ursprung der provenzalischen Lyrik* (Marburg, 1937).

52. Review, *RP, 4* (1950–51), 65.

53. Joseph Anglade, *Les Troubadours* (2d ed. Paris, 1919) devotes one paragraph to William, remarking on his grossness and passing on to the so-called founders of the doctrine of courtly love (p. 100).

on Crusade").[54] In that very dramatic poem, the Earthly Lord surrenders to the Celestial Lord—but not without a struggle. In the closing line, William hands over to God his "white fur, gray fur, and sables"; previously he had handed over his more abstract virtues, such as chivalry, pride, prowess, and joy. The way in which William enumerates the furs so lovingly in the closing line is a true indication of the very vital concern for reality that is the essence of the genius of Provençal poetry. Does William's fabliau cancel out his hymn? Does Chaucer's *Retraction* cancel out his *Miller's Tale?* Medieval literature constantly forces us to think in terms of opposites and to relate the three interlocking spheres of religion, romance, and realism.

Duke William has left the world two poems which employ spring landscapes, and one of these is so beautifully conceived that Scheludko is perhaps correct in stating that it is the prototype for the nature opening as a conventional beginning for the early Provençal love song:

> In the sweetness of the spring
> Woods are leafing, birds are singing,
> Each one in his Latin,
> According to the "verse" of his spring "chant";
> Then a man should ease himself
> With what he most desires.

> *Ab la dolchor del temps novel*
> *Foillo li bosc, e li aucel*
> *Chanton chascus en lor lati*
> *Segon lo vers del novel chan;*
> *Adonc esta ben c'om s'aisi*
> *D'acho don hom a plus talan.*[55]

54. *Les Chansons de Guillaume IX*, ed. A. Jeanroy (2d ed. Paris, 1927), no. 11, pp. 26–29. For his development, see Theophil Spoerri, "Wilhelm von Poitiers und die Anfänge der abendländischen Poesie," *Trivium*, 2 (1944), 255–77.
55. *Guill. IX*, no. 10, pp. 24–26, 1–6.

It is a delicate little picture, and obviously related to the contemporary Latin *tropes* (we might well use this Latin rhetorical term, since the noun "troubadour" or *trobaire* descends from the learned verb *trobar* or *trop-ar,* with the Ciceronian meaning "to invent," *invenire*).[56] But William's personal touches are striking; he converts his birds into worshipers through his interesting use of the word "Latin" for "talk" or "song" (the word also means simply "language" in Romance languages); he also uses the Latin word *vers,* already encountered in the hymn to Mary, to describe the musical arrangement of the warbling. Furthermore his word *chan* (from Latin *cantus*) has an ecclesiastical-rhetorical connotation. But William's birds are clearly not chanting hymns to Mary; they are singing songs to the goddess Natura. The birds are poets; they are singing love songs; it is spring; *ergo*—what else does one do in the spring? Classical poets coupled the spring and love centuries before. Now William does the same thing, in a Christian age, in a popular tongue, and in an accentual octosyllabic meter that descends from the iambic dimeter of hymnology. Both he and his birds are singing secular love songs in Church modes; the effect is delightful, having none of the oppressive features that sometimes crop up in the *Burana.* Everything is—natural, of course.

Discordant notes, however, creep into the second strophe. The lady has not sent him a letter with messenger and seal (*mesager ni sagel*) in reply to what he begged or asked for.

---

56. *Trobar* meant simply "to find" in common language (Fr. *trouver,* It. *trovare*); the meaning "to make a trope" also has a direct reference to liturgical literature; for discussion and bibliography, see Karl Young, *The Drama of the Medieval Church* (2 vols. Oxford, 1933), *1,* 565, n. 1; Scheludko, "Beiträge . . . ," *AR, 15* (1931), 137 ff.; Edmond Faral, *Les Arts poétiques du XIIe et du XIIIe siècle* (Paris, 1962). Both studies, citing such authors as Geoffrey de Vinsauf and John of Garland, have accounted for the practices of *trobar clus* ("obscure style"; from *clausum*) and *trobar leu* or *pla* ("clear style"; *leviter, plane*) entirely within the terms of the contemporary rhetorical tradition. In the twelfth century, Latin grammar and rhetoric were a basic part of the educational system.

The notion of the lover as letter-writer, and the love song as letter, is a continuing and much ignored factor in Provençal verse. Ovid's *Heroides* were read at that time with much more interest than they are today; Chaucer's adaptations in his *Legend of Good Women*, with his consistent use of the word "martire" to describe the agony of pagan lovers, demonstrate the continuity. William tells us that he cannot sleep or laugh because of his anxiety. Interior discord and exterior joy thus are first voiced in Provençal poetry by him.

The third strophe, one of the most famous in troubadour literature, was adapted by Dante in a more spiritual sense, but in William it is clearly a part of the terrestrial Paradise:[57]

> Our love moves onward
> Just like a hawthorn branch
> That stands on a trembling tree,
> At night exposed to rain and ice,
> Till morning when the sun shines
> Through the branches and green leaves.

> *La nostr'amor vai enaissi*
> *Com la branca de l'albespi*
> *Qu'esta sobre l'arbre tremblan,*
> *La nuoit, a la ploja ez al gel,*
> *Tro l'endeman, que.l sols s'espan*
> *Per las fueillas verz e.l ramel.*

Scheludko has found contrasting specimens of this image in hymns, but none of these samples can explain or account for William's invention.[58] For the purposes of this study, it is interesting to consider the alba-like qualities of this strophe; for William clearly makes no distinction here between dawn and spring; he uses both for the purpose of contrasting ideal-

57. *Inf.*, II.127–30, on hearing Vergil mention Beatrice. Dante also uses Bernart's lark (in a more idealized manner) in *Par.*, XX.73–76, comparing it with the Eagle in the Heaven of Jupiter.
58. "Ovid," p. 139, citing *An. Hymn. 48*, p. 312, and Anselm (*PL 158*, col. 705): "*Res huius mundi . . . sunt quasi flos agri, quem frigus et aura cremavit.*"

ized dream elements with a less pleasant reality. The third strophe repeats the mood and tone of the first, which was interrupted by the second. The fourth strophe develops quite naturally out of the mention of the morning sun, and leads to a reminiscence of past happiness; it is an alba in a highly abbreviated form, and works toward an erotic close:

> I still remember that morning
> When we put an end to our war,
> And she gave me that great gift:
> Her loving, and her ring.
> God, let me live some more
> To put my hands beneath her cloak!

> *Enquer me membra d'un mati*
> *Que nos fezem de guerra fi,*
> *E que.m donet un don tan gran,*
> *Sa drudari'e son anel:*
> *Enquer me lais Dieus viure tan*
> *C'aja mas manz soz so mantel!*

God is here invoked as a witness to a very Ovidian stanza. William's call to Him is exactly comparable to that of the lady in the *Oi Deus* poem. The word *drudaria* (loving) is of Germanic origin and has a very common-sounding ring; it never occurs in hymns as an alternate word for *amor*. It is a secular love-word.

The last stanza is beautifully balanced in terms of the idealized and sensual elements that have preceded it. William manages to hold both strains in balance:

> I don't need any strange talk
> That might part me from my Good Neighbor,
> For I know how words go
> In a quick talk that expands;
> Let others brag about their love:
> We've got the pestle and the bowl.

Qu'eu non ai soing d'estraing lati
Que.m parta de mon Bon Vezi,
Qu'eu sai de paraulas com van
Ab un breu sermon que s'espel
Que tal se van d'amor gaban,
Nos n'avem la pessa e.l coutel.　　　　　　　(25–30)

The *lati* that William rejects in line 25 is not the bird's Latin of the first strophe, the speech of nature, but any "foreign talk" that is not straightforward and clear—possibly even the Latin of the Church as it sounded to the illiterate. The lady's secret name, Good Neighbor, is about as Christian as one could imagine, although Jesus had no such love affair as this in mind when he urged people to love their neighbors. Similarly, the word *paraulas* in line 27 is based upon the religious word *parabolas* (from Greek, meaning "preachings" or "parables"). In William's day the word was already thoroughly secular, as it is in its modern verbal forms, *parler* in French and *parlare* in Italian; but on Sunday, the Latinized form would be heard in church with its purely religious meaning. Then too, the word *sermon* in the following line derives from Classical Latin, where it meant "conversation, talk," just as it does here. The Church gave the word a new meaning, that of the English word "sermon," but here the meaning is closer to Cicero than to Bernard of Clairvaux. The two symbols that close the poem are about as secular as one could expect. William is fond of sexual symbolism; Bernart preferred the creation of an erotic scene presented as dream. William's personality is far more masculine than Bernart's. Even when William is putting himself into the role of the love-servant, one can hear the voice of the duke speaking through the poetic artifice. Yet William shows in a franker form the very same contrasting rhetorical elements that Bernart shows. His parody of religious expression is a little more obvious than Bernart's, but his idealized metaphors are no less compelling, and his erotic moments in a blended lyric such as this are really not much cruder than Bernart's sneaking into his lady's chamber to view her Christmas-snow-white naked body.

William actually has three faces rather than two: the lecher of the fabliau; the polished lover who glorifies the things of this world without overlooking their physical entities; and the obedient Christian of the hymn at his death. If one thinks in terms of a doctrine of courtly love, he is out of place; if one thinks in terms of rhetorical elements, he is quite clearly and deservedly the father of the troubadour tradition. Later poets tended to soften or tone down his contrasts, but they did not necessarily improve upon his poetry.

The next poet whose work has survived is Cercamon (c. 1137–52; his name means Search-the-World). This troubadour has left us only seven poems, but what a variety of modes! He wrote the first great *planctus* for a man, rather than saint, in Provençal, on William X of Aquitaine's death. He wrote a debate poem (*conflictus* or *tenso*) with William, in which he complained to his patron about his purse and hinted that William paid him from other people's pockets. He also wrote two vicious little satires on "false lovers," in which human love is treated under the same system and terminology as the love of God:

> Telltales with nosey beaks
> Are worse than Judas,
>   who betrayed God.

> *Per lauzengiers qu'an bec malahuros,*
> *Qui son pejor que Judas,*
>   *qui Dieu trays.*[59]

and again:

> You'll be burned in the big fire
> With the pain that never passes,
> You false and lying cheaters!

59. *Les Poésies de Cercamon,* ed. A. Jeanroy (Paris, 1922), no. 5, pp. 14–18, 34–35.

El fuec major seretz creman
En la pena qe non trasvai,
Enganador fals e truan.[60]

It is significant perhaps that Cercamon used a spring opening for both these satirical poems, and also for a delicate lyric that shows the Sapphic "bitter-sweet" attitude toward love, one that seems to lie at the heart of lyric expression:

> Love is sweet when it walks in,
> And bitter when it walks out;
> One day it will make you weep,
> And another, laugh and sing.

> *Amors es douza a l'intrar*
> *Et amara al departir,*
> *Q'en un jorn vos fara plorar,*
> *Et autre jugar e hurdir.*[61]

Brilliant lines stated with classic simplicity. Perhaps those four lines represent the sum total of all the knowledge of human love that lyric poets have left us.

Cercamon wrote another poem that is so ambiguous that even Jeanroy, who was not kind toward the notion of ambiguity, labeled it *Chanson Pieuse* [?] in his quite excellent edition.[62] The question mark dramatically indicates the weakness of generic classification; the poem seems to be stated too materially to be written to the Virgin, and too mystically to be written to a virgin. Despite moments of clear-cut separation, the rhetoric of the Court or World and the rhetoric of the Church were still finely interwoven.

Cercamon was the teacher of the next troubadour, Marcabrun (c. 1130–48). Cercamon's satires found a fitting perpetua-

60. *Cercamon*, no. 4, pp. 11–14, 29–31.
61. *Cercamon*, no. 2, pp. 4–7, 36–39.
62. *Cercamon*, no. 3, pp. 8–10.

tor in the person of Marcabrun, who has long been famous for his hatred of women. Some of his most expressive lines are:

> Marcabrun, the son of Lady Bruna,
> Was born under such a moon
> That he knows how love crumbles
> —Listen!—
> He never loved any woman,
> And no woman ever loved him.

> *Marcabruns, lo fills na Bruna,*
> *Fo engendraz en tal luna*
> *Qu.el saup d'amor cum degruna*
> *—Escoutatz!—*
> *Que anc non amet neguna,*
> *Ni d'autra no fo amatz.*[63]

Yet Marcabrun is not Chancellor Philip. It would be unfair to call this witty poet (his name means Dark Spot; his mother is The Dark Lady!) an antifeminist, just as it is unfair to label Bernart de Ventadorn a eulogist of women. When he cared to, Marcabrun could portray the force of love very powerfully. This intellectual wrote what is perhaps the greatest pastourelle in Provençal literature: "At the fountain in the meadow" (*A la fontana del vergier*).[64] It opens with a spring landscape, where the scholastic narrator encounters a high-born woman whose knight has gone away on a crusade. Marcabrun (or the speaker) tries to console the lady by telling her that God is in Heaven, and her knight has done the right thing (a very fitting placing of the love of God over the love of man). Then, like the lonely woman of the *Levis exsurgit Zephirus*:

---

63. *Poésies complètes du troubadour Marcabru*, ed. J.-M.-L. Dejeanne, Bibliothèque méridionale, 12 (1909), Vida 2, p. 2; variant reading in no. 18, pp. 77–83, st. 12, from which the biographer extracted it. For Marcabrun's use of scriptural and patristic sources, see Errante, *Marcabru*.

64. *Marcabru*, ed. Dejeanne, no. 1, pp. 3–4.

"Lord," said she, "I do believe
That God will have mercy on me
In the other world, forever,
As he will to other sinners;
But *here* he's snatching the thing
That brings me joy; what do I care
When my man's so far away?"

"Senher, dis elha, ben o crey
Que Deus aya de mi mercey
En l'autre segle per jassey,
Quon assatz d'autres peccadors;
Mas say mi tolh aquelha rey
Don joys mi crec; mas pauc mi tey
Que trop s'es de mi alonhatz."   (st. 6)

Marcabrun knows the way to write a moral-immoral love poem. He accomplishes it through dialogue. In his poem there is a clear-cut distinction drawn between the things of this world and the things of the "other world" (*segle* from *saeculum*); between him and Him. Marcabrun supposedly asserts the superior, capitalized values; the lady takes the lower ones. Yet the voice of Marcabrun in this pastourelle is like the voice of Vergil in his tenth pastoral. Vergil urged Gallus to rise up and put love aside, exactly as the poet here tries to persuade the lady. If the lady and Gallus seem to have made a deeper impression upon humanity, this fact may tell us why such poems survive.

Alfred Pillet's brilliant study of the Romance pastourelle takes us back to those romantic, shadowy debate-lands of Vergil, Theocritus, and Ovid's *Metamorphoses*.[65] When the thirteenth-century biographer of Cercamon said that Marcabrun's teacher wrote pastorals "according to the old custom" (*a la usanza antiga*), Jeanroy and Paris assumed a whole body of lost pastourelles written by the people in the vulgar tongue;

65. "Zum Ursprung der altprovenzalischen Lyrik," *SKGG*, 5, 4 (1928), 345–65.

Edmond Faral suggests more plausibly the possibility that Cercamon wrote Latin pastorals "in the manner of antiquity."[66] Scheludko and Faral have cited many interesting pastorals in contemporary Latin literature, aside from those in the *Burana*. The Latin works are usually much more obscene, but contain the significant bit of information that many of the elements can be read allegorically: as dialogues between Reason and the Senses.[67] Fortunately, Provençal pastourelles never descend to the depths of North French and Latin poems of this nature; their dialectic is in-built, and does not require an hypostatized structure.

Marcabrun, like almost all these poets, knew his Medieval Latin and Classical Latin well. His famous crusade song begins with a call that might have issued from Bernard of Clairvaux: "*Pax in nomine domini!*" It is the wittiest crusade song ever written, because although Marcabrun is quite serious about summoning people to fight for God (indeed, it gives him an excellent chance to harangue everyone for his laziness), he describes the battle in which the warriors will bathe in the blood of the Lamb as a big washing-tub (*lavador*). Yet his debate with Uc Catola shows him in his most characteristic, antifeministic pose:

> Catola, Ovid shows us here
> And the course of events is traced
> How he never scorns a blonde or brunette,
> In fact, he's drawn to the most depraved.

> *Catola, Ovides mostra chai*
> *E l'ambladura o retrai*
> *Que non soana brun ni bai,*
> *Anz se trai plus aus achaïz.*[68]

66. "La Pastourelle," 241–42.
67. For Scheludko, see n. 15; Faral, 256–59, citing John of Garland's *Poetria*.
68. *Marcabru*, ed. Dejeanne, no. 6, pp. 24–26, 37–40. Dejeanne translates 38 "*et l'allure (des choses) le fait voir*" (p. 27). My translation is based upon a reading of *ambladura* as *ambulatura* ("the march of events").

Marcabrun is pointing to Ovid's *Art of Love* or possibly the poem *Amores* 2.4; his attitude toward that book is, on the one hand, that of a man quoting the Bible: "Ovid says here . . . ." Yet there is no concealing the fact that he also regards Ovid's work, in a playful way, as the Book of the Devil. His fellow debater, Catola, cites idealized arguments that might emanate from Ovid; Marcabrun cites debased ones. Marcabrun speaks from the point of view of the *Remedium Amoris;* Catola from the preliminary *Ars Amoris.* The point is: both conflicting statements come from Ovid's so-called treatise on love, and the very same contradictions can be pointed out in Andreas Capellanus' work or even the Arab Ibn Hazm's *Risāla* or *Dove's Neck-Ring.*[69] The very notion of a definitive treatise on romantic love is preposterous. In the dark years of the Provençal decadence, some bad poets but decent rhetoricians wrote a tract called the *Leys d'Amors* ("Rules for Writing Love Poems"; not "The Rules for Love Affairs," as it is sometimes misinterpreted).[70] These fourteenth-century poets, writing with the Inquisition around them, quite firmly put the *amor Dei* above the *amor mundi* in their opening chapter. Some poets continued to write saccharine love poems to women, but by this time the Virgin Mary, whose cult was established after the Albigensian Crusade, was once again the Prime Lady, as she had been in the beginning.

If Marcabrun's negative attitude toward human love seems to contrast with Duke William's frankly positive (except in his final hymn), a third, distinct voice appears in Provençal literature in the person of Jaufré Rudel. (I take Cercamon to be a

69. The renunciation in Andreas' *De amore* 3 (p. 418) is stated with inverse meanings given to the secular symbolism traced to that point: "*Cave igitur, Gualteri . . . ut, quum venerit sponsus, inveniat te vigilantem";* the groom is Christ, the vigil suddenly Christian. See also *Risāla,* tr. Nykl, pp. 152 ff., and the closing prayer, p. 221.

70. Misconstrued in De Rougemont, rev. ed., pp. 75, 198; cf. the purpose in *Leys d'Amors,* ed. J. Anglade, Bibliothèque méridionale, 17–20 (1919–20), *17,* 8: "*per dar bonas doctrinas e bos essenhamens, a lauzor et honor de Dieu nostre senhor e de la sua glorioza Mayre, e de totz los Sans de Paradis.*"

transitional figure; the corpus is too slim and varied to abstract a predominant attitude or tone.) Jaufré's poetry is clearly directed toward monistic idealism, but the exact nature of that idealism (Christian-religious; heretical-mystic; personal-symbolic; non-Christian, non-heretical mystic) has never been articulated. The legend that has grown up around his name, connecting him with a flesh-and-blood princess in Tripoli, is now generally accepted as the creation of the author of his biography in the chansonnières.[71] The man who wrote that vida deduced his information from Jaufré's poetry. Thus the poet's fiction supplied historical facts which were later turned by Petrarch, Heine, and Rostand into new poetic fiction. Poets may use their famous license to conjure up swooning ladies and knights on bended knees; critics should be more precise.

I have already cited the beginning of Jaufré's "When days are long in May" in the Introduction. There I noted that the poem begins with a spring landscape that changes suddenly into winter ice. In terms of the tradition thus far traced, we might expect a tragic, or basically paradoxical, poem. Indeed the poem ends with a godfather's curse against Jaufré's ever attaining his far-off love. Between the winter ice and the curse, Jaufré describes his lady in rather vague terms. Most of the poem tells of his desire to become a pilgrim in order to see her; he says that he would gladly serve as a slave among the Saracens if he could reach her, for her room and garden are like a magnificent palace. Then comes the godfather's curse, which Jaufré in turn curses.

It is obvious that this poem is constructed in a world removed from anything thus far considered in Provençal. Jaufré suppresses all the sensual elements that can be found in Bernart and William, thereby opening the door to any and every theory of mystical dogma. One can speak of the poem in terms of opposing tensions: distance-nearness, fantasy-reality, mind-

---

71. Jeanroy, *La Poésie lyrique, 1,* 104–27, dates most of the vidas after 1230; he admits the possibility of some historical facts, but dismisses the *vie amoureuse* of any poet as fiction.

matter, or, as Leo Spitzer has suggested in a seminal essay, possession and non-possession.[72] The Italian critic Mario Casella compared the paradoxes of this poem to a mystical view of the world in which life is an enigma and even the greatest human act, love, is but a deceptive shadow of a divine reality; he related the poem to a Provençal genre called the *devinalh* or riddle-poem, of which the first specimen was written by Duke William, and Spitzer later compared these secular works with common medieval mystical riddles:

What both is and is not? Nothing.

Quid est quod est et non est? Nihil.[73]

In general, Casella tended to make the poem too orthodoxly Augustinian. It is obvious that all of the troubadours in their *nature* openings may be said to be expanding the terms of Augustine's *amor naturalis* (natural love), Bernart's *joi natural*. Yet Rudel idealizes and damns love as natural act; Augustine never idealizes it, and at times openly damns it. The schematology may be said to be Augustinian; but the manipulation of the terms is not.

There seems to be little question that the body or matter in Rudel's poem can be interpreted as evil, whereas the soul is still capable of mystical flights. However, we must be very careful about labeling the terms of this opposition heretical-Catharistic. The notion of the body as prison of the soul, the *soma-sema* antithesis, is a part of Platonism and Neoplatonism, and hence, through Augustine and the early Church Fathers, part of the Church, however much Augustine himself denied it. I doubt that the poem is merely Christian allegory, as Grace Frank indicated: "his far-away love was no lady of flesh

72. *L'Amour lointain de Jaufré Rudel*, Univ. of No. Car. Studies in Romance Langs. and Lit., 5 (1944), 34, citing Friedrich Neumann, "Hohe Minne," *ZDK*, 39 (1925), 81.

73. Spitzer, *L'Amour lointain*, 25; Casella, "Poesia e storia," *ASI*, 96, pt. 2 (1938), 153 ff. Spitzer is critical of Casella's rigidly Augustinian interpretation.

and blood, but the ideal of so many men of the Middle Ages" (that is, the Holy Land).[74] It would seem to be more than a mere extension of Cercamon's ambiguous *Chanson Pieuse.* If generations of poets and critics pictured that far-off love as a princess in Tripoli, and if Spitzer and Casella incline toward the opposite notion that this "secular" love poem exists in a rarefied mystical atmosphere, then the poem must partake of the very essence of ambiguity. If I were forced to make a choice between interpretations, I would incline to the viewpoint of Casella and Spitzer simply because the literal interpretation is so feeble: who, for example, is that godfather? In metaphoric terms, he may be the jealous Christian God of the albas who frowns on the poet's adoration of the Lady Beautiful; or he may be Adam, the Father of Us All, who turned the original Earthly Garden of Bliss into Hell. Jaufré's far-off lady is too much a haunting vision of Beauty to be a mere princess in some far-off land. Jaufré knows that he can never reach her, but the quest haunts him. He curses his "earthbound" state, but his desire for union continues. His poetry is humorless, dignified, grave, and tragic. If William of Aquitaine stressed the lower values of Platonic correspondences, Jaufré insists upon the superior ones. Jaufré is a part of his age, but he stands apart from it because of his unique genius. His spiritual imitator is probably Dante, but the Italian erects the epic whole that Rudel craves for but is denied.

After Jaufré (c. 1150), we return to Bernart de Ventadorn and the question: did Bernart take anything from his poetic predecessors? Considering the very diverse attitudes of William, Jaufré, and Marcabrun, no exact answer could ever be stated. Did he take his ethereal flights from Jaufré, his vivid sensual images from William, his antifeministic poses from Marcabrun? When we add all these things together, we still do not have a delicate, witty, organically conceived poem like

---

74. "The Distant Love of Jaufré Rudel," *MLN*, 57 (1942), 533. Developed further by D. W. Robertson, Jr., "Amors de terra lonhdana," *SP*, 49 (1952), 566–82.

Can vei la lauzeta mover. Or, to state the same question in even broader terms: given the traditional love symbolism of Ovid and the mystical symbolism of Christianity, can we deduce Provençal poetry? Ultimately the answer is: no. The literature is too rich, too varied; the voices of the poets, despite their obvious borrowings and parodies, are too diverse and too original.

If Bernart learned anything from his predecessors, it may have been simply the notion of poetry as a dialogue composed of many voices or tones and existing on at least two levels: the ideal and the real. Bernart became the great troubadour or literary inventor because he never sacrificed the realistic elements in his poems, nor did he allow his mystical overtones to harden into dogma or doctrine. Did he eulogize women? In his debate with Peire d'Alvernha on the nature of love, Bernart joined Marcabrun in saying (I have used his words as the inscription for this chapter):

> Peter, a man who loves is mad,
> for the liars among the women
> have ruined joy and worth and merit.[75]

His very unreliable vida tells us that he ended his life in a monastery.[76] That fact, since it would be difficult to deduce from his extant poetry, may be true, and may help to point up a basic contention of this study: the two conflicting spheres in medieval poetry are the religious and the secular; ultimately the conflict is artificial, for there is a constant tendency to fuse. Most of the poets were educated in schools where they learned logic, Latin grammar, Latin rhetoric, music, and theology; after spending their youths in the world, they returned to the Church to die. The journey from religious idealism to "reality" was not so far as we in the modern world might imagine.

75. *Bernart: SL*, no. 2, pp. 11–12, 46–48.
76. *Bernart: SL*, p. xiv: *"en Bernartz abandonet lo mon e.l trobar e.l chantar e.l solatz del segle e pois se rendet a l'orden de Dalon; e lai el fenic."*

THE ACHIEVEMENT OF THE TROUBADOURS

> And so I've finished my Don't-Know-What-It-Is,
> And I'd like to baptize it;
> Since nobody ever heard the likes before,
> Let them call it by this name.
> And let them recite it when they've learned it by
> heart
> Whenever they want to be honored.
> And if anyone asks who wrote it, say: "A man who
> can do anything he wants, if he happens
> to feel like it."[77]
>
> Raimbaut, Lord of Orange and Corthizon

There is no way to account conceptually for a spontaneous act of creativity. A critic may no more enter into the mind of Duke William of Aquitaine when he sat down to compose the first extant modern vernacular love lyrics than he can penetrate the psychic state of Shakespeare before composing *Hamlet*. Through these portals another does not enter. A critic has only words and forms to deal with: the end-product of the creative act. He can relate these words and forms to other similar manifestations and draw certain deductions, yet he must never, in his *re*creation of an original creation, pretend that his conceptualizations constitute a perfect imitation of the work of art *in act (per accidens)*. In medieval terminology, we can say that the substances of poems may be defined; the essences, or true inner lives of the poems, are mysterious and elusive. Any system of criticism that relegates Provençal poetry to a conceptual pigeonhole, reducing its positive-negative love dialectic to a single-toned praise of women, commits aesthetic heresy for the sake of historical and philosophical continuity; such a procedure destroys the individual poem for the sake of the genus and ultimately reduces

77. Hill–Bergin, no. 35, pp. 51–53, 42–48.

the corporate entity of very diverse poems to an inclusive catch-word that in time becomes a hazardous cliché.

The limited vocabulary of the Old South French love lyric (barely four thousand basic words) leads us to envision some self-contained, hierarchic sphere of expression. If the scholars who opened up the world of Romance philology interpreted these words almost entirely upon a literal level, relating them to the courts in which the poets lived, they were not wrong; they were simply not entirely right. They ignored the mystical grandeur of the lady and the romantic glorification of agony that surely must have had some bearing upon the one great Passion that the western world has known. The sweet sickness of love, the unremitting service to a lord (not necessarily a lady) of love, and the torment or crucifixion of love—these basic tropes have no direct correspondence in the castle life or feudal organization of the twelfth century. They are, however, deeply rooted in one thousand years of antecedent Christianity.

Since the works of mythographic scholars such as Jessie Weston and Joseph Campbell have expanded the far narrower scopes of Romance philologists and medieval specialists, we now see Christianity as a great synthesizer, rather than innovator, of symbolism; the cross, the lance, the grail, and the chalice—these symbols are Indo-European and have existed from time immemorial.[78] They were taken from pagan religious and romantic epics and adapted to the one great Christian epic: the life of Christ. Similarly, the kiss or direct communion, the doctrine of service or faith, the pledge of secrecy, the willingness to undergo the agony of passion for an ideal—these terms were applied to the religious cults of pagan gods long before they were absorbed into Christianity; and they appear in secular pagan works such as Plato's *Symposium*, Ovid's *Art of Love*, and Hellenic romances in such an obvious way that their very existence is undeniable. Chris-

---

78. Weston, *From Ritual to Romance* (Cambridge, Eng., 1920); Campbell, *The Hero with a Thousand Faces* (N.Y., 1949).

tianity's achievement was not that it invented such symbolism; Christianity codified it and spiritualized it. The Church sanctioned a hermetic vocabulary; the court or world, in imitating the worship of Lord Jesus in the domain of an earthly lord, expanded its terms within the social context. But if, in reading this age-old symbolism, we see only the social or courtly context, then surely we are blind to the great achievement of the poets, for we thereby lose all sense of their courage and their wit.

Scholars naturally resent a phrase like "twelfth-century jazz" (although in his *De vulgari eloquentia* Dante indicates that many poems were danced to, especially the later Italian *ballata*, derived from *ballare*, "to dance or have a ball"). Yet I suspect that the phrase captures far more of the flavor of the dancing bears, the clashing cymbals, the wailing flutes, the clowns, and the *joglars* (the very word for the man who sang the poem is akin to the later derivate "juggler") than a bland term such as "courtly love." What we need, in describing this humanistic impulse, is not a term that connotes cultural history, but one that tells us something about the poetry itself. For this reason, the phrase "Christian secular" poetry is both more descriptive and less literal.

As for the question of origin, one needs only to look at a map of central and southern France. Given the widespread Platonizing influence there in the twelfth century, particularly at Chartres under the Bernards, we have perhaps the most important clue that history affords us in reconstructing the spiritual ethos of the age. Bernard Silvestris' magnificent epic, *De mundi universitate* ("On the Wholeness of the World"), outlined the Platonic scheme of the macrocosm *joined with* the microcosm.[79] After such humane writers as Bernard, who

79. Ed. C. S. Barach and J. Wrobel (Innsbruck, 1876). For the most plausible historical account of the period, emphasizing the fusion of Christian and classical elements within the feudal hierarchies of Germanic Europe, see Reto R. Bezzola, *Les Origines et la formation de la littérature courtoise en Occident, 500–1200* (2 vols., 3 pts. Paris, 1944–60). See also the penetrating comments of

loved nature description, it was possible to humanize deities if one wrote religious poetry or to deify humanity if one wrote secular poetry. The spheres interacted in almost perfect conjunction. The world was ready for Dante's magnum opus: the final epic vision of the whole.

Yet the lyric poets of Provence, Poitou, and Gascony were not Dante, and this is perhaps where mystically inclined critics such as Casella tend to overplay their hands. There is no formal philosophical vocabulary in troubadour poetry, such as the Italians used to bridge the worlds of spirit and nature: "essence," "accident," "substance," etc. The vocabulary is loosely Platonic in the Christian tradition of Augustine and Richard of St. Victor, but the object of worship is "my lady" (*ma domna*) and not Our Lady or Milady (*Madonna*). An enormous gap. Furthermore, the lyric ego destroys the basically idealized texture of the hymn, scattering negative statements ("She's robbed me," "I'm through with love," "All women are like that," "What a man forbids she does") among the positive, and sundering the monistic song of praise into the brilliant shards of the lyric. When Cercamon says that love is sweet when it walks in and bitter when it walks out, he joins hands with Sappho and Catullus, not Plato, Augustine, Mohammed, Celtic druids, or that arch-Catharist Pop Bogomil of Bulgaria.

The dialectic in Provençal poetry extends beyond conflicting statements and attitudes into the very ambiguity of the

---

Antonio Viscardi, "Le Origini della letteratura cortese," *ZRP, 78* (1962), 269-91, esp. 290: *"Il poeta—il grande poeta—è sempre non tanto l'interprete, quanto piuttosto il maestro del mondo in cui vive ed opera."* Bezzola has managed to dispel the romantic mist surrounding the period by tracing the fusion of pagan *humanitas* and Christian service in a society of warring nobles; his accounts of the Carolingian *laus* addressed to great ladies add another important factor in the evolution of the secular lyric, although this strain is muted or transcended in the Provençal tradition, where the poets profess to love their ladies. In the last analysis, despite the impressiveness of the technique, one cannot abstract a poem from a chronicle of lords.

individual word. Let us briefly cite a few of the important words touched upon in the previous sections, showing the twin sphere of religious-secular connotation. The double definitions cited are English equivalents of the definitions listed in the standard Provençal dictionary of Raynouard (supplemented by Levy and Appel); beneath these definitions are Classical and Medieval Latin words which show the source of this ambiguity in their Romance descendants:[80]

Provençal word	Secular meaning (Classical Latin ancestor)	Religious meaning (Medieval Latin ancestor)
merces	reward, pay (for soldier) (CL: merces)	mercy, grace (ML: merces)
dom(p)na	lady or mistress (CL: domina)	The Lady (ML: Domina)
precs	entreaty, petition (CL: prex, both meanings)	prayer (ML: prex, both meanings)
servir	serve or obey (a lord) (CL: servire)	serve or obey (the Lord) (ML: servire)
pascor	spring (CL: ——)	Easter (ML: Pascha, Semitic)
nou	young (physical); new (CL: novum)	new (spiritual), i.e. life after baptism, conversion (ML: novum)
dous	sweet (sensual) (CL: dulcis, both meanings)	sweet (abstract); humble (ML: dulcis, both meanings)
saber	taste (primarily sensual) (CL: sapere, both meanings)	know (primarily abstract) (ML: sapere, both meanings)

The list could be extended indefinitely.

80. F. J. M. Raynouard, *Lexique roman: ou, Dictionnaire de la langue des troubadours* (6 vols. Paris, 1838–44; rev. 1844); Emil Levy and Carl Appel, *Provenzalisches Supplement-Wörterbuch* (8 vols. Leipzig, 1894–1924); Levy–Appel, perhaps because it is later and hence more inclusive, is far more indicative of verbal ambiguity; see words cited. For a study of poetic ambiguity, see Eugen Lerch, "Trobadorsprache und religiöse Sprache," *CN, 3* (1943), 214–30; an interesting but less successful attempt by Charles Camproux, "A propos de 'Joi'," *Mélanges István Frank* (Saarbrücken, 1957), 100–17.

It is difficult to understand how one can ignore the conflicting meanings for these basic words, since any comprehensive Provençal glossary lists both diverse definitions. Translation from Provençal is an enormously complicated process, for it is almost impossible at times to select the proper meaning for even such a common word as *merces*. Then, when one considers the added dimension of metaphysical wit, by which the lady functions as *grace*-ful Mary, cold-cruel Eve, or graceful-graceless Lady-Lord, he has a general idea of why early Romance scholars could not acknowledge these religious overtones: if taken seriously, they might have sounded either openly sacrilegious or else too orthodoxly Christian; and so the scholars concluded that the poetry was operating in a sphere that was utterly divorced from Christianity; hence, they described it as "courtly" or secular. Finally, to account for what they interpreted as a hymn of praise to a woman, they went searching for feministic idealism in Arabia, southern Spain, the Celtic forests, Albigensian retreats, and the hovels of peasants—in fact, everywhere except the very place that they had singled out for its milieu: the courts of southern France, which existed side by side with monasteries and cathedrals. It is an ironically sad joke that the poets who composed delicate lyrics in the twelfth century have almost never been credited with writing beautiful poetry; instead, they have been credited with evolving a new attitude toward women, with initiating a new code of social behavior. However, since this code and this attitude are nowhere evident in histories of the period (which read like the blood-and-thunder accounts of any era and in which great ladies like Eleanor of Aquitaine are often treated like miserable pawns), the troubadours are thus believed to have adapted social or religious standards from some exotic culture or ideology. In short, the poets are no longer poets; they have become emancipators of women and the first formulators of the kind of etiquette that was proper (but not necessarily universally practiced) in Victorian England, but which seems to have disappeared at the end of the

Edwardian Age. In accepting this mystery-dogma theory, T. S. Eliot came to the following conclusion: "That mysterious people had a religion of their own which was thoroughly and painfully extinguished by the Inquisition; so that we hardly know more about them than about the Sumerians."[81] On the other hand, C. S. Lewis believed that: "French poets, in the eleventh century, . . . erected impassable barriers between us and the classical past or the Oriental present."[82] Both views are extreme. Bernart de Ventadorn and William of Aquitaine are in no way as esoteric as Eliot would have us believe; neither are Catullus and Ovid as pornographic as Lewis would make them. The difference between the two groups is obvious: the troubadours are Christian and address themselves primarily to the world of the spirit; Catullus and Ovid are pagans speaking directly from the paradoxes in the world of nature, with only a phantasmal screen of ideals. Most modern readers can understand either group, for the poets ultimately speak a common language, and can appreciate their similarities as well as their quite obvious differences.

We might now try to answer two basically unanswerable questions:

1. *Why was the spring motif not a conventional part of the classical love lyric?*

The most apparent reason would seem to be that the classical lyric, especially as treated by the Romans, descended abruptly from idealization to reality, and hence the setting of love in mankind's perennial dream of earthly bliss was hardly in keeping with this realistic attitude toward nature, love, and the creative act of writing itself. Furthermore, since there was no Church or group of theologians around to carp about the depravity of sex, an "animal" act, and romantic passion, the

81. "Dante," *Selected Essays* (new ed. N.Y., Harcourt, Brace and World, 1950), p. 235. Eliot admits: "I have not the knowledge to read them at first hand." He is to be commended for an honesty conspicuously lacking in numerous modern popularizers.
82. *Allegory of Love*, p. 4.

nature-trapping was not needed as a rationalization.[83] The Romans, however, left a sufficient body of spring poems to show that the advent of the mating season left a strong impression even upon their basically urban souls.

2. *Why did the spring motif in early Romance literature become not only a convention but almost an obsession?*

Latin literature from the Carolingian Revival to the *Carmina Burana* furnishes one primary key. For a period of about three hundred years the only secular poems of high artistic merit were nature poems built upon a conjoined dialectic. The Song of Songs is surely another important key, for that little book of love lyrics went everywhere the Bible went. It could be moralized, allegorized, and dogmatized, but eventually someone would see simply an earthly turtle-dove and an earthly maiden in its memorable passages about spring. Philosophically, the question can be answered perhaps more conclusively. The Augustinian phrase used by Casella to define love in the Provençal lyric, *amor naturalis,* was a sup-

---

83. The Church's response to the expression of romantic love has been best spelled out by the Oriental scholar Alan W. Watts, *Nature, Man and Woman* (N.Y., Pantheon: Random House, 1958), e.g., p. 149: "For from the earliest times the Church Fathers virtually equated sex with sin by identifying all sexual feeling and desire with the evil of lust." Writing from a Buddhistic-Confucian point of view, Watts avoids the anticlericalism of nineteenth-century scholarship and the Christian apologetics of the twentieth century. His inclination toward an Albigensian-origin theory is not substantiated: does one have to be a philosopher or heretic to feel that human love is a good or even noble thing? However, see his critique of De Rougemont, p. 174. Naturally when a poet is forced to rationalize about love (which has always been the primary theme of lyric poetry), he must idealize his context to some extent; however, in re-creating the experience, a poet creates a world in which, as Watts says (p. 159): "woman is always a mystery to man, and man to woman. It is in this sense that we must understand van der Leeuw's remarkable saying that 'the mystery of life is not a problem to be solved, but a reality to be experienced.'" One might say the same thing about poetry: a poem is not a set of symbols to be reconciled with a generic or conceptual classification, but a tissue of sounds, symbols, and sensations that is transmitted by the poet to his reader for a vicarious experience. The term "courtly love" no more explains the poetry of Bernart than the term "classical music" explains Mozart; the individual sonata and sonnet must be heard.

pressed, inferior term as used by Christian writers. When songs about human love were once again written after an extraordinarily long lapse, it was perfectly logical for a poet to proclaim that his love was natural. Nature (*Natura*) was finally given lip service after yielding for so many centuries to her creator, God.

The idealized romantic springs of the classical epic descended from the Olympian Golden Age into the bitter springs of the lyric; when poets of the twelfth century felt compelled to stress the idealized aspects of love, they reached out for the related notion of the Garden of Eden, which was itself a pastiche of the earlier ideal *locus amoenus;* they then transferred this garden of perpetual splendor into an earthly setting in time: a morning in April or May. If their obstreperous ladies tend to become cruel Eves who destroy their gardens of bliss, this fact is totally in keeping with lyric expression as defined in this study: the sweetness of idealism in constant tension with the bitterness of reality. In short, we should not praise these lyric inventors of Provence for discovering a hypothetically new species of love. We should praise them for the more obvious and unarguable fact that they *re*discovered poetry.

It was May (so I dreamed)
In the time of love, full of joy,
The time when everything is glad . . .
Happy and gay and full of joy
I found myself by a river . . .
It delighted me and pleased me so
To regard that pleasant place . . .

GUILLAUME DE LORRIS, *Roman de la rose*

*Matilda near the banks of River Lethe in the
Christian Earthly Paradise:*

Those who in times of old poetized
About the Golden Age and its happy state
Perhaps dreamed about this place on Parnassus.
Here the root of humanity was innocent;
Here spring was eternal, eternal every fruit;
This river is the nectar of which they all sang.

DANTE, *Purgatorio*

4 Diaspora and Diffusion: The Lyric Spring in Northern France and Italy

THE ALBIGENSIAN CRUSADE was highly effective in crushing whatever heresies were being bred in southern France in the first two decades of the thirteenth century, so effective that only scraps and fragments exist from which we can solve the perplexing problem: what was an Albigensian? Yet the crusaders did not crush poetry, although the North French did indeed crush the political power of southern France, thereby laying the framework for the modern nation of France in which the North French *langue d'oïl* replaced the South French *langue d'oc* as the vital language of communication; and the Church did indeed nurture the cult of the Virgin over the ruins of castles where ladies had been immortalized in songs. The troubadours themselves, however, survived, thereby pointing up the fact that poets and singers are seldom the primary targets of political tyranny; their "heresies" may be annoying, but their primary appeal to intellectuals nullifies their general effect. With many of the lords of southern France impoverished, several of the later troubadours such as Guiraut Riquer (1254–82) took refuge in Castile; others found havens in the untouched courts of Portugal, northern France, and Italy; some brave souls penetrated the hated country of the Alemanni and others went beyond that into the depths of medieval Hungary and Bohemia.

With these poets went joy, wit, gaiety, love songs, and that golden spring of the late Middle Ages that is timeless, placeless, forever a part of man's dream of earthly perfection. And after the troubadours came *trouvères, trovatori,* and *Minne-*

singer; in short, secular poetry returned to Europe in full force, and spring was blossoming throughout the frontierless world of Romania and nearby Germania:[1]

Thibaut, Count IV of Champagne, King I of Navarre (1201–c. 1253)
OLD NORTH FRENCH: *Contre le tems qui devise*
Yver et pluie d'esté ...

Walther von der Vogelweide (1170?–1230?)
MIDDLE HIGH GERMAN: *Dô der sumer komen was*
und die bluomen dur daz gras
wünneclichen sprungen ...

Giacomino Pugliese (middle 1200s)
OLD ITALIAN (SICILIAN): *Quando vegio rinverdire*
giardino e prato e rivera,
gli auscelleti odu bradire ...

Compiuta Donzella (latter 1200s)
OLD ITALIAN (TUSCAN): *A la stagion che il mondo foglia e fiora* ...

Alfonso XI (1312–50)
OLD CASTILIAN: *En un tiempo cogí flores*
del muy noble parayso ...

Anonymous (early 1300s)
MIDDLE ENGLISH: Bytuene Mersh and Averil
When spray biginneth to springe ...

Yet, sad to say, not all the imitative poetry attained the metaphysical wit that is the dominant feature of the classical Old Provençal love lyric. If one speaks in cultural terms, he says: the Provençal poets established the courtly-love tradition, and this tradition dominated European poetry for the next three hundred years; later poets wrote verse after verse in honor of their ladies, and this social aspect, the praise of an earthly woman, is ultimately more important than the poetry

---

1. For a general survey from the French point of view, see Jeanroy, *Origines,* pp. 127–338; for Italian, Francesco Torraca, *Studi su la lirica italiana del Duecento* (Bologna, 1902); for German, Hennig Brinkmann, *Entstehungsgeschichte des Minnesangs, DVLG 8* (1926); for a synoptic view from Great Britain to Byzantium, Bezzola, *Origines, 1,* pt. 2 (Paris, 1960).

itself, since all of the poetry tends to sound the same: *"mono-tone en son contenu"* (Jeanroy).[2]

This study, however, will continue to speak in rhetorical terms: the Provençal writers bequeathed a store of fixed images which had both religious and secular connotations; these two spheres tended ultimately to separate even in Provençal literature itself in the thirteenth and fourteenth centuries. The poetry could go upward into the clearly religious realm or downward into the world. We will see this diffusion dramatically illustrated in diverse ways by tracing the two primary streams which flowed out of the Provençal fountainhead: the North French and the Italian.

Northern France: The Court and the World Around Us

In a passage that has long been the bane of many a school-boy, Julius Caesar remarked rather perfunctorily that all Gaul is divided into three parts. Omitting Belgium, we can say that even in the late Middle Ages the land that we today call France was divided into two parts: the southern region of the *langue d'oc*, with the cavalier inhabitants of Aquitaine, the Côte d'Azur, and the castle valleys; and the northern land of the *langue d'oïl*, with the far more somber inhabitants of Brittany, Normandy, the Ile-de-France, and Alsace-Lorraine. One thinks of southern and central French culture radiating from the poetic Platonizing schools at Chartres, Bordeaux, Limoges, and Poitiers; of northern French culture radiating from the Aristotelian schools of Paris, which produced Abelard, Albertus Magnus, and a host of other great doctors who were analyzing the world in rational, nonpoetic terms. We might compare the jewel-like, self-contained, Romanesque splendor of St. Trophime at Arles with the mammoth, searching, Gothic systematization of Notre Dame of Paris.

Literarily, it has long been known that a curious kind of schism existed between southern and northern France. Schol-

2. *La Poésie lyrique,* 2, 94; cf. Spitzer, *L'Amour lointain,* pp. 40–44.

ars of the nineteenth century pondered two interesting and related questions:

1. Why did Provençal literature produce a wealth of lyric poetry and practically no epics or narrative romances?

2. Why, on the other hand, did North French literature produce a wealth of epics and narrative romances, yet almost no sophisticated lyrics which are not obvious imitations of the poetry of their southern neighbors?

Naturally, these questions admit of no absolute answers. In terms of the ideas developed in this study, one could say simply that the gulf between the epic and lyric sensibilities is an enormous one; only the greatest individual poets are capable of bridging that gap. When poets write in schools, as they frequently do, it is logical for a disciple to follow his master. The masters in northern France were the anonymous author of the *Chanson de Roland*, the romantic epic-writer Chrétien de Troyes, and finally Guillaume de Lorris and Jean de Meun, who together composed the influential *Roman de la rose*. The pace in southern France was set by William of Aquitaine, Cercamon, Marcabrun, and Bernart de Ventadorn, whose creations were written in a different key.

It is commonly believed that the seminal work of northern France, the *Roman de la rose*, is a fusion of both elements: from Provence, the notion of the adoration of woman, an ideological factor, and a doctrine of social service; from northern France, the tendency to allegorize and to organize an episodic narrative that works gradually toward a monistic conclusion. It is interesting to conjecture how the two men who wrote the *Roman* could ever have made such a complete fusion. However, only modern Christian apologists and anticlerical nineteenth-century scholars seem to think of the *Roman* as a treatise written in deification of women and love. The Wife of Bath, who was far closer to the work, considered it a dangerous piece of antifeministic propaganda; so did the fifteenth-century French-Italian poetess Christine de Pisan, who wrote a whole tract attacking the latter part of the *Roman*.

This curious disparity of opinion stems from the fact that the *Roman* was composed by two writers who ought never to have approached the same work: the first part, an idealized love vision by Guillaume de Lorris; the last, and by far the longest part, a religious encyclopedia composed by the sour-faced moralist Jean de Meun.

Guillaume's section is a secular treatise, a romantic conceptualization of the free-moving lyric symbolism of Provence whereby various abstractions are converted into characters. Bernart's "joy" and "jealousy" become Guillaume's Joy and Jealousy. This conceptualizing process is typically North French. For example, we can observe its beginnings in an early lyric poem by Gace Brulé:

> She has sweet manners
> And makes good company;
> She's wise among envious people—
> The girl who has power over my heart.
> She has good sense and beauty
> And she hates all villeinie . . .

> *Cele est de douz acointement*
> *Et de bone compaignie,*
> *Et sage entre envieuse gent,*
> *Qui de mon cuer est saisie.*
> *Sens et biautez en li s'estent,*
> *Et hait toute vilenie . . .* [3]

Here we have the woman treated entirely in social terms. This poem could refer only to an actual woman, because good company and the other facets of the etiquette of high society really have very little, if any, application to a deity. Furthermore, the tone is a bit pedantic; the man who is speaking likes

---

3. *De bien amer*, 9–14, *Poètes et romanciers du moyen âge*, ed. A. Pauphilet, new texts by R. Pernoud and A.-M. Schmidt, Bibliothèque de la Pléiade, 52 (Paris, Editions Gallimard, 1952), p. 883; hereafter cited as Pauphilet. Cf. *Chansons de Gace Brulé*, ed. G. Huet (Paris, 1902), pp. 13–16, with the inferior reading *enuieuse gent* (11).

to categorize and classify in a way that recalls a medieval ency-clopedist. We can already see personalized abstractions emerg-ing from this isolated strophe. We can envision a war of society in which the loved one stands on the side of Good Company, Wisdom, Good Sense, and Beauty; on the other side we have those primary religious and romantic villains Envie (Invidia) and Villeinie (Evil). All we need to do now is to add about forty more characters, chart an action, and, since we are con-ceiving what is basically a romantic epic, write the traditional happy ending. Here we have the general outline for Guil-laume's part of the *Roman*.

In the latter part, Jean took great liberties with Guillaume's Social Graces; he erected a religious structure to counter Guillaume's secular structure. He transformed the odorous rose in Guillaume's perpetual Garden of Delight back into a religious symbol, as it is in Dante. He converted the garden itself into an Earthly Paradise clearly cast in the shadow of a Celestial Paradise:

> Be loyal, be piteous
> And then you'll reach the Fields of Delight,
> By following the footsteps of the Lamb,
> Where there's living durability,
> And drink from the beautiful fountain
> That is always sweet and clear and healthful.[4]

Jean is like Prudentius recasting the romantic material of Vergil and Ovid. It is true that he quotes Vergil's "Love con-quers all" (*Amours vaint tout*, 21,332), summarizes Ovid's picture of the Golden Age (20,181 f.), and gathers his pagan rosebud while he may, but Jean's Dominican bent leads him to supply the religious overtone wherever it is possible to do so. After transforming the whole structure of Guillaume's vision, Jean finally supplies the happy ending of romance.

We now face a problem that is often ignored: what *is* the

4. *Roman de la rose*, ed. E. Langlois (5 vols. Paris, 1914–24), 5, 51 f., 20, 647–52.

Roman de la rose? The fact is, the *Roman* is as much a prey to the dialectic of love as is Andreas Capellanus' *De amore* or Ovid's *Ars Amoris.* It shows a curious return from romance (Guillaume) to ritual (Jean) that runs directly counter to the epic descent "from ritual to romance" in North French literature.[5] Yet Guillaume eventually carried the day. Guillaume's profeminism, social graces, and secular idealism subdued Jean's antifeminism, religious grace, and religious idealism, at least insofar as most later *poets* were concerned. Guillaume de Lorris' influence is heavily felt in the later works of Guillaume de Machaut, Eustache Deschamps, and Alain Chartier. All of these poets idealized the world around them; they sound very courteous, very polite, and very idolatrous of women. When we read the North French lyrics of the thirteenth and fourteenth centuries, we may form the impression that we are reading the works of a very well-bred, genteel, refined society in which *la belle dame sans merci* (the human counterpart of Mary, who is "the beautiful mistress with grace abounding") is forever hymned and praised by a suffering, noble, castrated knight on bended knee. Indeed, Huizinga informs us that this era, the so-called Waning of the Middle Ages, was "always vacillating between tearful piety and frigid cruelty, between respect and insolence, between despondency and wantonness, [and] could not dispense with the severest rules and the strictest formalism."[6] It was an age that embodied paradox, yet strove to maintain its idealism; as religious ceremonies deteriorated, they were replaced by rigid ceremonials.

This was the age in which the idealized love poem became a stifling convention, bereft of any but the faintest religious overtones. The term "courtly love," with its exclusion of superior elements, is indeed well suited to describe the romantic ethos of this period; yet the gap between the idealized behavior portrayed in the poems and the actual behavior in the world at large is obvious. North France was crying for a man of hon-

5. See Weston, *From Ritual to Romance.*
6. *The Waning of the Middle Ages* (N.Y., 1954), pp. 50–51.

esty who could portray the world as it was. That man came in the person of François Villon, who replaced fantastic illusion with brutal realism. Villon wrote about Fat Margaret and Rose and the scheming Chancellors whom he named by name; he also wrote about the Virgin Mary; in him, the spheres of religion, romance, and realism are all active and alive. He is the first really great lyric poet of northern France; and he is a cousin of William of Aquitaine, not Chrétien de Troyes.

Very few people have attempted to make a case for the beauty of North French lyric poetry as poetry; scholars such as Jeanroy and Paris freely admitted that the North French imitated the South French; they then went on to claim that the French people as a nation invented a new romantic and civilized attitude toward women and love. Their claims were nationalistic and historical; the aesthetic they conveniently ignored. Nor will the aesthetic be mentioned here at any length, for as the conceptual, secularized categories of Gace Brulé and his contemporaries prefigure the systematic codification of the *Roman*, which then established the secular nature of subsequent poetic composition, the poetry withered under the impact of formalism, mannerism, and dreary repetition of themes and symbols. Charles d'Orléans, who was capable of writing some very fine poems, varies the standard allegorical process by writing about the Chamber of Thought, the Ship of Good News, and the Forest of Long Awaiting; his characteristic tone, the result of dire misfortunes in his life, is one of tragic melancholy and world-weary indifference (*nonchaloir*).[7]

Charles wrote the most famous spring poem in French literature, and the simple earthly elegance of it shows how far from any complicated vision of life the fifteenth-century attitude toward nature had descended. The spring poem was no longer a love poem; it was now a manneristic portrait of na-

7. For allegorical poems, see Charles d'Orléans, *Poésies*, ed. P. Champion (2 vols. Paris, 1923-27), *1*, 47-48, 67-68, 165-66, 181-82; for *nonchaloir* poems, esp. *1*, 254, 178-79, etc.

ture, just as the love poem had become a manneristic portrait of an earthly lady—*objets d'art* meant to be placed on an early baroque mantelpiece:

> Time (*temps*)* has put aside his cloak
> Of wind and cold and rain,
> And has now put on an embroidery
> Of sunshine, bright, beautiful, and clear.
>
> There is not a beast nor a bird
> Who in his speech doesn't sing or shout:
> Time has put aside his cloak!
>
> River and pool and brook
> Carry in pretty livery
> Drops of smithied silver,
> Each one dressed in something new:
> Time has put aside his cloak.[8]

*Perhaps better "the weather" or "course of seasons."

The charming simplicity of Charles' portrait is really quite original. The accent is upon nature, which is personified in its many parts; yet there is no romantic melancholy in his portrait, not a trace of paradox. "God's in His Heaven—all's right with the world." God is never mentioned, but this omission can hardly be termed serious; perhaps his presence is so obvious that it does not need mention. If the poem has a baroque splendor, its tone is also strikingly Victorian. Nature to Charles, as later to Tennyson and Lowell, was hardly a phenomenon that aroused deep feelings of tragic despair. Nature had its place; so did God. Yet late medieval idealism, with its almost unconscious emphasis upon the world around us, led eventually to Renaissance humanism, where the Horatian paradoxes and pagan questions about nature and time were once again asserted. In succeeding generations, nature poetry tended to mirror the religiosity of the age. The modern popu-

8. Ed. Champion, 2, 307–08.

lar conventions about the romance of spring ("What is so rare as a day in June?"; "In the spring a young man's fancy . . ."; "O to be in England . . .") descend from nineteenth-century idealism and the circumambient glow of Victorian hymnology; the nineteenth century resuscitated medieval idealism, as we have had frequent cause to mention with reference to the scholarship of that period. The most effective use of the spring motif in the twentieth century, however, in Eliot's *Wasteland*, is a prelude to a realistic vision. Romantic mystery and classical realism contend for superiority in the literature of the modern world.

The bland optimism of Charles' spring poem is striking when compared to the earlier North French lyric, where the sensuality of the *Carmina Burana* can be detected in a poem by Le Châtelain de Coucy:

> The spring and May and the violet
> And the nightingale force me to sing,
> And my refined heart (*fins cuer*) makes me such a sweet gift
> Of a love that I dare not refuse it.
> Now may God let me rise to such honor
> That her in whom I place my heart and thought
> I may hold one time naked in my arms
> > Before I go overseas [i.e., on crusade]![9]

or where the more balanced presentation of the Provençal lyric is evident in a poem by Gace Brulé:

> In the sweetness of the beautiful season
> When everything shines with greenness
> And fields and bowers and groves are pretty
> And birds are singing on tops of flowers,
> Then I'd be happy if they'd all put aside their love,
> For I don't see any true lovers except *me*.
> *I alone* want to love; *I alone* want that honor.[10]

9. Pauphilet, p. 873, 1–8.
10. *A la douçor de la bele saison*, 1–7, Pauphilet, p. 881. Huet lists it among "doubtful pieces" (pp. 85–86).

Despite its derivative nature, North French poetry contains many fine poems in which the paradoxes and twin spheres of religious-secular connotation are beautifully harmonized, especially by the earlier poets such as Thibaut de Champagne, Conon de Bethune, and Colin Muset. Even at the time of Charles d'Orléans, the spheres were sufficiently interactive so that Charles could write a poem in which human love was treated as a mystical rite, and in which every important word has at least two possible meanings:

They speak about religion,
With its strict *governing*,
How through *ardent devotion*
One bears many a *hard penance*,
But since I have some *knowledge* about it
And it suits my *purpose*,
Above all things I have *compassion*
For *the observances of lovers*.

Always in their *contemplations*
They keep their *hearts ravished in trance*
So they can *rise through perfection*
To *the high Paradise of Pleasure;*
Hot, cold, hunger, thirst they suffer
With hope, in many a country:
Such is the *discourse*
Of *the observances of lovers*.

Barefooted, they *beg*
For *the alms of Consolation;* they want
No *pension for allegiance*,
Except *Mercy*—a poor pittance
In the satchels of *Remembrance*
For their meager *provisions!*
Is this not a *holy condition*
For *the observances of lovers?*

> I don't seek the acquaintance of *bigots:*
> I don't praise their *opinions;*
> But, through *affection,* I side
> With *the observances of lovers.*[11]

It is a magnificent and quite conscious exercise in double entendre. Yet even at the end of the medieval tradition, while ambiguity is still alive, we can hear a quiet, muted calm in Charles' poem. Perhaps the conscious turning of every single important word signifies the end. Poetry is probably at its best when it is subtle and elusive, as it was in Provence. In the main, the North French lyric exists as a kind of footnote to the North French epic. When Alain Chartier addresses his *belle dame,* he does so in what is clearly a social situation; and he speaks like one of the Arthurian knights in Chrétien's romances.[12] During its florescence, the North French lyric perpetuated the rich ambiguity of Provençal; for example, the very typically North French word *courtois (cortois)*—a word that is not at all important in Provençal—was applied to Christ and the Virgin Mary:

> Fructus ventris tui, from the fruit of thy womb,
> Who was so kindly, simple, sweet, and "courteous."

> Fructus ventris tui, *de ton ventre li fruis,*
> *Qui tant fu debonaires, simples, dous et cortois.*[13]

Yet because North French literature was primarily directed toward the *haut monde* and not "another world," it never produced the greatest epic of the Middle Ages. For the religious view of the whole, we must turn to Italy, where something very different was taking place.

---

11. Ed. Champion, *1,* 158–59.
12. Compare the speeches of the "amant" in *La Belle dame sans merci* with those of Yvain in Chrétien's *Yvain.*
13. Philippe de Beaumanoir, "Ave Maria," st. 5, 3–4, *Oeuvres poétiques,* ed. H. Suchier (2 vols. Paris, 1885), *1,* 301.

Italy: Heaven and the Aftermath

The first Italian poets wrote in the Provençal language in northern Italy, where they were more a part of the Provençal decadence than the Italian florescence. The spring landscape had already ceased to form a conventional opening for poems. But during the early 1200s, the Italian language itself was stretched over the Procrustean couch of Provençal paradoxes in the Sicilian court of Frederick II. Whatever is fresh in this poetry has long been described by literary historians as merely a restatement of old themes in a new and struggling language. For example, the spring opening which was cited earlier, taken from a poem by Giacomino Pugliese, is an obvious imitation of antecedent Latin and Provençal tropes. Yet the conventional scene withered fast in southern Italy too, and the effect on Italian poetry was salubrious.

Sicily was one of the principal gateways for the introduction into the western world of Latin cribs of Aristotle. Plato had long been known in Italy, and the effect of philosophy upon Italian rhetoric is evident from the very start. In his *De vulgari eloquentia* Dante noted that Sicily was the seat of a "courtly" idiom, but neither the Hohenstaufen court nor the Sicilian idiom dominated later Italian culture; for in that same treatise Dante noted that Italy did not have the kind of centralized court life that could be found in northern France, England, and Germany.[14]

Yet Italy's political loss soon became a poetic gain. Early Italian poetry grasps upward for superior values, is not content to reside in a social sphere. We can observe this phenomenon in a lyric by Giacomo da Lentino, who probably invented the sonnet:

> You surpass in beauty every other thing,
> just as the rose surpasses every other flower.

14. I.12; I.18.2: *"si aulam nos Ytali haberemus, palatinum foret";* he adds, however, *"Quare falsum esset dicere curia carere Ytalos, quanquam principe careamus: quoniam curiam habemus, licet corporaliter sit dispersa."*

> *passate di belleze ogn'altra cosa,*
> *come la rosa—passa ogn'altro fiore.*[15]

The rose here is no flower to be sniffed in a sensual garden of bliss, attended by Venus, Amor, and Good Entrée. Nor is Beauty a walking abstraction. These kinds of conceptualizations are absent from Italian poetry; it is nonallegorical, although it is clearly philosophical. The rose here is a living symbol of an ideal beauty, just as the woman is a living symbol of a perpetually enduring *idea*. In this poetry we encounter the macrocosmic-microcosmic sphere of Platonic correspondences, and this sphere becomes more pronounced and more elaborate until we reach the vision of the Rose Multifoliate at the end of Dante's *Paradiso*.

Let us look at the way, for example, Giacomo thinks about Paradise; it is no Earthly Paradise with green brooks and laurels and the dances of the Graces, but the Christian Paradise itself, without any of the metaphysical double entendre that characterized Charles d'Orléans' poem about the "observances of lovers":

> I've resolved to serve God
> So that I can go to Paradise,
> To the holy place that I've heard tell of,
> Where pleasure, games, and laughter reside.
> Without Milady, I wouldn't want to go there:
> She with the blonde head and shining face;
> For without her I wouldn't have any joy,
> Standing divided from my lady.

> *Io m'agio posto in core a Dio servire,*
> *com'io potesse gire im paradiso,*
> *al santo loco, c'agio audito dire,*
> *o' si mantien sollazo, gioco e riso.*
> *Sanza mia donna non vi voria gire,*

---

15. Canzone 6, 23–24, *The Poetry of Giacomo da Lentino*, ed. E. F. Langley (Cambridge, Mass., Harvard University Press, 1915), pp. 15–17.

quella c'à blonda testa e claro viso,
chè sanza lei nom porzeria gaudire,
estando da la mia donna diviso.[16]

Here we have a very close correlation of the spheres between which Bernart and William of Aquitaine hovered; here *mia donna* is stylistically the equivalent of Madonna. If the North French struck off the notion of a Celestial Paradise with Milady, preferring a happy nook in the woods with my lady, the Italians settled for nothing less than happiness, beauty, and peace eternal and enduring with their private goddesses.

It is amazing to see how the early Italians dote on the lower case abstraction:

> You have worth above
> all other women,
> and all wisdom;
> no man could ever
> reckon your value,
> for you're so beautiful.

> *Valor sor l'altre avete*
> *e tucta caunoscença,*
> *null'omo non poria*
> *vostro presio contare;*
> *Di tanto bella sete.*[17]

In this poem by Emperor Frederick II, we observe no social war, as in the lyrics of Gace Brulé and his contemporaries; here we encounter no abstract character named Value or Wisdom, but the abstract quality itself, which is not placed in juxtaposition with any opposing element. Here human love is exalted to the dizzy heights of religious idealism. The word *valor* in these lines of poetry has no close relationship to its kindred North French *valoir* and *vaillant*, where the meaning

16. Sonnet 15, 1–8, p. 73.
17. Canzone 2, 19–23, *Crestomazia italiana dei primi secoli*, ed. E. Monaci (Città di Castello, 1912), pp. 72–73.

often approaches the modern English "valor" or "excellence"; here the word means "worth" or "value," precisely what it means in a Latin philosophical treatise of the period.[18] The persistent attempts to link the early Sicilian vocabulary with the Provençal, though enlightening, have obscured the fact that the Italian vocabulary, even in its rudimentary stages of development, was awaiting the philosophical sanctions of Guido Guinizelli in Bologna and Dante and the *dolce stil nuovo* in Tuscany. Guittone d'Arezzo (c. 1225–94?) is usually considered a bridge between the Sicilians and Dante. Yet Dante himself detested Guittone's crude language and rhetorical trickery.[19] Guittone was an early-day Petrarch who loved to savor the melodious features of various sound combinations and also enjoyed dabbling in the age-old dialectic of love:

> Love, love, more bitter than poison.

> *Amore, Amor, più che veneno amaro.*[20]

The play on words between bitter (*amaro*) and love (*amore*) sounds like a desperate attempt to capture the flavor of Sappho's *glukuprikon;* here the conceit is far more successful than in Guittone's other Byzantine efforts. Guittone ended his life in a monastery hymning the Madonna, and his poems to the great lady of Christianity are far more moving than those he wrote to the hypothetical ladies of his *canzoni.*

18. For North French usage, see *Roman de la rose*, 5, 321; for Italian, *Le Rime di Guittone d'Arezzo*, ed. F. Egidi (Bari, 1940), p. 112, 36–38, where the context is ascetic and moral. However the word had ambiguous possibilities in both tongues; for the social usage in Dante, see *Inf.*, XVI.67.
19. *De vulg.*, I.13 and II.6.8; *Purg.*, XXIV.55–57, XXVI.124–26.
20. No. 14, 77, *Rime*, pp. 29–31. Other poets use the love-death paradox (*amor-mors*), as Guittone does in no. 7, 28, pp. 14–17: "*amore*" *quanto* "*ah, morte*" *vale a dire;* still others derived *amor* from *a-mors*, "deathless"; the North French connected their *amer* with the identical adjective meaning "mad, wild." Andreas Capellanus related *amor* to *hamus*, "hook" (*De amore*, 1.1), using Isidore as his source. Most of the meanings recall either Sappho's "death-less" or "bitter-sweet."

After the parenthesis that Guittone and his circle present, we have the incontestable appearance of the Italian genius in Guido Guinizelli (c. 1235–76?). His poem "Love always repairs to the gentle (noble) heart" is one of the most important lyrics ever written, for here the Christian-Platonic correspondences are fully spelled out in the opening stanza:

Love always repairs to the noble heart
as a bird nestles in the greenery of a wood;
nor did Nature make Love before noble hearts
nor noble hearts before she made Love.
For as soon as the Sun was made,
Then was its splendor brilliant:
A splendor that did not exist before the Sun.
So Love takes its place in nobleness
Exactly like the heat
In the clarity of fire.

Al cor gentil repara sempre amore
com'a la selva ausello 'n la verdura;
nè fe' amore anzi che gentil core,
nè gentil core anzi ch'amor, natura;
—ch'adesso com fo'l sole,
sì tosto lo splendore fo lucente,
nè fo davanti 'l sole—;
e prende amore 'n gentilezza loco
così propiamente
come calore 'n clarità di foco.[21]

In these lines, the medieval love birds have become mere metaphoric signs for the statement of a proposition that has far more than a purely natural application; human love is treated here under the same systematization as "the love that moves the sun and the other stars." Guido's poem is revolutionary; there is nothing quite like it in North French and

21. Text on pp. 31–35 of Mario Casella, "Al cor gentil repara sempre amore," *StR, 30* (1943), 5–53; cf. *Rimatori del dolce stil novo,* ed. L. di Benedetto (Bari, 1939), pp. 7–9.

Provençal literature, except perhaps Bernart's timid lines about "a wind from Paradise." Guido is not afraid of mentioning the Celestial Paradise (although at the end of the poem he retracts somewhat, apologizing a bit whimsically to God for mistaking his lady for an angel). The little birds warbling in the trees are natural symbols of a supernatural binding force that is the real subject of his poem. Guido later says:

> There shines in the Intelligences of Heaven
> God the Creator, more than the sun in our eyes;
> The Intelligence understands (intuits) its maker
>   beyond its heaven,
> And turning its own sphere obeys Him
> And obtains at once the blessed perfection
> That is willed to it by the just God.
> Likewise in truth, the beautiful lady
> Shining with noble power in the eyes of a noble man
> Should give pleasure to him who does not abandon her.
>
> (st. 5)

In reading these lines, we might well ask: what has happened to chivalry? where is the doctrine of social service? These "worldly service" elements merely vanish in the light of Christian mysticism; the poet is not a knight attending an earthly lady, as he is in a great deal of North French poetry, but not so often in the Provençal lyric; he is an intellectual worshiping an earthly reflection of a divinely perfect ideal. As Dmitri Scheludko has said, perhaps too exuberantly, of Guido's poem: "He takes over the whole Neoplatonic cosmology."[22] This cosmological tendency culminates with Dante's Beatrice; but even after Dante put his blessed one in a banquet with Mary and God, Petrarch continued to write of Laura in a way that emphasized her divine aspects as much as her social, physical

---

22. "Guinizelli und der Neuplatonismus," *DVLG, 12* (1934), 392: *"er übernimmt die ganze neuplatonische Kosmologie."* For an appreciation of Guido's originality, see E. G. Parodi, "La Lettura di Dante in Orsanmichele," *BSDI, 13* N.S. (1906), 241–70, esp. 247 f.

entity. The point is stated here merely to show that the social context in Italian poetry is of very little consequence. Italian literature does not begin with romantic epics and ladies conceived as mistresses of castles. It is not in any sense of the word "courtly." Italian literature begins with the erection of a philosophical system centered around human love, a system that was capable of challenging any other system that denied the glory of this human act. The eminent literary historian Francesco de Sanctis has said about Guinizelli: "The artist is a philosopher; he is not yet a poet."[23] Yet with Dante, who acknowledged Guinizelli's mastery,[24] the Italians found a man who could blend philosophical idealism with dramatic realism and thus create a medium in which he could write some of the world's most brilliant lines of poetry.

Yet it is difficult to speak of Dante without mentioning his close friend, Guido Cavalcanti. Guido was one of the last Italian lyricists to employ the spring motif in the medieval manner. He wrote a delicate, sensual pastorella which evokes some of the old splendor of Provence and culminates in a vision of the love god Amor.[25] Yet the pastourelle tradition never took hold in early Italian literature; it remained for the Renaissance poets, with their conscious working over of Vergilian and Ovidian themes, to evolve the standard Italian pastoral form.[26] Cavalcanti used the echoes of the nature-love poem in some of his lyrics which were conceived in the spirit of Guinizelli; one of these shows the exquisite, transcendental movement bequeathed by the Bolognese poet to the poets of Tuscany:

> You have in you the flowers and the greenery
> and all that's bright or beautiful to see.

23. *Storia della letteratura italiana*, ed. B. Croce (2 vols. Bari, 1912), *1*, 29: *"L'artista è un filosofo, non è ancora un poeta."*
24. *V.N.*, XX.3; *Purg.*, XXVI; *Conv.*, IV.20.7; *De vulg.*, I.15.6.
25. *Rime*, ed. G. Favati (Milan, 1957), p. 305.
26. E.g., Boiardo, *Canzoniere;* Lorenzo de'Medici, *Selve d'amore, Trionfo di Bacco e Arianna;* Poliziano, *Orfeo, Stanze.*

Avete 'n vo' li fior' e la verdura
e ciò che luce od è bello a vedere . . .[27]

Yet in the main Cavalcanti ignored the conventional setting. His poems to his "dark lady" express a hauntingly distrustful attitude toward woman and love. He has been labeled an Averrhoistic heretic, a Neoplatonist, an Aristotelian, and an orthodox Christian.[28] In the last analysis, since his poems have eluded all these tabs, he must simply be considered one of the greatest lyric poets of the Italian language, a man who was capable of describing the tragic bitterness of love as well as its grandeur and glory.

Dante tells us that Cavalcanti's mistress was nicknamed Lady Spring; she is the heroine of one of Guido's most lilting lyrics:

> Fresh, newborn (spring) rose,
> My pleasing Spring,
> Through field and river
> Gaily singing,
> Your noble worth I commit—to greenery.[29]

Yet during the course of the poem, Lady Spring moves out of the earthly setting into the broad expanses of heaven:

> An angelic likeness
> Rests in you, my lady;
> God, how good-fated
> Was my desire for you!
> Your joyous face,
> Since it passes and surpasses
> Nature and custom,
> Is a truly miraculous thing.
> Among themselves the ladies

27. *Rime*, p. 128, 1–2.
28. For a critical summary of the scholarship, see Shaw, *Cavalcanti's Theory*, pp. 147 ff.
29. *Rime*, pp. 125–26, 1–5.

Call you goddess, as you are:
You appear so well adorned
That I can't express it:
For who can describe—what's *beyond nature?* (19–31)

Cavalcanti brings us to the threshold of the *Vita Nuova*. Dante's work is itself a bridge between the earlier secular love poetry of Provence and the metaphysical poetry of Italy; his book ends precisely where his friend Cavalcanti's poem ends: with his beloved Beatrice having ceased to be a creature of flesh and blood and now existing as a divine abstraction, Beatitude or Bestower of Blessings. In fact, her transfiguration is stated dramatically in one of the final poems of the work, when Beatrice's name occurs in lower case: "She (Florence) has lost her beatitude" (*Ell'ha perduta la sua beatrice*).[30] In the very last poem, where the lady's transcendence is complete, Dante expresses his inability to recognize her as she appears to him in a heavenly vision; he stresses his ability to recall her only as she was on earth (XLI.12). Yet what connects him with her is a "new" intellectual power (*intelligenza nova*) created by a love that can yoke a pure spirit with a man who is still struggling with his desires on earth.

The word *nuova* or *nova* is perhaps the key to the whole transition. In the early parts of the work, the word frequently means "new" or "strange" (e.g., XIV.11; XV.1). In these sections, Dante, the young boy, experiences a typical romantic infatuation with a beautiful young girl. Much like the hero of the Provençal poetic novel *Flamenca*, he gazes at his beloved during mass at church (V.1–2); he swoons and becomes sick with the very thought of her beauty (IV, VII); he experiences nightmare visions in which Love appears symbolically as Death (III); he undergoes a frightful battle of the senses and

---

30. *V.N.*, XL.10, ed. M. Barbi, *Le Opere di Dante* (Florence, 1921), pp. 1–53. I am indebted to Enrico de'Negri for my interpretation; see his "Una leggenda nuova," *Wort und Text: Festschrift für Fritz Schalk* (Frankfurt am Main, 1963), 142–60.

the spirit, thinking alternately that love is evil and good (XIII–XIV).

Then, in the seventeenth chapter, he begins to treat "new and more noble material" (*matera nuova e più nobile*). Here the Provençal motifs begin to fade. The poem "Ladies who have intellect of love" (XIX.4) reveals the intellectual style of Guinizelli; here Dante's manner becomes more refined as his words become less secular and more religious. For example, in this seminal poem, he describes how God created Lady Beatrice in order to show mankind a "marvelous thing or operation" (*cosa nova*). From this point on, the word *nova* loses its negative, sensual meanings and acquires the positive, metaphysical meanings associated with the "miraculous new life" of Christian redemption from sin, as described by Augustine and St. Paul.[31]

In chapter XX, the poem "Love and the gentle heart are a single thing" is, as the poet himself confesses, an adaptation of Guinizelli's greatest work. Yet it remained for Dante to suffer the agony of Beatrice's death before he could thoroughly renounce the sensual side of love and embrace the spiritual; only when Beatrice herself became a pure spirit did the poet realize the true nature of love: it is not a pagan abstraction, even though Dante used the love god Amor as a symbol in his work; it is not merely a Neoplatonic force; it is a personal, felt power emanating from a created person, but originating with the Creator, and therefore capable of triumphing over death, the senses, indeed over life itself. In chapter XXIV, Dante makes this fusion of the natural and supernatural clear: Cavalcanti's lady, who was named Giovanna (feminine for John), often walked ahead of Beatrice through the streets of Florence, just as metaphorically John the Baptist preceded Christ. Giovanna was nicknamed Spring, and so, in terms of the underlying topos studied here, the somewhat pagan Spring of Cavalcanti (for Dante must have regarded her thus, pri-

31. *Civ. Dei* 12.20; *Serm.* 33, 336: *PL 38*, cols. 207, 1472; *Enarr. in Ps. 143: PL 37*, col. 1866; *Enarr. in Ps. 66, PL 36*, 808. *Rom.* 6:4; *Eph.* 4:24.

marily as a physical entity) preceded the redemptive Christian Spring of his own beloved lady. Even through the use of the ladies' secret names (and how mystical these names have become!), Dante begins the pagan-Christian fusion that accounts for the underlying methodology of his epic.

Dante as artist, Dante as philosopher—we must not ignore the double role. His love for Beatrice is the crowning point of medieval humanism, the affirmation of the splendor of human love that we do not find anywhere else, because the achievement is, as Eliot has suggested, "Dante's own."[32] After Gilson's book on the subject, it is possible to speak of Dante without slavishly citing St. Thomas Aquinas, except with reference to incidental teachings and turnings of plot.[33] To view Dante as the great perfector of "rhymed theology" is to ignore the fact that the *Comedy* (as well as the *De monarchia*) has always been a delicate matter with the Church itself, which prefers that people love Our Lady and not their own particular ladies. The philosophical side of the great poet abounds in originality; even given Guido Guinizelli, we cannot deduce Dante, although we may sense that Dante is the next, last step in the closing of the circle of medieval poetry: he entirely subsumes secular expression within religious expression in a way that was never done again.

For example, in terms of the topos studied here, he takes the spring of pastoral delight and baptizes it Christian:

> Those who in times of old poetized
> About the Golden Age and its happy state
> Perhaps dreamed about this place on Parnassus.
> Here the root of humanity was innocent;

32. "Dante," p. 235: "The system of Dante's organization of sensibility—the contrast between higher and lower carnal love, the transition from Beatrice living to Beatrice dead, rising to the Cult of the Virgin, seems to me to be his own." On the other hand, Dante's insistence upon the reality of the human condition and rejection of "vulgar spiritualism" has been brilliantly stated by Auerbach, *Dante: Poet of the Secular World*, tr. R. Manheim (Chicago, 1961).

33. *Dante the Philosopher*, tr. D. Moore (N.Y., 1949).

Here spring was eternal, eternal every fruit;
This river is the nectar of which they all sang.

Quelli c'anticamente poetaro
L'età de l'oro e suo stato felice,
Forse in Parnaso esto loco sognaro.
Qui fu innocente l'umana radice;
Qui primavera sempre, ed ogni frutto;
Nettare è questo, di che ciascun dice.

(*Purg.*, XXVIII.139–44)

In his *Qui primavera sempre,* Dante draws together the perpetual spring of Vergil's Golden Age in Italy (*Hic ver adsiduum*) and the Christian Paradise Lost; the age-old religious
dream of earthly perfection in a garden is extended to include
both cultures. The woman who speaks the lines is a Christian
nymph, Matilda, who weaves flowers on the banks of the rivers
of Purgatory and who is compared to the classical "nymph"
Proserpina.[34] Yet this "lovely place" is not a place for love,
as in Guillaume de Lorris' *Roman,* even though Dante's lady
soon appears here. Like Jean de Meun, Dante transforms the
natural setting into a religious tapestry permeated with Christian symbolism; a parade of the books of the Bible appears;
Beatrice the Blessed (representing the Celestial Paradise) appears; Vergil (representing the Earthly Paradise) vanishes in
the shadows. We advance to the true Paradise to come, which
is not a land of perpetual spring but a Christian cosmology of
harmony and light. Dante had little use for gardens of romantic adventure; he conceived of the Earthly Paradise as Polity,
and in this sense, Vergil, who immortalized the Empire of the
Caesars, is the most fitting guide to precede the angelic Beatrice, who steps down from the Empire of Christ.[35]

34. *Purg.*, XXVIII.49–51.
35. Stated in *De mon.*, II. Dante was perhaps the first person in the modern
world to read the *Georgics* seriously; his adaptation of Vergil's *Hic ver
adsiduum* is logical in a way that earlier Christian adaptations were not. For
a discussion of the religious elements, see Charles S. Singleton, *Dante Studies 2:
Journey to Beatrice* (Cambridge, Mass., 1958).

Having referred to Dante as a philosophical epic poet who evolved a framework of idealized human love *within a religious system*, we must now discuss Dante as a lyric poet and writer of tragedy. Dante himself, in his *De vulgari eloquentia*, paid far more attention to the lyrics of Provence than to the epics of northern France.[36] When we read the *Inferno*, we find the negative aspects of human love stated in poignant lyric monologues. For every person in modern Italy who can quote the idealized love dialogue between Dante and Beatrice (and very few can, simply because Beatrice is far more spiritual than real, awesome than lovable, and at times pedantic than compassionate), there are hundreds who can quote the lines describing the ill-fated love of Paolo and Francesca:

> *Amor, ch'a nullo amato amar perdona,*
> *Mi prese del costui piacer sì forte*
> *Che, come vedi, ancor non m'abbandona.*
>
> (*Inf.*, V.103–05)

And what was the spark that ignited this sensual flame? A book of Arthurian romance: *Noi leggiavamo . . . Di Lancialotto.*[37] Apparently the people of thirteenth-century Italy read those romantic epics in a way far different from that in which modern scholars read them; when a knight is bathed and lies with a woman in a North French romance, the people of the period (or at least such as Paolo and Francesca, who were otherwise quite noble) seem to have drawn a conclusion that most modern scholars will not accept. Even when Countess Beatriz of Dia cries out in a Provençal lyric, "O how I'd like to hold my knight naked one night in my arms!"[38] we are told that such

36. The focal point is contained in II.3.3: *"Horum autem modorum cantionum modum excellentissimum esse pensamus";* his reasons follow, with examples drawn largely from Provençal and Italian lyric poetry (5.4).

37. V.127–28. Francesca's condemnation contains the line *Galeotto fu il libro e chi lo scrisse!* (137). One need only think of Tennyson's *Idylls of the King* to note the difference in attitude.

38. Hill–Bergin, p. 53, 9–10.

affairs stopped short of complete possession because Andreas Capellanus tells us that they *ought* to. Of course, there are some who say that Francesca quoted the book merely to rationalize her "error"; however, if we examine the recesses of the Hell of Lust, we find Semiramis, Dido, Helen of Troy, and Tristan, the hero of what is probably the most famous of all medieval romances. Dante never confused the idealized rhetoric of romantic poetry with idealized behavior in external cultural history.

As for those who are only moderately stained by lust and who managed to maintain enough virtue to enter the road to salvation, we find Guido Guinizelli and the troubadour Arnaut Daniel. In their rung on Mount Purgatory, Guinizelli calls Provençal the "maternal tongue" of all poets: *parlar materno* (XXVI.117). It is here, perhaps even more than in the *De vulgari eloquentia,* that Dante's enormous respect for the lyric poets of southern France asserts itself. And it is in this enormous epic that their lyric outcries are corrected, idealized, and transcended.

After Dante had written, Italian poets faced an almost impossible problem: what was there left to do? Poetry could really take only one course: downward. The first step was taken by Petrarch, whose Laura is cast in the image of Beatrice, but who remains a living creature for a much longer period of time. While alive, Laura behaves like a *belle dame sans merci;* after her death, she becomes, like Beatrice, a *bella domina cum mercede.* Petrarch was fond of the Provençal dialectic; one of his finest poems, translated by Chaucer, shows his deft handling of paradox:

> If no love is, O God, what fele I so?
> And if love is, what thing and which is he?
> If love be good, from whennes cometh my woo?
> If it be wikke, a wonder thynketh me,
> When every torment and adversite

> That cometh of hym, may to me savory thinke,
> For ay thurst I, the more that ich it drynke.[39]

Petrarch determined the course of lyric poetry for the next few centuries; he is perhaps the complete poet in the sense that every image found in Ovid and the Provençal troubadours recurs somewhere in his *Rime*. But in resuscitating lyric poetry by divorcing it from the epic whole, Petrarch bequeathed to his successors a set of stock paradoxes that eventually led to a Petrarchan doctrine of rhetoric and to total decadence. His influence and achievement have been summarized by J. H. Whitfield:

> He was eclectic, open to the influences that lay within his view; and in this matter of techniques he put back into common circulation what else might have been buried with Guittone and the Provençals, something that was to remain an embarrassment until Marino (so much more successful than Petrarch in the matter of conceits, because they are for him the substance of poetic statement) sets the old frigidities alight in a baroque blaze of fireworks, thereby producing a new embarrassment.[40]

In other words, although paradox lies at the heart of lyric expression, Whitfield feels, quite rightly, that a poem must contain more than a mere statement of these contradictory elements. Many of Petrarch's poems do contain more than rhetorical artifice; but most of his imitators' poems do not. At any rate he, more than Dante even, strongly influenced subsequent lyric love poetry.

---

39. *Troilus and Criseyde*, I.400–06; in full, an imitation of Petrarch, *S'amor non è*, 1–6; text in *The Works of Geoffrey Chaucer*, ed. F. N. Robinson (2d ed. Boston, Houghton Mifflin, 1957), p. 393. Robinson notes (p. 815, n. 411): "The rhetorical figure of oxymoron in the description of love has been common in both ancient and modern literature."

40. *A Short History of Italian Literature* (Harmondsworth, Eng., Penguin Books, 1960), p. 29.

Meanwhile, in Giovanni Boccaccio, Italy found its François Villon far earlier than France had. In trying to bring Italian poetry back to earth, Boccaccio first attempted to create a romantic world in epic terms, after the model of northern France. His early efforts—*Il Filocolo, Teseida, Il Filostrato*— exist in that golden never-never land of adventurous forests and pleasurable gardens of love which dot the North French epic. Yet even in a long work such as the *Teseida,* elements of realistic laughter sometimes intrude to shake the mechanical workings of the robotlike characters. When Boccaccio consciously tried to duplicate the allegorical method of the *Roman de la rose,* as in painting his temples in the *Teseida,* he achieved Renaissance tableaux, as C. S. Lewis has pointed out,[41] and not a medieval philosophical tract. Perhaps Giovanni's failure boded well for the course of world poetry; it would have been fatal if he *had* been able to produce the twelfth-century achievements of France in fourteenth-century Italy.

In the last of his romantic productions, the *Ninfale Fiesolano,* Boccaccio shows some of the splendid mixture of styles which mark his unique place in literature; in telling the metamorphosis-like story of an Italian virgin nymph who is loved by a handsome shepherd, Giovanni blends Christian and pagan rhetoric, romance and realism, in a way that suggests Ovid more than any other poet. The finer features of the new paganism were moving abroad in the world, and the next step into the world of brutal reality had to be taken. Giovanni took it when he wrote the *Decameron,* where religious idealism can still be heard, romantic idealism is all but shattered, and most of the characters run rampant. Perhaps the most enormous gap in world literature lies between the closing line of the *Divine Comedy* and Boccaccio's description of his first protagonist, who loved life, wine, and women "the way a dog likes a tree."

41. *Allegory of Love,* pp. 174–76.

There is no point in indulging in that meaningless argument about the Renaissance or medieval quality of Boccaccio's work. Humanism and realism were implied in every way by the poems of William of Aquitaine, the father of the troubadour tradition. The word "Renaissance," with all its deceptively easy distinctions, is largely a product of Jakob Burckhardt and the nineteenth century; it is sometimes hard to tell the Late High Middle Ages from the Early Low Renaissance. Boccaccio stands somewhere between the two. At any rate, after Giovanni had written, the three major spheres of poetic inquiry all lay open for interpretation: the religious, the romantic, and the realistic. There is no point in analytically pursuing them further. The road lies open to Geoffrey Chaucer, with his singing bird parliaments, budding rose gardens, and pilgrims stirring restlessly but religiously under the warm breath of spring. Although many modern Chaucerians talk about Geoffrey in the same terms as are used for Augustine, Boethius, or a twelfth-century treatise writer, Chaucer comes later than they think. In fact, the Middle Ages itself, despite its constant *Grundriss,* shows phases of development which prepared the way for "modern" literature.

With Chaucer we enter a complex age, where poets have numerous choices: they may elect to write the supernatural vision, though few will do so after Dante; they may elect the intermediary world of romantic fiction, in which much of *Troilus and Criseyde* is written; or they may probe the essentially tragic world of the isolated individual, where Golias, Jaufré Rudel, Cavalcanti, and François Villon leave us. In terms of the topos studied here, they may write Easter hymns, as very few will do; may discover new hermetic landscapes of romance, as many will do, for Arcadia or the tropical island of Paul and Virginie are even more haunting for material, technological societies than they were to the urban Romans and Alexandrians; or they may explore the "real" world around them in the season of fruition. This last method is typically that of the modern lyric poet. William of Aquitaine is the literary kinsman of English poets who sport for a time with Amaryllis in the shade or gather rosebuds with Corinna, just as the lonely lady of the *Cambridge Songs* is related to Margaret grieving over autumnal wanwood, and the narrator of Chaucer's *Parliament of Foules* resembles Eliot's young-old narrator stumbling in the ruins of ideal gardens of present and past.

But if a Christian poet elects to write of the splendors of reality and sounds the inherently tragic grandeur of the lyric voice, he may, of course, eventually renounce Lady Tristan or Bel Vezer and hand his minks and sables over to God. He may return to that pastoral vision which has always been a part of the Indo-European literary tradition in which spring, the season of youth and love, is merely one of four seasons which form the great circle of fulfillment. For the lyric "I" and the epic "all" are never entirely removed from each other. Together they form the whole picture, just as the twisted frown of the tragic mask makes the wall look incomplete in the absence of the broad smile. The questions of life and love demand both responses, for these age-old *mysteries* may be resolved within *mysticism,* as in the epic, or they may be loosed on the wild winds of paradox, as in the lyric.

In the late Middle Ages, human love and human destiny emerged as questions out of the self-contained structure of mystical resolution which had been built over the shifting sands of the Greco-Roman paradoxical world view. The process of this emergence may be traced in the poetry which expressed it. This poetry quite naturally contains elements of high idealization; it moves with the metaphysical spirit of the age; indeed, the greatest poet of the age, Dante, could make the secular and the religious coincide. Yet to view this love poetry in its total form as a one-dimensional hymn to an earthly lady is to ignore both its provenance, which is religious, and its essence, which is ambiguous. For the "inventors" (*trobaire*) of Provence and their heirs speak about life and love in the bitter-sweet, major-minor modes that were first perfected in

Europe by the Ionian "makers" (*poietai*) of Greater Greece. Yet, at the same time, the poets of both these ages are not totally reconciled to the shadows of wintry death. These lyric voices speak from a romantic twilight that shrouds the shrines of Aphrodite, Persephone, Venus, and the Great Lady of Christianity, Mary, Star of the Sea. Their *twi*light essence suggests the total illumination of dawn; their unfulfilled schemata suggest fulfillment. In this sense, the greatest lyricists never stray entirely beyond the ken of hymnologists, just as the writers of secular romance paint their wandering heroes within the shadows of Olympus or the castle of the Grail. Together, these comic and tragic voices form the single, unified voice of the human psyche, that ambiguous entity that is common to all men for all time.

Appendix

A Comparison of Basic Tropes
Attached to the Spring-Youth-Romantic
Love Topos

I. LOVE CONQUERS ALL

1. Classical Latin (CL):
   Omnia vincit amor (Vergil, *Ecl.* 10.69)
   Positive voice in a love dialogue.

2. Medieval Church Latin (MCL):
   amor omnia Christi | vincit
   (Paulinus of Nola, *CSEL 30, 2,* no. 14, 79–80)
   Christian metaphoric raising; absolute monistic idealism.

3. Medieval Secular Latin (MSL):
   Vincit Amor omnia (*CB,* no. 56, st. 4, 17–18)
   Secular leveling; destruction of idealism; the poet asserts material love, but without tension.

4. Old Provençal (OP):
   amors . . . totas causas ventz
   (Arnaut de Mareuil, *Domna, genser* 212)
   Secular idealism; again no ambiguity. Arnaut shows the tendency of later Provençal verse to flatten into mere social panegyric. The classical troubadours avoid the sententia entirely.

5. Old North French (ONF):
   Amours vaint tout (*Roman de la rose* 21,332)
   The sentiment is very much a part of the North French epic-didactic tradition.

II. PERPETUAL SPRING (an ideal of religion and romance; the notion is conspicuously absent from lyric poetry)

1. CL: *Hic ver adsiduum* (Vergil, *Georg.* 2.149)
   The Golden Age, the lost ideal of Olympic religion, is applied to Augustus' Italy; the ideal is a reality.
   ver erat aeternum (Ovid, *Meta.* 1.107)
   Struggle to retain a religious ideal against a romantic outpouring of loss, but with comic overtones.
   vere fruor semper (*Fasti* 5.207)
   The goddess Flora as romantic heroine.
   pater . . . veris, | qui . . . regnas . . . | semper
   (Claudian, *De raptu* 73–75)

The conquest of romance; vital mysticism debased to romantic mystery; no application to reality; the Underworld knows spring too.

2. MCL: *Hic ver adsiduum* (Avitus, *De mundi initio* 222)
Eden, the lost ideal of Christianity, is based upon the Golden Age in rhetorical portraits. There is no application to reality, as in Vergil, nor any romantic subjectivism, as in Ovid. Similar treatment in Proba, Dracontius, Marius Victor, etc.
Ver ubi perpetuum redolet (Prudentius, *Cath.* 3.103)
The Christians also apply the rhetoric to the afterlife; the portrait is purely metaphysical; allegory in its early phases.

3. ONF: *Lors ireiz ou champ deliteus,*
Par trace l'aignelet sivant,
En pardurableté vivant,
Beivre de la bele fontaine (*Roman* 20,648–651)
The *Roman* contains both the new romantic garden of spring delight where Ovidian and Christian elements are fused in secular terms (Guillaume's part) and the standard Christian vision of pastoral bliss (Jean's part).

4. It: *Qui primavera sempre* (Dante, *Purg.*, XXVIII.143)
Brilliant combination of Christian and classical rhetoric in a purely religious sphere. The ancient pastoral tradition is, however, passed by, and Dante enters the abstract Christian-Neoplatonic cosmology.

III. THE DAWN

1. CL: *Quo properas, Aurora? mane!* ...
lente currite, Noctis equi! ...
invida, quo properas? (Ovid, *Am.* 1.13.3, 40, 33)
Aurora, a goddess and hence a particular agent of nature or reality, is envious of the poet's love; the lover despises nature and places the self above the cosmos.
detinenda tota nox est, perviglanda canticis (*Perv. Ven.* 46)
The night is meant for love and poetry; the darkness is good, and light is evil. The vigil is related to earthly love (*amor*).

2. MCL: *Tu rumpe noctis vincula ...*
   Vigilate, iam sum proximus
   (Prudentius, *Cath.* 1.98, 8)
   Night, darkness, and human love are negative factors in a
   traditional dualistic system inherited from earlier Stoic alle-
   gorizers and observable in Cleanthes; the dawn, light, and
   day are symbols of Christ. Each earthly dawn is but a *figura*
   for the One Dawn of Salvation. The vigil exists for the love
   (*caritas*) of Christ. (N.B. The old Latin word for dawn, *aurora*,
   is dropped because of the pagan mythic connotation; a new
   word, *lux* [light], is used.)

3. MCL? MSL?: *Fert aurora lumen terris tenue ...*
   OP: *L'alba par umet mar atra sol*
   (*Phebi claro* 2, 4)
   The blending of the Christian and pagan traditions is observable in the use of *aurora* and *alba* (the new Romance
   word meaning "white" which replaces Prudentius' "light" to
   describe the dawn). Is the poem religious? Secular?

4. OP: *Oi Deus, oi Deus, de l'alba! Tan tost ve!*
   (*En un vergier*, refrain)
   Return to the secular conditions of an Ovidian alba, but the
   Christian God's name (not his agent Nature's) is taken in
   vain. The poem shows the descent from religious to romantic
   idealism.

IV. THE VIRGIN

1. CL: *Virgo:* ambiguous: young girl? virgin?
   In Latin prose, it is best translated "young girl" unless the
   context demands the other meaning (i.e. Vestal Virgin). Ovid
   uses *puella* for his "girl" (*Ars Am.* 1.244; 2.673, etc.), since
   chastity or extreme youth are obviously evils to a lover.
   ipsa Laurentem puellam conjugem nato dedit:
   moxque Marti de sacello dat pudicam virginem.
   (*Perv. Ven.* 70–71)
   Diana (symbolic of Chastity) is driven away in favor of Venus
   (symbolic of Love in all its multiple phases). The poet makes
   a clear distinction between the "young girl, maiden" Lavinia

and the Vestal Virgin Rhea. The Vestals, though few in number, anticipated the Christian nuns.

2. MCL: *Ave, maris stella* . . .
   Virgo singularis   (*An. Hymn.* 2, no. 29, 1, 17)
   The word has begun to assume its purely idealized meaning, since Chastity is a Christian virtue. The goddess Venus lingers on as an evil power; the lower case *venus* is an abstraction meaning "lust"; in the *Perv. Ven.* 76, it meant "desire" in an idealized sense. The Virgin Mary replaces Diana as a symbol of chastity; Eve, who belongs to the Christian frame of reference, gradually replaces Venus, who is willed by Christian antifeminists to poets (who always worshiped her more than philosophers or priests in the first place). In the hearts of hymnologists, Mary is the ruler of the realm of Love.

3. MSL: *ave, decus virginum,*
   virgo gloriosa   (*CB,* no. 77, st. 8)
   A "young girl" who is later seduced is addressed in the rhetoric reserved for the Virgin.
   Magnetem verum iterat
   virgo mire perfecta   (Schmeller, no. 36, st. 12, 1–2)
   The technique is the same as in the above sample, but the context is far more serious; this young girl may *be* a virgin (i.e. an object worthy of veneration).

4. OP: The word *verge(na)* is restricted to hymns to the Virgin Mary, the first poems written in the language. The Romance word means simply "virgin"; it has only the idealized meaning, unlike Classical *virgo.* New words, often of Germanic origin, supply the neutral word for "young girl": *toza, piucella, ragazza, muchacha, jeune fille.* The beloved of the lyric poets is a *dom(p)na:* see The Lady. The troubadours do not call their loved ones virgins because Chastity meant no more to William or Bernart than it did to Ovid; as in the *Roman,* Chastity is an enemy of the secular lover. The troubadours are too subtle to employ the word for comic parody, as in the cruder *Burana.*

5. It: *Vergine Madre, figlia del tuo Figlio*   (*Par.,* XXXIII.1)
   Dante combines the great hymn to Mary with his love songs

to Beatrice, thus bringing the secular totally within the framework of the religious; after the *Comedy*, however, the strains diverge again.

V. THE LADY

1. CL: *arbitrio dominae tempora perde tuae!* (*Ars Am.* 1.504)
   sunt tibi cum domina signa ferenda tua (*Am.* 2.3.10)
   paruit imperio dominae Tirynthius heros
   (*Ars Am.* 2.221)
   Ovid developed the notion of the beloved as *domina* ("lady or mistress of the heart"). The Latin word was applied to the wives of plantation owners, who became the dukes of medieval estates, and the great ladies of the Roman aristocracy. The word was also applied to goddesses: to Venus by Ovid, Cybele by Vergil, etc. Ovid's poetry has a socioreligious frame of reference, but his *mystica fides* was not erected against the structure of a dogmatic religion. Ovid avoids the ordinary "woman" word, *femina*.

2. MCL: *Te Deum laudamus, te Dominum confitemur.*
   (*Te Deum* 1)
   o mater virgo . . .
   sponsa, columba, domus regina, fidelis amica
   (*Oxford*, no. 84, 28, 30)
   Ave, mater verbi summi . . .
   Angelorum domina. (*An. Hymn.* *54*, no. 218, 17, 20)
   Despite early reluctance on the part of the Church in encouraging Mariolatry, the Virgin Mary by the eleventh century had firmly become the Great Lady of Christianity; to some extent she rivaled the less tangible Holy Ghost as the dominant Spirit of Love. She was also the "friend" (*amica*) to mankind. Mary was a great humanizing force in Christianity; undoubtedly she helped to raise the general concept of womanhood, for she embodied the idealized feminine virtues.

3. MSL: *Ne miretur ducis tante*
   quis sublimitatem . . . (Schmeller, no. 36, st. 7, 1–2)
   mea dux,
   te mea lux (ibid., st. 29, 4–5)

The earthly woman is an earthly lord (*dux*). Is this an attempt to endow her with powers in the social sphere that she obviously did not have? Or is it simply comic? Ovid called his girl a friend in order to raise her to the level of masculinity; the *Burana*, however, often draw much of their inspiration from hymns to the great "friend" Mary:

> *singularem et pudicam*
> *te adoptabat in amicam.* (Schmeller, no. 158, st. 3, 3–4)

The *Burana* poets prefer the stronger word *virgo* to *domina;* the troubadours reverse the process.

4. OP: *D'aisso.s fa be femna parer*
ma domna, per qu'e.lh o retrai . . .

> (Bernart, *Can vei* 33–34)

My lady (*ma domna*) means, on the metaphysical plane, Madonna; on the physical plane, she is an earthly lady with political power (and hence akin to Ovid's *domina*). However, she can fall even farther and become a "mere woman" (*femna*). The lyric poets of Provence do not use the word *amiga* much because it is not sublime enough; they avoid the highly charged *vergena* and never praise chastity.

5. ONF: *A l'entrer fu bien recueilly*
Des dames et des damoiselles
Et de celles bien accueilly
Qui toutes sont bonnes et belles

> (Alain Chartier, *La belle dame* 65–68)

The North French lady is the Madame of high society. The poetry is directed toward the social or courtly sphere, and religious overtones are not emphasized.

6. It: *chè sanza lei nom porzeria gaudire,*
estando da la mia donna diviso.

> (Giacomo da Lentino, *Poetry*, p. 73, 7–8)

In Italian, *mia donna* becomes closely identified with Madonna. Secular rhetoric is raised to the height of religious idealism until Dante's Beatrice sits near Mary in the divine assembly.

VI. A Lover Is Like a Ship at Sea

1. CL: *auferor ut rapida concita puppis aqua.*   (*Am.* 2.4.8)
   The classic statement by Ovid.

2. MCL: *Navis nunquam turbata,*
   quamvis fluctibus tonsa   (*Oxford,* no. 50, 9–10)
   The conceit is denied by the Christians, whose love is steady
   and abiding.

3. MSL: *navicula*
   levis in equore,
   dum caret anchore subsidio
                         (Schmeller, no. 159, st. 3, 3–5)
   Reaffirmed by the *Burana* poets.

4. OP: *c'atressi.m ten en balansa*
   com la naus en l'onda   (Bernart, *Tant ai mo cor* 39–40)

   . . . sui plus despers
   Per sobramar
   Que naus, can vai torban per mar
   Destrecha d'ondas e de vens.   (Guiraut, *Can lo glatz* 35–38)
   Perpetuated by the troubadours.

VII. Love Is a Flame

1. CL: *fervida vicino flamma vapore nocet*   (*Am.* 1.2.46)
   tenuis sub artus
   Flamma demanat (Catullus, 51.9–10; adapted from Sappho)
   The classical statement—with awe and fear.

2. MCL: *O beatum incendium,*
   o ardens desiderium,
   o dulce refrigerium
   amare Dei filium.   (*Oxford,* no. 233, 113–16)
   Christians adore the flaming love of Jesus; however, they
   castigate the flames of earthly love (*Conf.* 3.1: *sartago fla-*
   gitiosorum amorum).

3. MSL: *Fave, Venus, tenero*
   ignem movens,
   ignem fovens,
   ne mori sit quod vixero   (Schmeller, no. 31, 43–46)
   The flame of secular love has now become idealized by the
   Burana poets.

4. OP: *m'eslaissei eu vas trop amar un jorn,*
   c'anc no.m gardei, tro fui en mei la flama
   (Bernart, *Be m'an perdut* 10–11)
   No.m meravilh s'ieu n'aflam   (Rudel, *Quan lo rius* 16)
   The troubadours regard the flame with mixed emotions; Ber-
   nart attributes it to excessive love.

5. It: Dante uses the flames of the Christian Purgatory (XXV,
   XXVI) to purify the troubadours of their worldly desires.

VIII. The Lover Is a Servant or Slave Who Acts in Faith

1. CL: *accipe, per longos tibi qui deserviat annos,*
   accipe, qui pura norit amare fide! ...
   non mihi mille placent, non sum desultor amoris:
   tu mihi, siqua fides, cura perennis eris.
   (*Am.* 1.3.5–6, 15–16)
   Siquis erit, qui turpe putet servire puellae,
   illo convincar iudice turpis ego   (*Am.* 2.17.1–2)
   Ovid evolved and documented the "doctrine," half comically,
   half seriously, allowing later ages to interpret it as they would
   (note that the conceit is an underlying principle of his *Art of
   Love*).

2. MCL: *O Deus, miseri*
   miserere servi.
   Tu me, Domine, fecisti,
   Ut servirem tibi ...   (*An. Hymn. 50,* no. 170, st. 2)
   Ergo cave, ne suave
   Iugum spernas Domini,
   Nec abiecta lege recta
   Servias libidini.   (*An. Hymn. 50,* no. 323, st. 14)
   The Christian serves God, not a lady, with his love and faith.

3. MSL: *Psallo tibi soli,*
   despicere me noli,
   per me precor velis coli (Schmeller, no. 158, st. 8, 1–3)
   The *Burana* poet serves and worships a lady.

4. OP: *Bona domna, re no.us deman*
   mas que.m prendatz per servidor,
   qu'e.us servirai com bo senhor
   (Bernart, *Non es meravelha* 49–51)
   ... don tant m'azaut
   Qu'al sieu servir
   Sui del pe tro c'al coma.
   (Arnaut Daniel, *L'aura amara* 32–34)
   The doctrine of service is given new dogmatic secular authority by the troubadours, who combine the social-religious connotations of such words as "faith," "service," "servant," etc.

5. For the North French secularization of the rhetoric and the Italian idealization, see Chapter 4.

IX. LOVE INVOLVES DEATH

1. CL: *Vota mori mea sunt, cum te peccare recordor* (*Am.* 2.5.3)
   tunc amo, tunc odi frustra, quod amare necessest;
   tunc ego, sed tecum, mortuus esse velim.
   (*Am.* 3.14.39–40)
   Ovid stated the conceit impressively in terms of a cruelly enigmatic earthly lady.

2. MCL: *Ab omni mortis impetu*
   Tuum defendas populum.
   (*An. Hymn. 51,* no. 83, st. 7, 3–4)
   Iesus cum sic diligitur,
   hic amor non extinguitur;
   nec tepescit nec moritur (*Oxford,* no. 233, 117–19)
   A Christian's love of Christ leads to the triumph over death (*mors mortis*); however, secular love is entirely a death: *ita duae voluntates meae, una vetus, alia nova, illa carnalis, illa spiritalis, confligebant inter se* (*Conf.* 8.5).

3. MSL: *Amare crucior, morior*
     vulnere, quo glorior. (Schmeller, no. 42, st. 2, 9–10)
   The *Burana* poet transfers idealized spiritual love to the love
   of an earthly lady. His love-death has the glory of the martyr
   about it.

4. OP: *cen vetz mor lo jorn de dolor*
     e reviu de joi autras cen.
     (Bernart, *Non es meravelha* 27–28)
   mor se.l vostr'amaire! . . .
   gran mal me faitz traire! (*Tant ai mo cor* 54, 60)
   S'elha no.m vol, volgra moris
     (Cercamon, *Quant l'aura doussa* 43)
   The conceit is much more complicated: at times, it has the
   new Christian martyr ring; at other times, it embodies the
   love-death, grief-joy paradoxes of classical poetry.

5. It: *"amore" quanto "ah, morte" vale a dire*
     (Guittone, *Rime*, p. 14, 28)
   Moral Christian poets continue to regard earthly love as a
   prelude to death; Dante, however, made Beatrice the angelic
   guide to perpetual life, thus rejecting the secular dilemma.
   With Petrarch the hell of human love is again dramatically
   stated, but always with reference to Dante's *Paradiso*.

X. LOVE IS WAR (IT MAY THUS BE: A. DESTRUCTIVE; OR B. GOOD FOR THE SOUL)

1. CL: *Militat omnis amans, et habet sua castra Cupido*
     (*Am.* 1.9.1)
   credibilest et te sensisse Cupidinis arcus:
   in me militiae signa tuere tuae! (*Am.* 1.11.11–12)
   quid me, qui miles numquam tua signa reliqui,
   laedis, et in castris vulneror ipse meis?
   cur tua fax urit, figit tuus arcus amicos? (*Am.* 2.9.3–5)
   A. Ovid describes the horrors of war under Lord Cupid.
   militis officium longast via: mitte puellam,
   strenuus exempto fine sequetur amans . . .
   Ergo desidiam quicumque vocabat amorem,
   desinat: ingeniist experientis amor. (*Am.* 1.9.9–10, 31–32)

(*Amor odit inertes*):
si rota defuerit, tu pede carpe viam . . .
militiae species amor est; discedite, segnes!
non sunt haec timidis signa tuenda viris;
nox et hiemps longaeque viae saevique dolores
mollibus his castris et labor omnis inest.

(*Ars Am.* 2.229–30, 233–36)

B. But he also sang, sometimes tongue in cheek, about its glory.

2. MCL: *Inferni claustra penetrans,*
      Tuos captivos redimens,
      Victor triumpho nobili
      Ad dextram patris residens

(*An. Hymn. 51,* no. 89, st. 3)

Sacratissimi martyres summi Dei,
bellatores fortissimi Christi regis,
potentissimi duces exercitus Dei,
victores in caelis Deo canentes: Alleluia.

(*Oxford,* no. 52, 1–4)

The Christian soldier fights for the love of Christ, and his suffering is *entirely* glorious. The negative side of the dialectic would, however, be applied to mortal love, as in Augustine's *Confessions.*

3. MSL: *Ergo militemus*
      simul Veneri,
      tristia vitemus
      nos qui teneri   (Schmeller, p. 184, 12–15)

The *Burana* poets transfer the glory of the Christian soldier's fight back into the realm of Venus and Cupid.

4. OP: *Enquer me membra d'un mati*
      Que nos fezem de guerra fi

(William, *Ab la dolchor* 19–20)

Truan, mala guerra
Sai volon comensar
Domnas d'esta terra

(Raimbaut de Vaqueiras, *Truan, mala guerra* 1–3)

Et es tan greus
La guerra devas totas partz
                    (Guiraut de Bornelh, *Can lo glatz* 44–45)
. . . *d'amor son gran poder,*
Per so car vens princes, ducs e marques
                    (Guiraut de Calanso, *Celeis cui am* 4–5)
The old horror and the glory are once again voiced in the brilliant lines of the troubadours.

5. It: *Amor, pur vincer creo,*
   combattendo per Deo;
   ed ho le mie battaglie sì ordinate:
   contra disamor, fede;
   contr'orgoglio, merzede;
   e contra di ferezza, umilitate
                    (Guittone, *Rime,* p. 51, 61–66)
   Guittone clearly applies standard Christian terminology in describing his war to win his lady.

Select Bibliography

CHAPTERS 1 AND 2

Allen, Archibald W., "Elegy and the Classical Attitude toward Love: Propertius I, 1," *YCS, 11* (1950), 253–77.

Allen, P. S., "Mediaeval Latin Lyrics," *MP, 5* (Jan. 1908), 423–76; *6* (July 1908), 3–43, (Oct. 1908), 97–180, (Jan. 1909), 385–406.

———, *Mediaeval Latin Lyrics,* Chicago, 1931.

Analecta Hymnica Medii Aevi, ed. G. M. Dreves, C. Blume, H. M. Bannister, 55 vols. Leipzig, 1886–1922.

Auerbach, Erich, *Dante: Poet of the Secular World,* tr. R. Manheim, Chicago, 1961.

———, "*Passio* als Leidenschaft," *PMLA, 56* (1941), 1179–96.

———, *Typologische Motive in der mittelalterlichen Literatur,* Krefeld, 1953.

———, Review, *RP, 4* (1950–51), 65–67.

Beare, William, *Latin Verse and European Song: A Study in Accent and Rhythm,* London, 1957.

Bezzola, Reto R., *Les Origines et la formation de la littérature courtoise en Occident (500–1200),* 2 vols., 3 pts. Paris, 1944–60.

Biese, Alfred, *Die Entwicklung des Naturgefühls im Mittelalter und in der Neuzeit,* 2d ed. Leipzig, 1892.

Bowra, C. M., *Greek Lyric Poetry from Alcman to Simonides,* Oxford, 1936.

Breul, Karl, *The Cambridge Songs,* Cambridge, Eng., 1915.

Brinkmann, Hennig, *Entstehungsgeschichte des Minnesangs, DVLG, 8* (1926).

———, *Geschichte der lateinischen Liebesdichtung im Mittelalter,* Halle, 1925.

Bulst, Walther, *Carmina Cantabrigiensia,* Heidelberg, 1950.

Bury, J. B., "On the *Perv. Ven.*," *CR, 19* (1905), 304.

Carmina Burana, ed. W. Meyers, A. Hilka, and O. Schumann,

2 vols., 3 pts. (incomplete) Heidelberg, 1930–41 (see also Schmeller).

Chandler, Albert R., "The Nightingale in Greek and Latin Poetry," *CJ, 30* (1934), 78–84.

Clementi, Cecil, *Bibliographical and Other Studies on the Perv. Ven.,* Oxford, 1913 (see also *Perv. Ven.*).

Copley, Frank O., *Exclusus Amator: A Study in Latin Love Poetry,* Philol. Monographs of Am. Philol. Ass., 17 (1956).

Cornford, F. M., *From Religion to Philosophy,* N.Y., 1957.

Corpus Scriptorum Ecclesiasticorum Latinorum, ed. Academia Litterarum Vindobonensis (Scientiarum Austriaca), 78 vols. Vienna, 1866–date.

Cumont, Franz, *Oriental Religions in Roman Paganism,* N.Y., 1956.

Curtius, Ernst Robert, *European Literature and the Latin Middle Ages,* tr. W. R. Trask, Bollingen Series, 36, N.Y., 1953.

Dodds, E. R., *The Greeks and the Irrational,* Berkeley–Los Angeles, 1951.

Duckett, E. S., *Alcuin, Friend of Charlemagne,* N.Y., 1951.

Frank, Erich, *St. Augustine and Greek Thought,* Cambridge, Mass., 1942.

Fränkel, Hermann, *Ovid: A Poet between Two Worlds,* 2d ed. Berkeley–Los Angeles, 1956.

Ganzenmüller, Wilhelm, *Das Naturgefühl im Mittelalter,* Leipzig, 1914.

Hanford, J. H., "The Progenitors of Golias," *Speculum, 1* (1926), 38–58.

Hughes, Dom Anselm, ed., *New Oxford History of Music, 2: Early Medieval Music up to 1300,* 2d ed. Oxford, 1955.

Jackson, W. T. H., *The Literature of the Middle Ages,* N.Y., 1960.

Jaeger, Werner, *Paideia: The Ideals of Greek Culture,* tr. G. Highet, 2d ed. 3 vols. N.Y.–Oxford, 1943–45.

Lewis, C. S., *The Allegory of Love,* N.Y., 1958.

Lieberg, Godo, *Puella Divina: Die Gestalt der göttlichen Geliebten bei Catull im Zusammenhang der antiken Dichtung,* Amsterdam, 1962.

Luck, Georg, *The Latin Love Elegy,* London, 1959.

Mackail, J. W., "The *Perv. Ven.,*" *JP, 17* (1888), 179–91.

Manitius, Maximilian, *Vagantenlieder aus der lateinischen Dich-*

tung des 12 und 13 Jahrhunderts: Carmina Burana, Germ. tr.
R. Ulich, Jena, 1927.

Monumenta Germaniae Historica: Auctores Antiquissimi, 15 vols.
Berlin, 1877–1961.

Monumenta Germaniae Historica: Poetae Latini Aevi Carolini,
6 vols. Berlin, 1881–1951.

Neumann, Erich, *Amor and Psyche: The Psychic Development of
the Feminine (A Commentary on the Tale by Apuleius),* tr. R.
Manheim, Bollingen Series, 54, N.Y., 1956.

Nicolson, Marjorie Hope, *Mountain Gloom and Mountain Glory:
The Development of the Aesthetics of the Infinite,* Ithaca, 1959.

Ovid, *Opera,* ed. R. Merkel and R. Ehwald, 3 vols. Leipzig, 1910–
14.

Oxford Book of Medieval Latin Verse, ed. F. J. E. Raby, rev. ed.
Oxford, 1959.

Parry, Adam, "Landscape in Greek Poetry," *YCS, 15* (1957), 3–29.

Patrologiae cursus completus: Series Latina, ed. J. P. Migne, 221
vols. Paris, 1844–80.

Pervigilium Veneris, ex editione Petri Pithoei, cum eius et Iusti
Lipsii notis; itemque ex alio codice antiquo, cum notis Cl.
Salmasii et Pet. Scriverii; accessit ad haec Andr. Rivini com-
mentarius . . ., Hagae Comitum, 1712.

———, *Poetae Latini Minores, 3,* ed. J. Wernsdorf, Altenburg, 1782.

———, ed. F. Bücheler, Leipzig, 1859.

———, *Poetae Latini Minores, 4: Anthologia Latina,* ed. E. Bährens,
Leipzig, 1882.

———, *Catullus with the,* ed. S. G. Owen, London, 1893.

———, ed. and tr. C. Clementi, Oxford, 1911.

———, *in Quatrains,* ed. J. A. Fort, preface J. W. Mackail, Oxford,
1922.

———, ed. and tr. C. Clementi, 3d ed. Oxford, 1936.

———, *La Veillée de Vénus,* ed. R. Schilling, Paris, 1944.

———, *Aphrodite: The Homeric Hymn to Aphrodite and the,* tr.
F. L. Lucas, Cambridge, Eng., 1948.

———, *Catullus, Tibullus and,* tr. J. W. Mackail and others, Loeb
Classical Library, rev. ed. London, 1962.

Poetae Melici Graeci, ed. D. Page, Oxford, 1962.

Poetarum Lesbiorum Fragmenta, ed. E. Lobel and D. Page, Oxford, 1955.

Prudentius, *Carmina*, ed. T. Obbarius, Tübingen, 1845.

Quinn, Kenneth, *The Catullan Revolution*, Melbourne, 1959.

Raby, F. J. E., *A History of Christian–Latin Poetry from the Beginnings to the Close of the Middle Ages*, 2d ed. Oxford, 1953.

——, *A History of Secular Latin Poetry in the Middle Ages*, 2 vols. Oxford, 1934.

——, "Philomena praevia temporis amoeni," *Mélanges Joseph de Ghellinck*, 2 vols. Gembloux, 1951, 2, 435–48 (see also *Oxford Book*).

Rahner, Hugo, *Greek Myths and Christian Mystery*, tr. B. Battershaw, London, 1963.

Rand, E. K., *Founders of the Middle Ages*, Cambridge, Mass., 1928.

——, "Sur le *Perv. Ven.*," *REL, 12* (1934), 83–95.

Reitzenstein, Erich, "Das neue Kunstwollen in den *Amores* Ovids," *RMP, 84* (1935), 62–88.

Robertson, D. S., "The Date and Occasion of the *Perv. Ven.*," *CR, 52* (1938), 109–12.

Schmeller, J. A., ed., *Carmina Burana: Lateinische und deutsche Lieder und Gedichte . . .*, 3d ed. Stuttgart, 1894; 4th ed. 1907.

Segal, Charles Paul, "Nature and the World of Man in Greek Literature," *Arion, 2*, pt. 1 (1963), 19–53.

Snell, Bruno, *The Discovery of the Mind*, tr. T. G. Rosenmeyer, Oxford, 1953.

Strecker, Karl, *Die Cambridger Lieder (Carmina Cantabrigiensia)*, *PLAC*, Suppl., Berlin, 1926.

Sullivan, J. P., ed., *Critical Essays on Roman Literature: Elegy and Lyric*, Cambridge, Mass., 1962.

——, "Cynthia Prima Fuit: A Causerie," *Arion, 1*, pt. 3 (1962), 34–44.

Süssmilch, Holm, *Die lateinische Vagantenpoesie des 12 und 13 Jahrhunderts als Kulturerscheinung*, Leipzig, 1917.

Taylor, Charles H., Jr., ed., *Essays on the Odyssey: Selected Modern Criticism*, Bloomington, 1963.

Unger, Hermann, *De ovidiana in Carminibus Buranis*, Strassburg, 1914.

Vuolo, Emilio P., "Iam, dulcis amica, venito," *CN, 10* (1950), 5–25.

Waddell, Helen, *Mediaeval Latin Lyrics*, 5th ed. London, 1948.

——, *The Wandering Scholars*, 7th ed. London, 1949.

Whicher, George F., tr., *The Goliard Poets*, N.Y., 1949.

CHAPTERS 3 AND 4

Andreas Capellanus, *De amore*, ed. S. Battaglia, Rome, 1902.
Anglade, Joseph, *Histoire sommaire de la littérature méridionale au moyen âge*, Paris, 1921.
———, *Les Troubadours*, 2d ed. Paris, 1919.
Appel, Carl, ed., *Provenzalische Chrestomathie*, 6th ed. Leipzig, 1930 (see also Bernart).
Axhausen, Käte, *Die Theorien über den Ursprung der provenzalischen Lyrik*, Marburg, 1937.
Bartsch, Karl, *Chrestomathie provençale*, 6th ed. rev. E. Koschwitz, Marburg, 1904.
Beck, J.-B., *Die Melodien der Troubadours*, Strassburg, 1908.
Becker, Philipp August, "Vom christlichen Hymnus zum Minnesang," *HJGG, 52* (1932), 145–77.
Bernart de Ventadorn, *Ausgewählte Lieder*, ed. C. Appel, Halle, 1926.
———, *Seine Lieder*, ed. C. Appel, Halle, 1915.
———, *The Songs of*, ed. S. G. Nichols, Jr., J. A. Galm, and others, Univ. of No. Car. Studies in Romance Langs. and Lit., 39 (1962).
Burdach, Konrad, "Über den Ursprung des mittelalterlichen Minnesangs, Liebesromans und Frauendienstes," *Vorspiel: Gesammelte Schriften*, 2 vols. Halle (1925–26), *1*, pt. 1, 253–333.
Cantera, Francisco, "Versos españoles en las *muwaššaḥas* hispanohebreas," *Sefarad, 9* (1949), 197–234.
Casella, Mario, "Al cor gentil repara sempre amore," *StR, 30* (1943), 5–53.
———, "Poesia e storia," *ASI, 96*, pt. 2 (1938), 3–63, 153–99.
Cercamon, *Poésies*, ed. A. Jeanroy, Paris, 1922.
Chailley, Jacques, "Les premiers Troubadours et les versus de l'école d'Aquitaine," *Romania, 76* (1955), 212–39.
———, "Notes sur les troubadours, les versus et la question arabe," *Mélanges . . . à la mémoire d'István Frank*, Saarbrücken, 1957, pp. 118–28.
Charles d'Orléans, *Poésies*, ed. P. Champion, 2 vols. Paris, 1923–27.
Chaytor, Henry John, *The Troubadours*, Cambridge, Eng., 1912.
Dante Alighieri, *La Divina Commedia*, ed. C. H. Grandgent, rev. ed. Boston, 1933.

——, *Le Opere,* ed. M. Barbi, E. G. Parodi, and others, Florence, 1921.

De'Negri, Enrico, "Una leggenda nuova," *Wort und Text: Festschrift für Fritz Schalk,* Frankfurt am Main, 1963.

Denomy, A. J., *"Fin'Amors:* The Pure Love of the Troubadours, Its Amorality, and Possible Source," *MS,* 7 (1945), 139–207.

De Rougemont, Denis, *Love in the Western World,* tr. M. Belgion, N.Y., rev. ed. 1956.

Diez, Friedrich, *Die Leben und Werke der Troubadours,* ed. K. Bartsch, 2d ed. Leipzig, 1882.

——, *Die Poesie der Troubadours,* 2d ed. Leipzig, 1883.

Errante, Guido, *La Lirica romanza del primo secolo,* N.Y., 1943.

——, *Marcabru e le fonti sacre dell'antica lirica romanza,* Florence, 1948.

Faral, Edmond, *Les Arts poétiques du XIIe et du XIIIe siècle,* Paris, 1962.

——, "La Pastourelle," *Romania, 49* (1923), 204–59.

Frank, Grace, "The Distant Love of Jaufré Rudel," *MLN,* 57 (1942), 528–34.

Frank, István, ed., *Trouvères et minnesänger,* Saarbrücken, 1952.

Garcia, E. G., "Más sobre las *'jarŷas'* romances en *'muwaššaḥas'* hebreas," *Al-A., 14* (1949), 409–17.

Gaspary, Adolf, *Die sicilianische Dichterschule des 13 Jahrhunderts,* Berlin, 1878.

Gennrich, Friedrich, *Lo gai Saber,* Darmstadt, 1959.

——, "Zur Ursprungsfrage des Minnesangs," *DVLG,* 7 (1929), 187–227.

Giacomo da Lentino, *The Poetry,* ed. E. F. Langley, Cambridge, Mass., 1915.

Gilson, Etienne, *Dante the Philosopher,* tr. D. Moore, N.Y., 1949.

Guittone d'Arezzo, *Le Rime,* ed. F. Egidi, Bari, 1940.

Hill, R. T., and T. G. Bergin, *Anthology of the Provençal Troubadours,* 3d ed. New Haven, 1957.

Hoepffner, Ernst, *Les Troubadours dans leur vie et dans leurs oeuvres,* Paris, 1955.

Huizinga, Johan, *The Waning of the Middle Ages,* tr. F. Hopman, N.Y., 1954.

Jaufré Rudel, *Les Chansons,* ed. A. Jeanroy, 2d ed. Paris, 1924.

Jeanroy, Alfred, *Les Origines de la poésie lyrique en France au moyen âge*, 3d ed. Paris, 1925.

——, *La Poésie lyrique des troubadours*, 2 vols. Paris-Toulouse, 1934.

Lerch, Eugen, "Trobadorsprache und religiöse Sprache," *CN, 3* (1943), 214–30.

Levy, Emil, and Carl Appel, *Provenzalisches Supplement-Wörterbuch*, 8 vols. Leipzig, 1894–1924.

Lewent, Kurt, Review, *ZRP, 43* (1923), 657–74.

Leys d'Amors, ed. J. Anglade, Bibliothèque méridionale, 17–20 (1919–20).

Lommatzsch, Erhard, *Leben und Lieder der provenzalischen Troubadours*, music by F. Gennrich, 2 vols. Berlin, 1959.

Lot-Borodine, Myrrha, "Sur les Origines et les fins du *service d'amour*," *Mélanges Jeanroy*, Paris (1928), 223–42; repr. in *De l'Amour profane à l'amour sacré*, preface E. Gilson, Paris, 1961.

Lote, Georges, *Histoire du vers français: le moyen âge*, 3 vols. Paris, 1949–56.

Mahn, K. A. F., *Gedichte der Troubadours in provenzalischer Sprache*, 4 vols. Berlin, 1856–73.

Marcabrun, *Poésies complètes du troubadour Marcabru*, ed. J.-M.-L. Dejeanne, Bibliothèque méridionale, 12 (1909).

Mélanges . . . à la mémoire d' István Frank, Saarbrücken, 1957.

Menéndez Pidal, Ramón, *Poesía juglaresca y juglares*, Madrid, 1924.

Monaci, Ernesto, *Crestomazia italiana dei primi secoli*, Città di Castello, 1912.

Neumann, Friedrich, "Hohe Minne," *ZDK, 39* (1925), 81–91.

Nostredame, Jehan de, *Les Vies des plus célèbres et anciens poètes provençaux*, ed. C. Chabaneau and J. Anglade, Paris, 1913.

Nykl, A. R., *Hispano-Arabic Poetry and Its Relations with the Old Provençal Troubadours*, Baltimore, 1946.

——, tr., Ibn Hazm al-Andalusī, *A Book Containing the Risāla Known as the Dove's Neck Ring*, Paris, 1931.

Paris, Gaston, "Lancelot du Lac: Le Conte de la Charrette," *Romania, 12* (1883), 459–534.

——, *La Littérature française au moyen âge*, 6th ed. Paris, 1922.

——, Review, *JS* (1891), 674–88.

Parodi, E. G., "La Lettura di Dante in Orsanmichele," *BSDI, 13* N.S. (1906), 241–70.

Pillet, Alfred, "Zum Ursprung der altprovenzalischen Lyrik," *SKGG, 5,* pt. 4 (1928), 345–65.

Poètes et romanciers du moyen âge, ed. A. Pauphilet, new texts by R. Pernoud and A.-M. Schmidt, Bibliothèque de la Pléiade, 52, Paris, 1952.

Pollmann, Leo, "Dichtung und Liebe bei Wilhelm von Aquitanien," *ZRP, 78* (1962), 326–57.

Pound, Ezra, *The Spirit of Romance,* Norfolk, Conn., 1952.

Rajna, Pio, "Guglielmo conte di Poitiers, trovatore bifronte," *Mélanges Jeanroy,* Paris (1928), 349–60.

Raynouard, F. J. M., *Choix des poésies originales des troubadours,* 6 vols. Paris, 1816–61.

——, *Lexique roman: ou, Dictionnaire de la langue des troubadours,* 6 vols. Paris, 1838–44; rev. ed. 1844.

Rimatori del dolce stil novo, ed. L. di Benedetto, Bari, 1939.

Robertson, D. W., Jr., "Amors de terra lonhdana," *SP, 49* (1952), 566–82.

——, "The Doctrine of Charity in Mediaeval Literary Gardens," *Speculum, 26* (1951), 24–49.

——, *A Preface to Chaucer: Studies in Medieval Perspectives,* Princeton, 1962.

Rodrigues Lapa, Manuel, *Lições de literatura portuguesa, época medieval,* 2d ed. Coimbra, 1943.

Roncaglia, Aurelio, "Laisat estar lo gazel," *CN, 9* (1949), 67–99.

Scheludko, Dmitri, "Beiträge zur Entstehungsgeschichte der altprovenzalischen Lyrik: Klassisch-lateinische Theorie," *AR, 11* (1927), 273–312.

——, "Beiträge . . .: Arabische Theorie," *AR, 12* (1928), 30–127.

——, "Beiträge . . .: Volksliedertheorie," *ZFSL, 52* (1929), 1–38, 201–66.

——, "Beiträge . . .," *AR, 15* (1931), 137–206.

——, "Guinizelli und der Neuplatonismus," *DVLG, 12* (1934), 364–99.

——, "Ovid und die Trobadors," *ZRP, 54* (1934), 129–74.

——, "Die Marienlieder in der altprovenzalischen Lyrik," *NM, 36* (1935), 29–48.

——, "Religiöse Elemente im weltlichen Liebeslied der Trobadors," *ZFSL, 59* (1935), 402–21; *60* (1937), 18–35.

——, "Zur Geschichte des Natureinganges bei den Trobadors," *ZFSL, 60* (1937), 257–334.

——, "Über die Theorien der Liebe bei den Trobadors," *ZRP, 60* (1940), 191–234.

Schläger, Georg, *Studien über das Tagelied,* Jena, 1895.

Schlegel, August Wilhelm, "Observations sur la langue et la littérature provençales," *Essais littéraires et historiques,* Bonn (1842), 211–340.

Schmidt, Johannes, "Die älteste Alba," *ZDP, 12* (1881), 333–41.

Schrötter, Wilibald, *Ovid und die Troubadours,* Halle, 1908.

Schultz-Gora, Oskar, Reviews, *ASNS, 136* (1917), 322–27; *ZRP, 42* (1922), 350–70.

Shaw, J. E., *Essays on the Vita Nuova,* Princeton, 1929.

——, *Guido Cavalcanti's Theory of Love: The Canzone d'Amore and Other Related Problems,* Toronto, 1949.

Singer, Samuel, *Arabische und europäische Poesie im Mittelalter, APAW, 13* (1918).

Singleton, Charles S., *Dante Studies,* 2 vols. Cambridge, Mass., 1954 58.

Spanke, Hans, "Beziehungen zwischen romanischer und mittellateinischer Lyrik," *AGWG,* III Folge, *18* (1936).

——, "St. Martial-Studien . . .," *ZFSL, 54* (1930), 282 317, 385 422; *56* (1932), 450–78.

——, "Untersuchungen über die Ursprünge des Minnesangs: Marcabrustudien," *AGWG,* III Folge, *24* (1940).

——, "Zur Formenkunst des ältesten Troubadours," *SM, 7* (1934), 72–84.

Spitzer, Leo, *L'Amour lointain de Jaufré Rudel et le sens de la poésie des troubadours,* Univ. of No. Car. Studies in Romance Langs. and Lit., 5 (1944).

——, "The Mozarabic Lyric and Theodor Frings' Theories," *CL, 4* (1952), 1–22.

Spoerri, Theophil, "Wilhelm von Poitiers und die Anfänge der abendländischen Poesie," *Trivium, 2* (1944), 255–77.

——, Review, *ZRP, 60* (1940), 302–04.

Stern, S. M., "Les Vers finaux en espagnol dans les *muwaššaḥs* hispano-hebraiques," *Al-A., 13* (1948), 299–346.

Torraca, Francesco, *Studi su la lirica italiana del Duecento*, Bologna, 1902.

Valency, Maurice, *In Praise of Love*, N.Y., 1958.

Viscardi, Antonio, "Le Origini della letteratura cortese," *ZRP, 78* (1962), 269–91.

Vossler, Karl, *Aus der romanischen Welt*, Karlsruhe, 1948.

——, "Die Kunst des ältesten Trobadors," *Miscellanea Attilio Hortis*, 2 vols. Trieste (1910), *1*, 419–40.

——, *Mediaeval Culture*, tr. W. C. Lawton, N.Y., 1929.

——, *Der Minnesang des Bernhard von Ventadorn*, Munich, 1918.

——, *Die philosophischen Grundlagen zum 'süssen neuen Stil,'* Heidelberg, 1904.

Watts, Alan W., *Nature, Man and Woman*, N.Y., 1958.

Weston, Jessie L., *From Ritual to Romance*, Cambridge, Eng., 1920.

William IX, *Les Chansons de Guillaume IX*, ed. A. Jeanroy, 2d ed. Paris, 1927.

Zorzi, Diego, *Valori religiosi nella letteratura provenzale: la spiritualità trinitaria*, Milan, 1954.

Zumthor, Paul, "Au Berceau du lyrisme européen," *Cahiers du Sud, 40*, pt. 326 (1954), 3–61.

Index